Honours & Awards:
The South Staffordshire Regiment 1914-1918

Honours & Awards: The South Staffordshire Regiment 1914-1918

by
J. C. J. Elson

First published in Great Britain, 2003
by
Token Publishing Ltd., Orchard House, Duchy Road, Honiton, Devon EX14 1YD
Telephone: 01404 46972   Fax: 01404 44788
e-mail: info@tokenpublishing.com   Website: http:/www.tokenpublishing.com

British Library Cataloguing in Publication data:
A catalogue for this book is available from the British Library
ISBN 1 870 192 58 3

Printed in Great Britain by Goodman Baylis, Worcester

CONTENTS

FOREWORD

THIS book is the end product of research into the awards of the South Staffordshire Regiments for the Great War 1914-1918. I originally put together details of the awards mentioned in regimental histories, but this left gaps for those battalions without an official written history, entries made in the respective war diaries were also added. It soon became apparent that there were many incorrectly described awards. So to enable as complete a record as possible, I undertook to put together this record.

It covers awards located in the *London Gazette*, as well as private and regimental records, together with articles found in local newspapers. Each type of award has its own section and where an individual received more than one award it will be necessary to cross reference these sections, for example Sergeant John Eades of the 1st Battalion, was awarded the Distinguished Conduct Medal, Military Medal & Bar and a Mention in Despatches. There are also awards which do not appear in any records, but the medal has been seen with a group, an example is that of Lieutenant George Bygrave MC who has a French Croix de Guerre but there is no mention of it in the *London Gazette*. Where it has been possible officers and men who served in the South Staffords who were attached or transferred to other formations have also been included, there are two Victoria Crosses amongst these awards.

There are some short biographical details on some of the officers and men, many of these have come from friends who have an interest in the South Staffordshire Regiment during the Great War.

On my many trips to the battlefields of France & Flanders (Belgium) I visited most of the sites where the battalions fought and where the deeds which produced these awards took place. I was struck by the open nature of the landscape, especially on the battlefield of Loos where both the Regular and Territorial Battalions fought between 23rd September and 13th October 1915.

This book is dedicated to all the officers and men of the South Staffordshire Regiment whose deeds are recorded here and to those that went unrecorded.

If I have omitted any awards I apologise and if notified I will ensure that the master copy is amended. In all some 82,130 pages of the *London Gazette* were checked to locate the awards in this book.

17 Battalions of the South Staffordshire Regiment existed during WW1. Not all of them saw active service and due to changes in the structure of the army some of them were disbanded or transferred to other units before the end of the war. They served in various operational areas including Belgium, Egypt, France, Ireland, Gallipoli and Italy.

Jeffrey Elson
Rugeley, 2003

ACKNOWLEDGMENTS

I WOULD like to thank all those who have helped me with either allowing access to records, photographs or other information, especially the *London Gazette*, the Trustees and Staff at the R.H.Q. Regimental Museum of The Staffordshire Regiment (The Prince of Wales's) past and present, Major R.D.W. MacLean, Major E. Green, Olive Wear, Helen Rayson, Neville Ferris, Sarah Elsom, Will Turner, Captain (Retd); P.H. Starling, Royal Army Medical Corps Museum, Simon Moody of The Royal Air Force Museum, Jake Whitehouse, David Baldwin, Terry and Barbra Reece, Geoff Thursfield, Maurice Holland, Iain Fathom, Peter Lead, Tracy Williams, Paul Richardson, Tony Watkiss, Hendrick Meersschaert, Michael Shakeford and Keith Steward FRGS for the loan of photographs and other material; Staff at Rugeley Library who put up with my constant requests for copies of the *London Gazette* and staff at the Local History Centre in Essex Street, Walsall for allowing me to copy photographs from the *Walsall Observer;* and *South Staffordshire Chronicle*. Billy Mahoney for second checking some of the awards at the Public Record Office; Hank Watson who at very short notice assisted with keeping my computer working and advising me on how to use the more complicated applications. Also to Janet my wife who kept me supplied with drinks and food whilst updating the files and not complaining when I needed to go out and collect photographs and research material at short notice. Also to Philip Mussell at Token Publishing for helping me to get the work into print. Finally my daughter Kirsty for being patient when she wanted to use the computer.

THE VICTORIA CROSS

THE Victoria Cross was instituted by Royal Warrant dated 29th January 1856 and was made available to officers and men alike. It was deemed by Queen Victoria that the cross should be simple in design and was to be made from the bronze cannon captured during the Crimean War.

It was in 1916 that a miniature of the cross was added to the ribbon in undress uniform to make it more distinctive, and in 1918 the crimson ribbon was adopted by all the services, as prior to this the Navy had been using a blue ribbon. Only three Victoria Crosses have been issued with a second award bar.

17114 Private Thomas BARRATT VC
7th Battalion South Staffordshire Regiment
Killed in Action 27.07.1917
(London Gazette 06.09.1917 Page 9260)

"For most conspicuous bravery when as a scout to a patrol he worked his way towards the enemy line with the greatest gallantry and determination, in spite of continuous fire from hostile snipers at close range. These snipers he stalked and killed. Later his patrol was similarly held up and again he disposed of the snipers. When during the subsequent withdrawal of the patrol it was observed that a party of the enemy were endeavouring to out flank them. Private Barratt at once volunteered to cover the retirement, and this he succeeded in accomplishing. His accurate shooting caused many casualties to the enemy and prevented their advance. Throughout the enterprise he was under heavy machine gun and rifle fire, and his splendid example of coolness and daring was beyond all praise. After safely regaining our lines, this very gallant soldier was killed by a shell."

Thomas Barratt was the third son of James and Sarah Ann Barratt; he was born on the 5th May 1885 and lived at Foundry Street, Coseley. His mother died whilst he was quite young and as a result of his father suffering with paralysis he became an inmate of the Dudley Workhouse Infirmary with his father. Thomas ran away from the workhouse and was eventually given permission to live with his grandmother at 35 Dark House Lane. He attended the Church Day schools until the time when he had to commence work, finding his first employment at the Cannon Foundry at 1 shilling a day (5 pence). He moved from there to Messrs Thompson Brothers, Lower Bradley Street, Bilston where he was employed until the 14th January 1915 when he enlisted into the South Staffordshire Regiment, at Bilston. He was called back and commenced his training on the 19th January. At an unknown date sometime later and before his award of the Victoria Cross he had been wounded and on his return to fitness was posted to the 7th Battalion South Staffords, who by this time were in France.

Essex Farm Cemetery, Boezinge,
Iper, Belgium, Plot 1, Row Z, Grave 8

On the afternoon of the 27th July he was a member of a platoon which was sent out to probe the German defences. Following the actions mentioned in his citation for the Victoria Cross he was killed along with some other men from his unit in a communication trench in the British lines when a shell burst right in the trench and buried them under a bridge killing them all instantaneously. They are buried together in Essex Farm Cemetery, which is near the original position where the action took place.

His grandmother received many letters relating to Thomas Barratt, including one from Brigadier General A.C. Daly, 33rd Infantry Brigade Commander. Thomas Barratt had been a regular attendor of the bible class meetings at Ebenezer Street Chapel. His brother James received Thomas's Victoria Cross from the King at Buckingham Palace. There is a block of flats and a street named after him, the flats being in his hometown and the street on Boley Park, Lichfield. The memorial to him at Coseley Parish Church was moved to the Garrison Church at the Army Training Regiment, Whittington Barracks, near Lichfield.

Captain John Franks VALLENTIN VC
1st Battalion South Staffordshire Regiment
Killed in Action 07.11.1914 aged 32
(London Gazette 18.02.1915 page 1700)

"For conspicuous bravery on the 7th November at Zillebeke. When leading the attack against the Germans under a heavy fire he was struck down, and on rising to continue was immediately killed.

The capture of the enemy's trenches which followed was in great measure due to the confidence which the men had in their captain, arising from his many previous acts of bravery and ability."

Ypres Memorial Gate

John Franks Vallentin was the son of Grimble and Lucy Ann (Finnis) Vallentin and was born in Lambeth on the 14th May, 1882. He was educated at Wellington College and at the age of 17 years obtained a commission into the 6th Militia Battalion of the Rifle Brigade as a Second Lieutenant, dated 9th August 1899, promotion to Lieutenant followed on the 25th July 1900. He transferred to the 3rd Militia Battalion Royal Sussex regiment and served with them in South Africa during the Orange River operation April-December 1901 and the Transvaal 1902. He then transferred to the Royal Garrison Regiment at Standerton, Transvaal as a 2nd Lieutenant, 27th July 1903 and transferred to the South Staffordshire Regiment 7th June 1905, promoted to Lieutenant 7th September 1907 and served on the North West Frontier. Promotion to Captain followed on 12th June 1909.

He continued to serve the 1st Battalion apart from short spells at the Regimental Depot and with the 3rd Battalion.

On the outbreak of war he went with his battalion to France on the 5th October 1914 and the unit was heavily involved in the First battle of Ypres (now Iper) Belgium. He greatly distinguished himself in the early battles around Gheluvelt and was wounded and was hospitalised. He rejoined his battalion and lead his men into the attack on the 7th November, 1914 being wounded almost immediately. He continued to lead his men until he was cut down and killed by a burst of machine gun fire. The attack was followed through and the position was captured.

His mother whose address is given as 116 Albert Place Mansions, Battersea Park, London was presented with the Victoria Cross by the King at Buckingham Palace on the 16th November 1916. There is a memorial to him at St Leonard parish church, Hythe and in the Garrison Church, Army Training Regiment, near Lichfield, Staffordshire. John Franks Vallentin has no known grave and is commemorated on the Ypres (Menin Gate), Iper, panel 35-37.

Captain Arthur Forbes Gordon KILBY VC, MC
2nd Battalion South Staffordshire Regiment
Killed in Action 25.09.1915 Aged 30
(London Gazette 30.03.1916 page 3409

"Captain Kilby was specially selected, at his own request, and on account of the gallantry which he had previously displayed on many occasions to attack with his company a strong enemy redoubt. The company charged along a narrow tow path headed by Captain Kilby, who, though wounded at the outset, continued to lead his men right up to the enemy wire under a devastating machine gun fire and a shower of bombs. He was shot down, but although his foot had been blown off, he continued to cheer on his men and to use a rifle. Captain Kilby has been missing since the date of the performance of this great act of valour, and his death has now been presumed."

Arthur Forbes Gordon Kilby was born on the 3rd February, 1885 and was the only son of Mr and Mrs Sandford Kilby of Lillington Avenue, Leamington. He was educated at Bilton Grange, Winchester College and privately by Mr Geidt of Frankfurt-am-Main.

He obtained a commission into the 1st Battalion South Staffordshire Regiment as a Second Lieutenant on the 16th August 1905, promoted Lieutenant 31st October 1907 and Captain 1st April 1910. He transferred to the 2nd Battalion South Staffords in December 1910 and commanded "E" Company. He was the only officer in the army qualified as an interpreter in German and Hungarian, he was also fluent in French and Spanish. He had many interests including Architecture and Ornithology.

Along with his battalion he was posted to France on the 24th September 1914. On the 12/13th November 1914 when the French had to retreat, he along with another officer supervised the filling of the gap. He was wounded in the right arm and lung in the action and evacuated to England. He was awarded the Military Cross for his actions (London Gazette 18.02.1915 page 1694). On recovery from his wounds he was posted to the 8th Battalion in March 1915 before returning to the 2nd Battalion in France, May 1915. He was recommended for the Distinguished Service Order on 24th September 1915, and twice mentioned in despatches, but events were overtaken the next day when he was awarded the Victoria Cross for leading his men along a tow path. Being wounded at the outset, he had his foot blown off by a bomb, but bravely cheered on his men, and was last seen using a rifle. Parties were sent out to recover his body but it could not be located amongst the dead and he was presumed missing.

His father received the Victoria Cross from the King at Buckingham Palace on the 11th July 1916.

It was some years later on 19th February, 1929 that his remains were located and laid to rest in the Arras Road Military Cemetery, Plot 3, Row N, Grave 27. The inscription at the base of the headstone reads "Thou hast given him his heart's desire".

There are memorials to him in York Minster and at the Garrison Church, Army Training Regiment, Whittington barracks, near Lichfield, Staffordshire.

Lieutenant Alan JERRARD VC
Royal Air Force
(Late 5th Battalion South Staffordshire Regiment)
London Gazette 01.05.1918 page 5287

"When on offensive patrol with two other officers he attacked five enemy aeroplanes and shot one down in flames, following it down to within 100 feet of the ground. He then attacked an enemy aerodrome from a height of only 50 feet from the ground, and engaging single handed some 19 machines, which were either landing or attempting to take off, succeeding in destroying one of them, which crashed on the aerodrome. A large number of machines then attacked him, thus fully occupied he observed that one of the pilots of his patrol was in difficulties. He went immediately to his assistance, regardless of his own personal safety, and destroyed a third enemy machine. Fresh enemy patrols continued to rise from the aerodrome, which he attacked one after another, and retreated, still engaged with five enemy machines, only when ordered to do so by his patrol leader. Although apparently wounded this very gallant officer turned repeatedly and attacked single handed the pursuing machines, until he was eventually overwhelmed by numbers and driven to the ground."

Alan Jerrard was born at Lewisham on the 3rd December 1897, and was initially educated at Bishop Vesey's Grammar School, Sutton Coldfield, where his father was the headmaster. He attended Oundle school and in 1915 Birmingham University. At the close of 1915 he volunteered to join the army and obtained a commission as a 2nd Lieutenant in the 3/5th battalion of the South Staffordshire Regiment, with seniority of 2nd January 1916.

Life as an infantry officer was short lived as he transferred to the Royal Flying Corps and began training on the 16th August that same year at the Military School Aeronautics, Oxford. Initial flying training was at Thetford before moves to 9 (Reserve) and to 59 Squadron at Narborough who were about to move to France. Illness prevented him from going with them and he remained with the 50 (Reserve) Squadron until he was fully fit. He graduated as a RFC pilot on the 14th June 1917. After several other postings in England he finally made it to 19 Squadron on the 24th July. On one of his first patrols he lost the remainder of his flight and was flying low trying to obtain his bearings when he came across a German convoy which he strafed with his machine guns. His bad luck continued and his engine cut out and his Spad, A8830 crashed head on into a railway embankment near St Marie Cappel. He had his nose and jaw broken in several places and other injuries which necessitated his removal to hospital. He was sent back to England to recover and on completing a refresher course was declared fit to fly. He was posted to 66 Squadron in Italy, arriving there on 22nd February 1918.

He claimed his first victory on the 27th February 1918 by shooting down a Berg single seater scout plane. He then destroyed an enemy observation balloon on 7th March and two Berg scout planes on the 11th March. On the 30th March 1918 he took off with two other pilots in their Camels. Jerrard was flying B5648, "E". What followed led to his award of the Victoria Cross, of which the citation is a brief condensation of the events.

Alan Jerrard was shot down by Oberleutnant Benno Fiala von Fernbrugg who was the Commanding Officer of the German Squadron 51J. Alan Jerrard's Camel crashed in a meadow north of di Molino, hitting a tree, tipped onto its nose and perched on its engine cowling. There was no fire and Alan Jerrard was pulled from the wreckage by Austrian Infantrymen. Von Fernbrugg landed his own plane and went by car to the crash site. There were a total of 163 bullet holes or marks found on Alan Jerrard's Camel, 16 bullets had penetrated the engine and 27 had hit the fuel tank, which probably saved him from being burnt in the crash. He had taken off in his flying suit with only his pyjamas underneath. The Germans sent a message to his Squadron and they in turn dropped two parcels of uniform, etc on an Austrian airfield. Following his interrogation he was taken to a prisoner of war camp at Salzburg. After the war he was repatriated to England and received his Victoria Cross at Buckingham Palace on the 5th April 1919. He remained in the RAF and served in Russia and other stations until his health deteriorated and he retired in 1933 with the rank of Flight Lieutenant.

Alan Jerrard died on the 14th May 1968 in the Buckfield Nursing Home, and was buried with full military honours at Lyme Regis on the 17th May 1968.

Captain John Leslie GREEN VC
Royal Army Medical Corps
(Formerly Medical Officer 1/5th Battalion South Staffordshire Regiment)
London Gazette 05.08.1916 page 7743

"For most conspicuous devotion to duty. Although wounded himself he went to the assistance of an officer who had been wounded and was hung on the enemy's wire entanglements and succeeded in dragging him to a shell hole, where he dressed his wounds notwithstanding that bombs and rifle grenades were thrown at him the whole time. Captain Green then endeavoured to bring the wounded officer into safer cover and had nearly succeeded in doing so when he was himself killed."

Upon the outbreak of the First World War John Leslie Green joined the RAMC. In 1916 whilst serving he married another doctor, Miss Edith Mary Moss MB, BS, on the 1st January 1916. She was the daughter of Mr F.J. Moss of Stainfield Hall, Lincolnshire. He was first attached to the 1/5th Battalion South Staffordshire Regiment between 2nd and 29th March 1915, where his brother was also serving, and following this to the 1/2nd North Midland Field Ambulance, 46th North Midland Division. It was whilst serving with the Sherwood Foresters that he met his death at Fonquevillers, France on the 1st July 1916, whilst attending Captain F.B. Robinson.

His wife continued to work at a military hospital in London. She received her late husband's Victoria Cross from King George V at Buckingham Palace on the 14th October 1916.

OTHER AWARDS

CONTAINED within this chapter are the awards of Knighthood, Order of the Bath, Order of St Michael & St George, Order of The British Empire: (MBE, OBE), the Albert Medal, Distinguished Flying Cross and Territorial Decoration.

Albert Medal (2nd Class)

KCMG Breast Star

CBE

KCB

ORDER OF THE BRITISH EMPIRE
KNIGHT COMMANDER MILITARY DIVISION (KBE)

Major & Brevet Lt Col (Temp Col) Vernon George Waldergrave KELL CB

London Gazette 09.06.1919 page 7426
(RP, RoO)

ORDER OF THE BATH
MILITARY DIVISION OF 3RD CLASS OR COMPANION (CB)

Lt Col C.S. DAVIDSON   London Gazette 18.02.1915 page 1694
2nd Bn

Major & Brevet Lt Col (Temp Col) Vernon George Waldergrave KELL

London Gazette 24.01.1917 page 924
(RP, RoO)

ORDER OF THE BATH
CIVIL DIVISION, THIRD CLASS, OR COMPANION

Captain Henry Littleton WHEELER DSO,   London Gazette 01.01.1918 page 80
(RP, Secretary Staffordshire Territorial Force Association.)

ORDER OF ST MICHAEL & ST GEORGE OR KNIGHT COMMANDER SECOND CLASS OR (KCMG)

Major (T/Lt Col) John Sedley Newton de JOUX London Gazette 01.01.1918 page 8.

ORDER OF ST MICHAEL & ST GEORGE THIRD CLASS OR COMPANION (CMG)

Major & Brevet Lt Col (Temp Brig Gen) Lionel Boyd BOYD-MOSS

London Gazette 03.06.1919 page 5559
King's Birthday Honour

Major & Brevet Lt Col (Temp Colonel) Stephen Seymour BUTLER DSO

London Gazette 03.06.1919 page 6792
King,s Birthday Honour

Major & Brevet Lt Col Percy Ryan Conway COMMINGS DSO

London Gazette 01.01.1919 page 4
New Years Honour

Major (Temp Lt Col) John Sedley Newton de JOUX

London Gazette 01.01.1918 page 8
New Years Honour

Major & Brevet Lt Col (Temp Brig General) Rosslewin Westropp MORGAN DSO
2nd Bn.

London Gazette 01.01.1919 page 4
New Years Honour

Lt Col Robert Montgomery OVENS   London Gazette 18.02.1915 page 1694
1st Bn   & London Gazette 16.03.1915 page 2622

Major (Temp Lt Col) Robert Richard RAYMER DSO
1/5th Bn   London Gazette 03.06.1919 page 6791

Major Henry Ernest WALSHE (R.P.)   London Gazette 23.06.1915 page 6114
1st Bn   King's Birthday Honour for 03.06.1915

ORDER OF THE BRITISH EMPIRE
COMMANDER, MILITARY DIVISION (CBE)

Colonel (Hon Brig General) Edward Kaye DAUBENEY DSO
S.Staffs (late)   London Gazette 01.01.1919 page 83
                                             New Years Honour

Lt Col Ivone KIRPATRICK   London Gazette 03.06.1919 page 6981
SSR (RP)   King's Birthday Honour

Ivone Kirpatrick was born 22nd May 1860 at Donacomper, County Kildare. He was an Ensign in the South Staffordshire Regiment, date of commission is given as 23rd October 1880.

He served during the Egyptian campaign and received the bars Nile & Kirbekan. He went on to command the 2nd Battalion South Staffordshire Regiment between 1907 and 1911 whilst the unit was stationed in South Africa. He retired from active service in 1911 and was founder of The Old Comrades Association for the South Staffordshire Regiment.

On the outbreak of WW1 he rejoined and commanded the 6th Battalion Royal Inniskilling Fusiliers. He became the embarkation Staff Officer in Dublin. He has no Great War Medals but was Mentioned In Despatches twice and received the C.B.E. in the London Gazette of 3rd June 1919. His full medal entitlement is CBE, Egypt Medal Bars Nile & Kirbekan and the Khedives Star.

Lieutenant Col Ivone Kirpatrick died on the 20th November 1936, at Buckhurst Hill, Essex.

Lt Col & Bt Col George JONES-MITTON   London Gazette 12.12.1919 page 15451
3rd Bn

Major & Brevet Lt Col (Temp Lt Col) Morris Boscawan SAVAGE DSO
2nd Bn   London Gazette 03.06.1919 page 6982
                                             King's Birthday Honour

Temp Lt Col Robert STEPHENSON DSO   London Gazette 03.06.1919 page 6938
                                             King's Birthday Honour (Italy)

Major & Brevet Lt Col Bertie Harry Waters TAYLOR
                                             London Gazette 01.01.1919 page 52
                                             New Years Honour (Egypt)

ORDER OF THE BRITISH EMPIRE
OFFICER, MILITARY DIVISION (OBE)

Captain Francis BROADWOOD   London Gazette 17.09.1918 page 4977
SSS (late)   (07.06.1918)

Temp Captain William Tom CARTER   London Gazette 03.06.1919 page 6985
                                              King's Birthday Honour

Captain (T/Lt Col) Eldon Anneslo CRUMP TD   London Gazette 03.06.1919 page 6986
King's Birthday Honour

Major Humphrey Percival GAMON   London Gazette 01.01.1919 page 8
5th Bn att from 5th Bn NSR   New Years Honour

Lieut (Acting Captain) Robert Heaton LIVINGSTONE
London Gazette 03.06.1919 page 6801
King's Birthday Honour

Captain (T/Major) Harry Leslie Bache LOVATT MC
6th Bn & R.E.   London Gazette 01.01.1919 page 9
New Years Honour

Lt Col Thomas Enoch LOWE TD   London Gazette 03.06.1919 page 6990
6th Bn   King's Birthday Honour

Captain (Acting Major) John MacArthur NICHOLLE
3rd Bn   London Gazette 03.06.1919 page 7028
King's Birthday Honour

Major (Temp Lt Col) Francis Hearle PARKIN
London Gazette 03.06.1919 page 6991
King's Birthday Honour

Major (Quartermaster) James PENKETH   London Gazette 03.06.1919 page 6991
Kings Birthday Honour

Captain (Temp Major) George William Robert STACPOOLE DSO
London Gazette 01.01.1919 page 10
New Years Honour (DSO S.A. War)

Lieut (A/Captain) Ernest Raymond STANLEY London Gazette 03.06.1919 page 6805
King's Birthday Honour

Major Sidney Chaytor WELSHMAN   London Gazette 12.12.1919 page 15454
Substituted for MBE dated 03.06.1919 page 7002

ROYAL VICTORIAN ORDER
(MEMBER FOURTH CLASS)

Lieutenant Colonel Alfred Henry Cotes JAMES DSO
London Gazette 18.06.1916 page 8149

ORDER OF THE BRITISH EMPIRE
MEMBER, CIVIL DIVISION (MBE)

Captain John McGEVOR   London Gazette 07.06.1918
(Upgraded see below)

2nd Lieut Henry Edward MERRY   London Gazette 07.06.1918 page 6735
(Upgraded see below)

ORDER OF THE BRITISH EMPIRE
MEMBER , MILITARY DIVISION (MBE)

2 Lieut Glenney Franklin BANNERMAN	London Gazette 12.12.1919 page 15455
Captain Charles Burnley BELT MC	London Gazette 03.06.1919 page 7028 King's Birthday Honour
Captain Derrick Ansell CLARKE 5th Bn	London Gazette 03.06.1919 page 6997 King's Birthday Honour
Captain (Quartermaster) John McGEVOR	London Gazette 15.04.1919 page 4988
2nd Lieut Henry Edward MERRY 6th Bn	London Gazette 15.04.1919 page 4988
Major Sidney Chaytor WELCHMAN	London Gazette 03.06.1919 page 7002 King's Birthday Honour
Temp Lieut Richard Linsley YOUNG 9th Bn	London Gazette 01.01.1919 page 65 New Years Honour (Italy)

DISTINGUISHED FLYING CROSS

Lieut (Honorary Captain) Percival James SLATER 6th Bn	London Gazette 03.12.1918 page 14325 (France)

"During operations in September at every advance this officer went forward with his balloon across difficult country, keeping up with, and often in front of, our artillery. Subjected to heavy bombing, shell fire, and frequent attacks by enemy aircraft, Captain Slater, with cool courage and marked ability, continued to carry out observations for the artillery, his balloon at times being severely holed."

THE ALBERT MEDAL (2ND CLASS)

Lieutenant Charles Edward Cox BARTLETT 4th Bn	London Gazette 19.05.1916 page 4971

"On the 22nd February 1916, at St Peters Barracks Jersey, one of the men under instruction at a bombing class, of which Lieutenant Bartlett was in charge, was practising with a catapult bomb thrower, and had removed the safety pin from a bomb, holding back the lever with his finger. In placing the bomb in the sling he dropped it, and in a fright ran backwards, colliding with Lieutenant Bartlett, who had started to pick up the bomb. Lieutenant Bartlett, however, succeeded in reaching the bomb in time to throw it over the parapet into the air, where it exploded harmlessly. The bomb was timed to explode five seconds after the lever was released. This Officer has already been awarded the Military Cross."

TERRITORIAL DECORATION

Major Percy D. BARLOW 6th Bn	London Gazette 13.03.1919 page 3396
Major Thomas Edward BARNETT	London Gazette 04.06.1917 page 5614
Captain (Temp Lt Col) Eldon Annelso CRUMP	London Gazette 27.02.1918 page 2573

Major Frank C. HUGHES
5th Bn

London Gazette 13.03.1919 page 3396
(Retired)

Lt Col Thomas Enock LOWE
6th Bn

London Gazette 04.06.1917 page 5614

Captain Frank M. NORMAN
6th Bn

London Gazette 13.03.1919 page 3397

Lieutenant Colonel Ivone KIRPATRICK CBE (RP)

Captain H.P. GAMON OBE
5th Bn North Staffords attached 5th Bn South Staffords

THE DISTINGUISHED SERVICE ORDER

THE DSO was instituted in 1886 as no adequate award for distinguished service was available to junior officers apart from the Victoria Cross, and in the case of Majors the CB. It was originally issued in gold and enamel, the award was made in silver gilt and enamel. Bars may be issued for further awards.

Temporary Captain Albert George ALLEN MC. London Gazette 01.01.1919 page 17. (General List)

No Citation. New Years Honour.

Temporary Major Alec Hutchinson ASHCROFT. 7th Battalion. London Gazette 01.01.1919 page 17.

No Citation. New Years Honour.

Lieutenant (Acting Captain) George Herbert BALL. 1/5th Battalion. London Gazette 08.03.1919 page 3225. Citation London Gazette 04.10.1919 page 12220.

"On September 27 to 28, 1918, north of Bellenglise he by a counter attack ejected the enemy, who had bombed their way into newly captured trenches. Later being short of ammunition and bombs, he was forced to fall back, showing great courage and stubbornness, and inflicting heavy casualties on the enemy. Next day he made a reconnaissance with a small patrol, and with two men went forward and captured sixteen enemy and two machineguns. He did fine work."

Temporary Major William Arthur John BARKER. 8th Battalion. Citation London Gazette 30.03.1916 page 3423.

"For conspicuous gallantry and devotion to duty. When organising a counter attack he was wounded in four places by a bomb, but continued to command his battalion throughout the three following days until it was relieved."

2nd Lieut Charles BATES MC, DCM. 4th Battalion. Citation London Gazette 26.07.1918 page 8742.

"For conspicuous gallantry and devotion to duty. He went forward, through a heavy barrage to a commanding position, and lay there under fire for three hours, sending back valuable information. Then, returning to his platoon, he altered his

dispositions and held up the enemy, in spite of repeated efforts to turn his flank. Although twice wounded, he stayed with his command, which withdrew the following day, when he again stopped the enemy's advance by getting a Lewis Gun into position on a railway embankment and firing it himself until all ammunition was exhausted. He was then able to withdraw."

Captain & Brevet Major Archibold Bentley BEAUMAN DSO. 1st Battalion. Citation London Gazette 06.09.1915 page 8840.

"For conspicuous gallantry and ability at Festubert on 16th May 1915, when commanding the leading company of his battalion in the attack. He handled his men with great skill, clearing the trenches to his right with his Company and bombers and, after reaching the line allotted to the battalion, entrenched himself and held on under heavy artillery fire during the 16th, 17th and 18th May."

Archibold Bentley BEAUMAN DSO, Bar to DSO London Gazette 26.11.1917 page 12315, Citation London Gazette 06.04.1918 page 4195

"For conspicuous gallantry and devotion to duty. When the troops on the right were in difficulty and communications with Brigade HQ broken down, he made dispositions with his own battalion and other troops which ensured the security on the division front. He proved himself to be a leader of exceptional ability."

Captain Norman Pellen BIRLEY MC. 1st Battalion. London Gazette 01.01.1918 page 18.

No Citation. New Years Honour.

Lieutenant Colonel Singleton BONNER. 1st Battalion, attached Royal Fusiliers. Died of Wounds 01.05.1917. Citation London Gazette 03.07.1915 page 6534.

"For particularly good and gallant services rendered at Festubert from the 16th to 18th May, 1915 when he showed a fine example in coolness bravery and power of command."

Major & Brevet Lieutenant Colonel (Temporary Brigadier General) Lionel BOYD-MOSS CMG. 2nd Battalion. London Gazette 01.01.1918 page 18.

No Citation. New Years Honour.

Captain (Temporary Major) Edward Charles Phillip BRIDGES. 7th Battalion (33 Brigade MGC Officer). London Gazette 02.02.1916 page 1337.

No Citation.

Temporary Major Lawrence Newman Beverley BULLOCK DSO. 9th Battalion. London Gazette 15.02.1917 page 1596 (Canadian Engineers attached).

No Citation. (For 01.01.1917)

Laurence Newman Beverley BULLOCK DSO, Bar to DSO, Citation London Gazette 01.02.1919 page 1601 (Italy)

"For conspicuous gallantry and devotion to duty. Prior to the operations on the River Piave, from 23rd to 27th October 1918, he was entrusted with arrangements for transfer of troops from the right bank to the island of Grave de Papadopli, maintenance of the passage, and control of the crossing of further men and material. His duties were most ably carried out under difficult conditions and considerable shell fire. The success of the division was to a great extent due to his resource and untiring energy."

Temporary Major (Acting Lt Col) Richard Parry BURNETT MC. 8th Battalion, attached 7th Battalion Royal Fusiliers. London Gazette 03.06.1919 page 6817.

No Citation. King's Birthday Honour.

Captain (Acting Lieutenant Colonel) Charles Sidney BURT. 1st Battalion. London Gazette 03.06.1918 page 6495 (Italy).

No Citation. King's Birthday Honour.

Major Stephen Seymour BUTLER CMG. 1st Battalion. London Gazette 04.06.1917 page 5468.

No Citation. King's Birthday Honour.

Temporary Captain (Acting Lieutenant Colonel) John Jackson CAMERON MC. Attached 23rd Battalion Royal Fusiliers. London Gazette 18.01.1918 page 954. Citation London Gazette 25.04.1918 page 4987.

"For conspicuous gallantry and devotion to duty. He made a thorough reconnaissance of the ground on which his battalion were able to assemble and advance in support of an attack. He guided his battalion to the position, which he found was being heavily shelled, and assembled them successfully in another position. He showed the greatest ability and skill throughout."

Lieutenant (Temporary Major) William Henry CARTER MC. Royal Warwicks, attached 7th Battalion. Citation London Gazette 20.10.1916 page 10170.

"For conspicuous gallantry during operations. He commanded the battalion after his C.O. was wounded, and displayed great skill and personal courage. He went about everywhere encouraging his men and making personal reconnaissance during three days of heavy fighting. He set a fine example to his command."

William Henry CARTER MC. Bar to DSO. London Gazette 02.04.1919 page 4316. Citation London Gazette 10.12.1919 page 15280

"For skilful leading of his battalion during the operations November 8 and 9, 1918, in the advance from Autreppe to Geognies Chaussee. On November 8 he by his drive and initiative kept his battalion going forward through heavy enemy opposition, and by a personal reconnaissance reported his exact dispositions at the end of the day. He has at all times set a very fine example to those under him."

Captain & Brevet Major (Temporary Lieutenant Colonel) John Clervaux CHAYTOR MC. 2nd Battalion. London Gazette 08.03.1918 page 2793 for London Gazette 01.01.1918.

No Citation. New Years Honour.

Major (Temporary Lieutenant Colonel) John William Jervoice COLLAS. 2nd Battalion. Citation London Gazette 25.08.1917 page 8802.

"For conspicuous gallantry and devotion to duty when the enemy had gained possession of our assembly trenches by means of counter attack. He led his battalion against them under heavy fire, and recaptured the line, which he held later on, in spite of numerous bombing attacks, with great coolness and determination."

Major (Temporary Lieutenant Colonel) Percy Ryan Conway COMMINGS CMG. 1st Battalion. London Gazette 14.01.1916 page 572 for London Gazette01.01.1916.

No Citation. New Years Honour.

2nd Lieutenant William Horace CURRY. 3rd Battalion attached 1st Battalion. Citation London Gazette 26.05.1917 page 5177-8. Killed in Action 25.10.1917.

"For conspicuous gallantry and devotion to duty. He collected men from three different companies and led them forward as far as it was possible to advance. Later, although nearly surrounded by the enemy, he succeeded in consolidating and maintaining his position. On another occasion he took command of two companies and handled them in a most able manner."

2nd Lieutenant Frank DAVIS. 4th Battalion. Citation London Gazette 24.09.1918 page 11277.

"For conspicuous gallantry and devotion to duty. When the left flank of the battalion was in the air, with the enemy working round in great strength, he kept his men steady, and by his coolness enabled an orderly withdrawal to be effected. Shortly afterwards, when the battalion was almost surrounded, he formed a rearguard with the remaining men of his company, and by skilful leadership of his men enabled the remainder of the battalion to withdraw successfully. Next day he hung on to an important position with great ability and resolution, though losing many men from heavy shell fire and being wounded himself. Throughout these two days of fighting his personal courage was most marked, and his skilful handling of his men saved the battalion on two occasions."

Captain & Brevet Major George DAWES MC. 2nd Battalion. London Gazette 18.02.1918 page 2156. Citation 18.07.1918 page 8440. (Commanding 21st Bn London Regiment).

"For conspicuous gallantry and devotion to duty during lengthy operations. He took over an important line and established a strong position. He rendered prompt assistance to a battalion on his left in a successful attack. Later, he organised and directed the withdrawal of the battalion with such skill that hardly any casualties were suffered, and all ammunition and tools were moved back. His courage and cheerfulness never failed, though he was constantly under heavy fire, and was suffering from gas."

George DAWES DSO MC, Bar to DSO, Citation London Gazette 26.07.1918 page 8736.

"For conspicuous gallantry and devotion to duty. With his battalion and some other troops he covered the retirement of the division, maintaining his ground for eight hours, until nearly surrounded, when he fought his way out. On another occasion, when the enemy outflanked his left, he saved the situation, reorganised the line under heavy machine gun fire."

Second Bar to DSO
Citation London Gazette 11.01.1919 page 577.

"For conspicuous gallantry and able leadership. When the enemy attacked the flank of the battalion, which had been uncovered owing to the retirement of other troops, and there appeared to be an imminent danger of their break through at this spot, which was the key of the position, Colonel Dawes went up under an intense fire, and rallied the men by his splendid example of courage and saved the line by his able and determined leadership."

Captain Joseph Leslie DENT MC. 2nd Battalion.
Citation London Gazette 01.12.1914 page 10187. Killed in Action 11.04.1917.

"On October 7th located an enemy's trench by daring scouting at night subsequently rushing it with two sections and driving the enemy away."

Major Ralph DUCKWORTH. 1st Battalion (Assistant Quartermaster General 46th North Midland Division). London Gazette 01.01.1918 page 20.

No Citation. New Years Honour.

Lieutenant (Acting Lieutenant Colonel) William Richard ENGLISH-MURPHY MC. 1st Battalion. London Gazette 02.04.1919 page 4317 (Italy). Citation London Gazette 10.12.1919 page 15286.

"In the attack across the Piave on October 27, 1918 and following days he handled his battalion with conspicuous gallantry and skill. Seeing the leading battalion in difficulties owing to the swiftness of the river and the wire on the river bank, he on his own initiative moved his battalion up on the flank of the leading battalion, and gave most valuable assistance in the capture of the first objective at a somewhat critical period. He then reorganised his battalion and led them rapidly forward, capturing the villages of Smichele Di Piave and Tezze, with hundreds of prisoners and several guns. Throughout operations he set his men a splendid example of fearlessness and dash, which materially helped to insure the great success achieved."

Lieutenant (Temporary Captain) Walter George FLUKE. 2nd Battalion. Citation London Gazette 20.10.1916 page 10170.

"For conspicuous gallantry during operations. He got up to the support line through a heavy barrage, and reorganised the line when all the officers had become casualties. On another occasion he led a bombing attack, although his company were much exhausted, and forced his way along the enemy trenches in an endeavour to reach a party of men who had been cut off. He showed utter disregard of personal safety."

Temporary Major William GIBSON MC. 8th Battalion attached 10th Battalion West Yorkshire Regiment. Citation London Gazette 02.12.1918 page 14210.

"For conspicuous gallantry and initiative when in command of his battalion during five days operation. He reorganised the battalion after an attack with great skill, pursued the retreating enemy, and assisted in the capture of further enemy positions. His coolness and determination inspired his men throughout and contributed largely to the success of the operations."

Captain & Brevet Major Guy de Coursey GLOVER MC. 2nd Battalion. London Gazette 03.06.1918 page 6459.

No Citation. King's Birthday Honour.

Lieutenant Frank Hugh GUNNER. 2nd Battalion. Citation London Gazette 01.12.1914 page 10187.

"For conspicuous and consistent good work in charge of the machine gun section 12th September to 4th November almost continually in action, displayed greatest courage, coolness and judgement in difficult and dangerous situations."

Captain (Temporary Major) Henry Alexander Augustus Francis HARMAN. 4th Battalion. London Gazette 04.06.1917 page 5470.

No Citation. King's Birthday Honour.

Lieutenant (Acting Captain) Ladas Lewis HASSELL MC. 1st Battalion. London Gazette 26.11.1917 page 12316. Citation London Gazette 06.04.1918 page 4198.

"For conspicuous gallantry and devotion to duty in leading his company forward through a heavy barrage. In spite of severe casualties, the relief was very little delayed. He pressed home an attack with great ability, captured his objective, and formed a defensive flank when troops on our right were giving way. Though buried by a shell for ten minutes, he continued in command of two companies in the front line till relieved twenty-four hours later."

Captain Alfred Henry Cotes JAMES. London Gazette 18.02.1915 page 1687 London Gazette 24.03.1915 page 2939.

No Citation. For meritorious service

Captain (Acting Major) Samuel Gordon JOHNSON MC. 2nd Battalion attached Royal Engineers. London Gazette 03.06.1918 page 6459.

No Citation. King's Birthday Honour.

Lieutenant (Acting Captain) Frederick Arthur KENDRICK MC. 1st Battalion. London Gazette 02.04.1919 page 4317 (Italy). Citation London Gazette 10.12.1919 page 15287.

"During operations October 27-29 1918, he showed the greatest gallantry, coolness and devotion to duty. On October 27th he pushed forward rapidly with his company, and captured the village of Tezze, three field guns and 240 prisoners. Again on October 28, his company was first to reach the objective, and he reorganised the battalion front for defence. On October 29, at Cimetta, he was given charge of two front line companies of the battalion. At the beginning of this operation he had one arm broken by a machine gun bullet, but continued to lead the attack through very difficult country and under heavy machine gun fire. Before reaching his objective he was again hit in the other arm, but insisted on continuing to lead the advance, finally clearing the village and capturing a large number of prisoners and machine guns. He only consented to leave after consolidation was complete. By his absolute fearlessness, disregard of his wounds and skilful leadership, he ensured the success of a difficult operation and set a splendid example."

Lieutenant (Acting Lieutenant Colonel) James LAMOND MC. 2nd Battalion Royal Scots attached 1/5th Battalion S.S.R. (TF). London Gazette 01.01.1919 page 19.

No Citation. New Years Honour.

Major (Temporary Lieutenant Colonel) Frederick William Bernarding LAW TD. 6th Battalion. London Gazette 03.06.1916 page 5568.

No Citation. King's Birthday Honour.

Captain (Acting Lieutenant Colonel) Cecil LISTER MC. Northumberland Fusiliers attached 1/6th Battalion S.S.R. London Gazette 08.03.1919 page 3226. Citation London Gazette 04.10.1919 page 12224.

"His battalion had been allotted the difficult task of storming the St Quinten Canal and capturing the village of Bellenglise on the further bank. Amongst the defences he had to attack was a tunnel system. On the 29th September, 1918, he achieved a complete success with slight casualties, and this was great measure to his careful preparation of the assault and the determination with which he personally inspired all ranks serving under him during the action."

Cecil LISTER DSO MC. Bar to DSO. London Gazette 01.01.1919 page 17

No Citation. New Years Honour.

Temporary Captain William MACKENZIE MB, Royal Army Medical Corps attached 9th Battalion S.S.R. London Gazette 01.01.1919 page 66. (Italy)

No Citation. New Years Honour.

Temporary Lieutenant Albert Basil MILLER MC. 4th Battalion. Citation London Gazette 16.09.1918 page 10869.

"For conspicuous gallantry and devotion to duty during an attack. After his senior officers had become casualties he led the battalion with great dash and determination, killing a large number of the enemy and taking 70 prisoners. When the withdrawal became necessary, he got his men back to the front line in perfect order. His courage and leadership were of a high order, and he turned a doubtful situation into a brilliant success."

Major Rosslewin Westropp MORGAN CMG. 2nd Battalion. London Gazette 14.01.1916 page 573 (For 01.01.1916).

No Citation. New Years Honour.

Rosslewin Westropp MORGAN CMG. Brevet Lt Colonel (Temp Brigadier General). Bar to DSO. Citation London Gazette 20.10.1916 page 10173.

"For conspicuous gallantry during operations. When the C.O. and second in command of another battalion had become casualties, he took command of both battalions, organised his defences, and held his own against counter attack and during heavy bombardment. He has always displayed the greatest bravery, and has set a fine example to his command."

Captain (Temporary Major) Robert John MORRIS. 1st Battalion. Citation London Gazette 11.12.1916 page 12101. (Also 4th Battalion)

"For conspicuous gallantry in action. He personally rallied men of other battalions, who were near by and reinforced his own battalion, at a critical time, enabled them to capture the village. He displayed the greatest courage and initiative throughout."

Captain & Brevet Major (Acting Lieutenant Colonel) Robert Francis Brydges NAYLOR MC. 1st Battalion. London Gazette 03.06.1919 page 6819.

No Citation. King's Birthday Honour.

Captain (Temporary Major) Richard PERSSE MC. 9th Battalion. London Gazette 03.06.1918 page 6995 (Italy).

No Citation. King's Birthday Honour.

Temporary 2nd Lieutenant John POTTER. 1st Battalion. Citation London Gazette 27.07.1916 page 7429. Died of Wounds 24.07.1916.

"For conspicuous gallantry. During the storming of an enemy position he was the first man to enter it, and then with his platoon captured and held under heavy fire till reinforced an hour later a point of great tactical importance. Later he took part in an assault on another position which was taken owing to his personal gallantry and fine leadership."

Major (Temporary Lieutenant Colonel) Robert Richmond RAYMER CMG. 1/5th Battalion. London Gazette 03.06.1916 page 5569.

No Citation. King's Birthday Honour.

Captain Morris Boscawen SAVAGE CBE. 2nd Battalion. London Gazette 18.02.1915 page 1694. (See also London Gazette 24.03.1915 page 2941).

No Citation.

Lieutenant Colonel Francis Savage Nesbitt SAVAGE-ARMSTRONG. 1st Battalion attached 11th Battalion Royal Warwicks. London Gazette 23.06.1915 page 6123. Killed in Action 23.04.1917.

No Citation.

Major (Temporary Lieutenant Colonel) Douglas Thorne SECKHAM. 7th Battalion. London Gazette 01.01.1917 page 26.

No Citation. New Years Honour.

Captain (Temporary Major) William John Townsend SHORTHOSE. 2nd Battalion attached Kings African Rifles. London Gazette 01.01.1918 page 26.

No Citation. New Years Honour.

Lieutenant (Acting Major) Joseph SNAPE MC. 1st Battalion attached H.A.C. London Gazette 03.06.1918 page 6995 (Italy).

No Citation. King's Birthday Honour.

Temporary Lieutenant Colonel Robert STEPHENSON CBE. 9th Battalion (Formerly Northumberland Fusiliers). London Gazette 04.06.1917 page 5474.

No Citation. King's Birthday Honour.

Lieutenant Colonel Frederick Joseph TRUMP. 6th Battalion. London Gazette 01.01.1917 page 27. Killed in Action 02.12.1917.

No Citation. New Years Honour.

Lieutenant Colonel B.F. WATERHOUSE TD. (Monmouth Regiment) attached 6th Battalion SSR. London Gazette 08.03.1918 page 2973. (For 01.01.1918)

No Citation. New Years Honour.

Captain (Acting Lieutenant Colonel) Arthur WHITE. 4th Battalion East Surrey Regiment attached 1/5th Battalion SSR (TF). London Gazette 08.03.1919 page 3266 (For 01.01.1918). Citation London Gazette 04.10.1919 page 12229. (Amendment London Gazette 12.07.1920 page 7429 read A/Lt Col Alfred White).

"On the 28th September 1918 his battalion on the day previous to the general attack on the St Quinten Canal, was heavily attacked by the enemy in our outpost line near Bellenglise. During the succeeding night he reorganised his battalion and completed with three companies preparations for an attack which was organised for four companies. He led his battalion to the attack, and its success was largely due to his forethought in preparation and coolness in action."

Major George Arthur Secombe WILLIAMS. 2nd Battalion. London Gazette 01.01.1918 page 27.

No Citation. New Years Honour.

Captain (Temporary Major) and Acting Lieutenant Colonel William Allsop WISTANCE MC. 1/5th Battalion. London Gazette 17.12.1917. Citation 23.04.1918 page 8456. Killed in Action 25.04.1918.

"For conspicuous gallantry and devotion to duty when in command of his battalion during an attack. He maintained complete control of the situation under extraordinarily difficult conditions."

Major (Acting Lieutenant Colonel) George Alexander YOOL. 7th Battalion attached Leicester Regiment. (Second supplement of London Gazette of 03.06.1918 page 6461) Amendment London Gazette 04.09.1918 page

10499 Major A/Lt Col George Alexander YOOL SSR att Lincolnshire Regiment.

No Citation. King's Birthday Honour.

SELECTED PERSONAL DETAILS
Details of other recipients can be found on p.177 et seq.

Lieutenant Colonel William Henry CARTER DSO & Bar, MC & Bar

William Henry Carter enlisted into the South Staffordshire Regiment prior to WW1 and had previously served in the South African War 1899 - 1902. He went with his unit to France in August 1914, as the signal sergeant. He received a commission and because of good work on the 24th November 1915 he was awarded the Military Cross. A bar to the Military Cross was awarded in June 1916. It was commented on at the time in the battalion that "hardly a day passes without his name being brought to notice for some act of devotion or gallantry".

The award of the DSO came out of work in connection with Delville Wood, July 1916. He received a slight wound but it was due to his courage that two hostile bombing attacks were repulsed and that consolidation could take place when he was himself bombing the enemy position. Twelve months previously he was the recipient of the Russian Order of St Stanislaus.

He received an engraved silver sword from the Borough of Wolverhampton on the 21st February 1918. The sword was inscribed "Borough of Wolverhampton Presented to Lt Col W.O.H. Carter by his fellow townsmen in recognition of his distinguished military services to the King and country".

He was the second son of Mr W.F. Carter of Maxwell Road, Wolverhampton, formerly of Blakenhall. His brother George Carter served in the Army Service Corps attached to the 3rd North Field Ambulance.

Major (Temporary Lieutenant Colonel), John William Jervoice COLLAS DSO

Lieutenant Colonel Ralph DUCKWORTH DSO

Ralph Duckworth was born on 13th November 1876, at Murtrey Hill, Buckland Dinham, Frome, Somerset, the second son of Russell Duckworth JP and Barrister at Law, and Jeanette Duckworth formerly Clutterbuck.

The family seat was Orchardleigh Park, Frome, Somerset, but Ralph's father being the second son, lived at The Cloister, Bath. Ralph spent most of his boyhood at Orchardleigh, to which he was greatly attached throughout his life. He was educated at Bath College for six years and entered Magdalen College, Oxford in 1895, gaining a B.A. He excelled in all forms of sport but in later years forsook all for golf and was well known on many of the English and Continental links.

He was commissioned 2nd Lieutenant from the Militia on 9th December 1899 into the 2nd Battalion South

Staffordshire Regiment. The battalion was stationed in Calcutta, India where he joined them and served at several stations.

On 9th June 1904, he married Elvira Ledgard, the only daughter of Major N.P. Ledgard of the Worcestershire Regiment. The battalion was posted to South Africa before returning to England in 1911, where in 1912 they took up duties at Windsor Castle.

On the outbreak of WW1 he, along with the battalion, were sent to France on 13th August 1914, landing at Havre. On 1st September he was involved in a rearguard action at Villers Cotterets and the fighting on the 10th September at the River Marne. At 8.45am the brigade surprised a column of Germans near Hautevesnes and following the action some 450 Germans were taken prisoner. During the action he was wounded. He was shipped back to England and whilst in hospital at Farnborough he was visited by King George V.

On recovery from his wounds he returned to France and took command of the 1st South Staffords on the 26th December 1914. He was ill between 15th February and 11th May 1915. Promotion to Major followed on the 1st September 1915 and shortly after he was posted to the staff of the 1st Army Corps. He did manage to visit his old battalion on the 27th October 1915. Ralph Duckworth remained on the staff for the remainder of the war. He received the award of the Distinguished Service Order in the New Years Honours list 1918 and three mentions in Despatches, 1.1.1916, 11.12.1917 and 5.7.1919. On the 14th September, 1918 he was promoted to Lieutenant Colonel and appointed Assistant Adjutant & Quartermaster General of the 46th North Midland Division. At the end of hostilities he retired from the army and was granted the rank of Brevet Lieutenant Colonel.

Ralph Duckworth had no fixed home in England and spent most of the winters abroad. Whilst on a visit to Monte Carlo he was taken ill with pneumonia and died on the 13th January 1924, aged 47.

Lieutenant (Acting Captain) Ladas Lewis HASSELL DSO, MC

Captain (Temporary Major) Robert John MORRIS DSO

Major George Archer Secombe WILLIAMS DSO

Major George Archer Secombe Williams DSO, 2nd Battalion, South Staffordshire Regiment, late Major 4th Battalion, late Lieutenant, South Nigeria Regiment, West African Frontier Force; late Royal Fusiliers, was born in the Falkland Islands at Port Stanley on 6th April 1874.

George Williams spent the better part of 20 years in uniform; five years and nine months in West Africa, an undetermined period of time in East Africa and three years from 1916 to 1919 or 1920 in France and Belgium. He was twice Mentioned in Despatches in West Africa during the years 1900 and 1906, and four times during the First World War. He was also awarded the DSO (London Gazette, 1st January 1919). He was undoubtedly resilient physically, hard working and competent yet he started and finished the First Word War as a Major. The explanation is perhaps to be found in his WW1 File, where he is shown as serving with the Regiment until 1st August 1916. He was then appointed Deputy Assistant Provost Marshall. It is likely that a year in the trenches at forty years of age was quite enough, when he was probably still suffering from recurring bouts of malaria, the consequence of his years in West Africa. Major Williams is shown as being finally demobilised on 1st April 1921.

George William was the third child of Charles Henry Williams, a solicitor from Cheltenham who had emigrated in about 1860 to the Falkland Islands to try sheep farming. George was educated in England, at the aratory school Baylis House. In 1885 he entered Stoneyhurst College . Little is known about him between 1890 and 1900 other than he had been in America and Western Australia. His appointment as Lieutenant, 3rd Battalion South Nigeria Regiment is dated 26th June 1901. He was awarded six clasps to his Africa General Service Medal. He applied for a transfer to the Civil Police, was transferred to the "Civil" as an Assistant District Commissioner but did not remain long, resigning on the 16th February 1906 and in April the same year was gazetted a Captain in the 4th Battalion South Staffordshire Regiment. He commanded a detachment of the Regiment for duty at the Coronation of King George V on 22nd-23rd June, 1911. He married Miss Alice Lock, the daughter of Brigadier General F.A.E. Lock CB, late Indian Army. Promotion to Major followed on 12th June 1912. He first saw service during WW1 with the B.E.F., 27th December 1915. He joined the 2nd battalion on 10th January 1916, as second in command. He was in command of the unit on the occasions when the commanding officer was absent on leave or courses. On the 1st August he was appointed Assistant Provost Marshall, this appointment he kept until he was demobilised in 1921. Major Williams died on the 19th February 1935 aged 60 years. A Requiem mass was held at "Our Lady of Victories", Kensington, followed by burial at Kensal Green. For a full account of his life and army career see article "A Falkland Islander DSO" by Keith Steward F.R.G.S. in the O.M.R.S. journal summer 2000.

THE MILITARY CROSS

THE Army, unlike the Royal Navy, who possessed the Distinguished Service Cross, did not have a gallantry award for issue to junior commissioned officers or warrant officers at the beginning of the First World War. The demands for such an award made it necessary to institute the Military Cross by Royal Warrant dated 28th December 1914.

The Military Cross is very simple in design being a cross of silver having on each arm the Imperial Crown and in the centre the Sovereign's cipher. The ribbon is distinctive, being three equal stripes of white, purple and white. Bars may be added for further awards.

Temporary 2nd Lieutenant Albert George ALLEN. Citation London Gazette 26.09.1916 page 9422.

"For conspicuous gallantry during operations. He carried out a very dangerous reconnaissance, crawling out twice by daylight close up to the enemy's position. He was heavily sniped at, but located the enemy in a trench previously reported as unoccupied."

Temp 2nd Lieutenant Harry APPLEBY. 4th Battalion attached 2nd Battalion. Citation London Gazette 24.09.1918 page 11287.

"For conspicuous gallantry and devotion to duty in carrying out a very daring reconnaissance under intense rifle and machine gun fire until he could observe the enemy dispositions and return with information enabling a position to be taken which held up a further advance by the enemy."

2nd Lieutenant (Temporary Lieutenant) John Alfred ARMSTRONG. 1st Battalion attached 8th Battalion. London Gazette 26.11.1917 page 12318, Citation London Gazette 06.04.1918 page 4206.

"When the commanding officer and all company officers had become casualties he took command of the battalion under the most difficult conditions. He organised the defence of the ground won, and set a splendid example of courage and devotion to duty."

2nd Lieutenant (Temporary Lieutenant Charles Henry ASBURY. 3rd Battalion attached Machine Gun Corps. Citation London Gazette 26.05.1917 page 5179.

"For conspicuous gallantry and devotion to duty. He handled his machine guns with great skill, silencing a hostile machine gun and inflicting heavy casualties on the enemy. He set a splendid example to his men."

2nd Lieutenant (Temporary Lieutenant) Cyril A. ASHFORD. 1/6th Battalion. London Gazette 27.06.1916 page 7444. Citation London Gazette 19.08.1916 page 8227.

"For conspicuous gallantry. He volunteered for and led a raid on the enemy's trenches, but at their parapet all his party except himself became casualties. He then, with the assistance of a wounded officer and some wounded men, brought back the seriously wounded and dead to our lines."

Lieutenant Harry Guiselin ATKIN. Attached Yorkshire Regiment. London Gazette 17.12.1917 page 13181. Citation London Gazette 23.04.1918 page 4860.

"When the advance was held up he had reached an advanced position with a handful of men. He held on in spite of heavy rifle and machine gun fire from both flanks until the consolidation was complete, and skilfully withdrew his remaining men when almost surrounded. It was largely due to his actions that the gains of the day were held."

2nd Lieutenant (Acting Captain Robert Henry ATKINSON. 3rd Battalion Special Reserve attached 2nd Battalion. London Gazette 08.03.1919 page 3236. Citation London Gazette 04.10.1919 page 12268.

"He was in command of a company near Havrincourt on the night September 27/28, 1918 by personal reconnaissance he was enabled to take up a second outpost line, from which he advanced to the attack on Cantaing line at dawn the next morning. In this attack he showed great gallantry and skill, his company accounting for many of the enemy, besides capturing several machine guns, in which he took a prominent part."

Temporary Captain Eric BACHE. 1st Battalion. Citation London Gazette 26.07.1918 page 8772.

"For conspicuous gallantry and devotion to duty in command of his company and later the battalion, when his CO became a casualty. He made a personal reconnaissance, when the situation was obscure, getting with 15 yards of the enemy, and later extricated his battalion from a difficult position without loss."

Temporary 2nd Lieutenant John BAKER. Attached 1/6th Battalion. London Gazette 08.03.1919 page 3236. Citation London Gazette 04.10.1919 page 12268.

"In the operations at Bellenglise on September 29th, 1918, he showed great gallantry and leadership in getting his platoon across the canal by compelling a prisoner to lead the way and test the depth of water, and afterwards pulling his men after him by means of a rope."

Lieutenant (Acting Captain) George Herbert BALL DSO. 1/5th Battalion. London Gazette 08.03.1919 page 3236. Citation London Gazette 04.10.1919 page 12269.

"On October 12, 1918, east of Bohain he led an attack on the south west edge of Riqueval Wood. The enemy barrage disorganised the attack, and drove it back temporarily. He reorganised his company, and with the help of part of another company, he again attacked, gaining the edge of the wood occupying a line some 200 yards into the wood. His great gallantry and devotion to duty won the admiration of his men."

Lieutenant (Temporary Captain) Joesph Alloysius BALLION. Attached 7th Battalion. London Gazette 02.04.1919 page 4324. Citation London Gazette 10.12.1919 page 15315.

"As adjutant during the advance through Abancourt on the afternoon 9th October, 1918, he frequently under heavy fire,

proceeded in advance of the battalion in order to find the route. Both before and after this event he carried out his duties regardless of his personal safety under the most adverse conditions, and often under heavy artillery fire."

2nd Lieutenant David Crawford Gordon BARDSLEY. 3rd Battalion attached 1st Battalion. London Gazette 18.01.1918 page 995. Citation London Gazette 25.04.1918 page 4995.

"For conspicuous gallantry and devotion to duty. He led the right flank of his brigade in an attack to the exact position of the final objective. He frequently exposed himself to heavy fire to take compass bearings."

Captain Harold BARKWORTH. 9th Battalion. Citation London Gazette 14.11.1916 page 11045.

"For conspicuous gallantry in action. He dug a communication trench under very heavy fire, displaying great courage and determination; he set a splendid example to his men."

Temporary 2nd Lieutenant Osborn BARLOW. 8th Battalion. Citation London Gazette 18.07.1917 page 7720. (Died of Wounds 14.04.1918)

"For conspicuous gallantry and devotion to duty. He commanded a platoon, which was held up by enemy wire. Despite a galling fire from machine guns he walked up and down urging and directing his men. Though wounded in both arms, he remained at duty."

Lieutenant E.C. BARTLETT. 1st Battalion. London Gazette 18.02.1915 page 1694.

No Citation.

2nd Lieutenant Charles BATES DSO, DCM. 4th Battalion. Citation London Gazette 16.09.1918 page 10918.

"For conspicuous gallantry and devotion to duty in repelling an enemy attack by the skilful use of his Lewis Guns, and reorganising the right flank, when he succeeded in keeping the enemy back all day. On the following day although the position was almost surrounded, he held on till late in the evening, and then extricated himself and his men from a very awkward position. His energy and courage were most conspicuous throughout several day's fighting."

Temporary 2nd Lieutenant Richard BAXTER. 2nd Battalion. Citation London Gazette 17.04.1917 page 3678.

"For conspicuous gallantry and devotion to duty. He rendered invaluable service in rallying and reorganising the remnants of the companies and taking out parties for the repair of our wire. He has on many previous occasions done fine work."

Lieutenant (Temporary Captain) Ernest BELL. 1st Battalion. Citation London Gazette 03.03.1917 page 2191.

"For conspicuous gallantry in action. He led his company in the attack with great gallantry. Later although severely wounded, he continued to encourage his men. He has previously done fine work."

2nd Lieutenant Arthur BELLERSON. 2nd Battalion. Citation London Gazette 02.12.1918 page 14229.

"For conspicuous gallantry and devotion to duty during an attack. He was instrumental in the capture of several machine guns and trench mortars, and although wounded, he remained with his platoon and was of great assistance in the reorganisation of his position after capture. His courageous bearing and fine example were most marked."

Captain Norman Pellew BIRLEY DSO. 3rd Battalion Special Reserve. London Gazette 26.09.1917 page 9973. Citation London Gazette 09.01.1918 page 587.

"For conspicuous gallantry and devotion to duty under trying circumstances, in visiting the HQ of two units when the

situation had become obscure, on both occasions passing through heavy hostile barrage and machine gun fire. Throughout the day he set a splendid example of coolness and cheerfulness under fire."

Temporary 2nd Lieutenant Walter Geoffrey BOLDERO. 11th Battalion attached Machine Gun Corps. Citation London Gazette 18.07.1917 page 7222.

"For conspicuous gallantry and devotion to duty. He handled two machine guns with great skill and initiative at a very critical period. By his prompt action and good leadership, he succeeded in driving off several parties of the enemy who were trying to turn the flank."

2nd Lieutenant William Evelyn BOOT. Royal Lancs Regt attached SSR. Citation London Gazette 16.09.1918 page 10923.

"For conspicuous gallantry and devotion to duty. He led battalion headquarters with great determination and dash in a counter attack against the enemy, driving them through a village and fields beyond, and finally capturing a company commander. Later at a critical moment, he used a Lewis gun so effectively as to save the situation. He did fine service."

2nd Lieutenant (Temporary Lieutenant) Eustace Walter BOOTH. 1st Battalion. London Gazette 01.01.1917 page 31.

No Citation. New Years Honour.

Lieutenant (Acting Major) Norman Sandeman BOSTOCK. 6th Battalion. London Gazette 03.06.1918 page 6463.

No Citation. King's Birthday Honour.

Norman Sandeman BOSTOCK MC. Bar to MC. London Gazette 03.06.1919 page 6822.

No Citation. King's Birthday Honour.

2nd Lieutenant John Frederick BOURNE. 2/5th Battalion "A" Company. London Gazette 17.12.1917 page 13181 Citation London Gazette 23.04.1918 pages 4681-2

"For conspicuous gallantry and devotion to duty when conducting pack animals to a forward position. When the enemy put down a heavy barrage on the track he off loaded the loads of his animals that had been killed and succeeded in delivering them, himself leading pack animals through the barrage several times to take them up. By this action he prevented further casualties."

2nd Lieutenant (Acting Captain) George Edward BRADBURY. 1/5th Battalion. Citation London Gazette 16.09.1918 page 10925.

"For conspicuous gallantry and devotion to duty. Leading the left company in an attack, he took all his objectives and relieved the right company which was held up, ensuring the success of the attack, and being instrumental in the capture of 54 prisoners and 5 machine guns. He did splendid service."

Quartermaster & Honorary Lieutenant Samuel BRADBURY. 1st Battalion. London Gazette 14.01.1916 page 586 (For 01.01.1916).

No Citation. New Years Honour.

Lieutenant (Acting Captain) Reginald BRIARS. 1/5th Battalion. London Gazette 03.06.1919 page 6824.

No Citation. King's Birthday Honour.

2nd Lieutenant Ernest Bertram BROWN. 1/5th Battalion. Citation London Gazette 11.05.1917 page 4589.

"For conspicuous gallantry and devotion to duty. He led two platoons into the enemy's lines and maintained his position until ordered to retire. He assisted to bring in several wounded men under heavy fire and throughout set a splendid example to his men."

Temporary 2nd Lieutenant Wilfred Ben BROWN. Attached 1/5th Battalion. London Gazette 08.03.1919 page 3237. Citation London Gazette 04.10.1919 page 12275.

"On September 29, 1918, north of Bellenglise, he showed marked gallantry and determination. Collected men from different units, he plunged into the canal, and with some twenty men secured the high bank of the opposite side, capturing four machine guns and crews who attempted opposition. Having secured his post, he returned into the water and remained waist deep in it for nearly an hour, having hauled men across, and then finally reorganising them for the next advance."

TEMPORARY Captain Edgar Lionel BROWNING MC. 9th Battalion. London Gazette 01.01.1917 page 31.

No Citation. New Years Honour.

Edgar Lionel BROWNING MC. Bar to MC. London Gazette 27.10.1917 page 11108. Citation London Gazette 18.03.1918 page 3418.

"For conspicuous gallantry and devotion to duty. He was detailed to construct two strong points and two tracks in an advanced position, and by skilful organisation completed the work in the face of great difficulties. Later, when entrusted with a most important piece of wiring, in spite of continuous heavy shelling by his splendid example of courage and leadership he completed the allotted task, and also wired an additional length of trench, thereby helping considerably to consolidate the captured position."

Lieutenant Leslie Colyn BULL. 2nd Battalion. London Gazette 04.06.1917 page 5477.

No Citation. King's Birthday Honour.

Temporary 2nd Lieutenant Percy William BURGESS MM. 6th Battalion. London Gazette 26.11.1917 page 12318. Citation London Gazette 06.04.1918 page 4208.

"For conspicuous gallantry and devotion to duty in an attack on an enemy post. While he was cutting the wire the enemy attempted to escape. He immediately rushed past and turned them back into a sap, where five were killed and one taken prisoner. He himself shot two, and it was entirely due to his splendid dash and careful previous reconnaissance that the encounter terminated successfully."

Lieutenant (Temporary Captain) Edward Percival Sevier BURNETT. 3rd Battalion seconded to 11th Battalion Tank Corps. London Gazette 02.04.1919 page 4325. Citation London Gazette 10.12.1919 page 15321.

"On the 8th October 1918, at Villers Outreaux he effected liaison with the infantry when they seemed hesitating to follow the tanks. By his personal direction on that occasion the formidable series of trenches and defences were captured at small cost to the infantry. His courage and leadership inspired all the crews of his section and was the means of bringing the infantry on to their correct objectives at a minimum cost."

Temporary Captain Richard Parry BURNETT. 8th Battalion. London Gazette 01.01.1917 page 31.

No Citation. New Years Honour.

2nd Lieutenant Leslie Frederick BURTON MM. 1/5th Battalion London Gazette 18.01.1918 page 995, Citation London Gazette 25.04.1918 page 4997.

"For conspicuous gallantry and devotion to duty. He pushed forward a fighting patrol through the enemy's wire, and cut a

gap in the face of heavy rifle fire and bombing. While in the wire he wounded two of the enemy. Entering the trench with four men he forced the garrison to evacuate their post, except for one man, whom, he shot, and brought back an identification."

2nd Lieutenant (Temp Captain) John Ford BYGOTT. 1st Battalion. Attached HQ 91st Infantry Brigade. London Gazette 03.06.1919, page 6940. (Italy)

No Citation. King's Birthday Honour.

2nd Lieutenant George BYGRAVE. 1st Battalion. Citation London Gazette 03.03.1917, page 2192.

"For conspicuous gallantry in action. He made several journeys backwards and forwards from the front line under heavy fire, and sent back most valuable information. Later, he greatly assisted in reorganizing and consolidating the position."

8860 Company Sergeant Major Frank BYTHEWAY DCM. 1st Battalion. Citation London Gazette 27.07.1916 page 7443. Killed in Action 14.07.1916.

"For conspicuous gallantry when assisting his company commander to rally and lead on his men. When his company commander became a casualty he took command and was conspicuous in the successful assault of an enemy position."

2nd Lieutenant Edmund Barry CAHUSAC. Attached Royal Flying Corps. Citation London Gazette 11.05.1917. page 4590.

"For conspicuous gallantry and devotion to duty. He carried out a successful artillery observation on a hostile battery in very adverse weather. He worked for two and a half hours at a height of 1,500 and 3,000 feet under very heavy fire. On another occasion whilst engaged in photography, he drove off three hostile scouts and completed his work."

2nd Lieutenant Stanley CALDWELL. 4th Battalion (attached 2nd Bn) South Staffordshire Regiment. Citation London Gazette 24.06.1916 page 6298.

"For conspicuous gallantry during a successful raid on the enemy's trenches. He commanded one party in the assault, made his way through strong wire, bombed several trenches, and saw all of his men out before leaving the enemy's trench. He showed great coolness and initiative."

Temporary Captain (Acting Major) John Jackson CAMERON DSO. Attached 23rd Battalion Royal Fusiliers. London Gazette 01.01.1918. Page 32.

No Citation. New Years Honour.

Lieutenant Hugh Clay CARTER. 6th Battalion Attached 2nd Battalion. London Gazette 03.06.1918 page 6464.

No Citation. King's Birthday Honour.

Lieutenant William Henry CARTER. 2nd Battalion Citation. London Gazette 23.12.1915 page 12799.

"For consistent good work throughout the campaign, notably on 24th November, 1915. The enemy exploded a mine under Gibson's Crater, south of the La Basse road, killing and wounding most of the garrison. Lieutenant Carter at once went up and commenced reorganizing the defences of the crater. He was slightly wounded, but remained at his post, and it was mainly due to his courage and example that two hostile bomb attacks on the crater were repulsed. He also organized a bomb attack on the enemy, thus keeping them quiet for four hours while the position was being consolidated."

William Henry CARTER. Bar to MC. Citation London Gazette 09.09.1916 page 8872.

"For conspicuous and consistent gallantry. Hardly a week passes without his name being brought to notice for some act of

devotion and gallantry. Lately he carried out a most gallant rescue work under fire after a night raid. He arrived in France in August, 1914, as signalling sergeant of the battalion, and has been with it in every action. Nothing effects his courage and nerve."

Temporary Captain Robert CHARLTON. 7th Battalion. Died of Wounds 05.10.1917. London Gazette 18.10.1917 page 10708. Citation London Gazette 07.03.1918 page 2909.

"For conspicuous gallantry and devotion to duty. During an attack he made a reconnaissance of the position under enemy fire, and brought back valuable information. Subsequently, when the posts held by his company were being heavily shelled, he continually went from post to post under heavy rifle fire and machine gun fire, encouraging his men and supervising the work of consolidation."

Captain (Acting Major) Cecil Ernest Wells CHARRINGTON. 4th Battalion Attached 2nd Battalion. Citation London Gazette 26.07.1918 page 8786.

"For conspicuous gallantry and devotion to duty in command of his company. When the enemy broke through on the right of his line he changed the front of his command and met the new conditions with great coolness, reorganizing the whole of his defences under heavy fire. Subsequently he conducted the retirement with great skill, being the last man to leave the vicinity."

Captain J.C. CHAYTOR. 2nd Battalion. London Gazette 23.06.1915 page 6123.

No Citation. King's Birthday Honour (For 03.06.1915).

Temporary Captain Edward James CLARK MB RAMC. Attached 7th Battalion SSR. London Gazette. 17.12.1917 page 13181. Citation London Gazette 23.04.1918 page 4863.

"For conspicuous gallantry and devotion to duty as medical officer to a battalion. Though continuously under heavy shell fire he moved about in the open attending to the wounded, and undoubtedly saved many lives."

Temporary Lieutenant Cecil Vandepeer CLARKE. 9th Battalion. London Gazette 03.06.1919 page 6940.

No Citation. King's Birthday Honour.

Temporary Captain Guy Cecil Richard COLERIDGE. 1st Battalion, attached 8th Battalion. London Gazette 01.01.1917 page 32.

No Citation. New Years Honour.

Temporary Lieutenant William Cockayne CONLEY. 1st Battalion. Citation London Gazette 03.03.1917 page 2192. (Killed in Action 26.10.1917 attached to 91 T.M.B.)

"For conspicuous gallantry in action. He carried on his work of consolidation with great energy under heavy fire. He pushed forward advanced posts and sent back most valuable information. He set a splendid example throughout."

2nd Lieutenant Meynell Frederick Bentley CORNFORTH. 3rd Battalion Special Reserve Attached 9th Battalion. London Gazette 02.04.1919 ,page 4326 (Italy). Citation London Gazette 10.12.1919 page 15325.

"For conspicuous gallantry and devotion to duty on the night 31st October/ 1st November, 1918, at Sacile. Under direct hostile machine gun and rifle fire, he succeeded after two attempts in throwing a footbridge across the River Livenza, thus enabling the attacking infantry to continue their advance. His coolness and personal gallantry were an inspiration to all ranks and materially assisted in the success of the operations."

7502 Company Sergeant Major William COX. 2nd Battalion. Citation London Gazette 13.02.1917 page 1544.

"For conspicuous gallantry in action. Although wounded he continued to lead his men with great courage and determination. Later, he rendered most valuable assistance in organizing the defence of the position."

2nd Lieutenant Percy COZENS. 1/5th Battalion. Citation London Gazette 16.08.1917 page 8363.

"During a raid upon an enemy trench his platoon was held up by wire before reaching the trench. With complete disregard of personal safety, although already wounded, he crawled to the trench, and conducted a bombing attack upon the enemy, thereby preventing them from bombing that portion of the raiding party that had succeeding in doing this."

Captain Leslie Charles CRICK. 6th Bn Lincolnshire Regiment attached 7th Battalion. London Gazette 02.04.1918 page 4326. Citation London Gazette 10.12.1919 page 15326.

"He did exceptionally fine work on the night 6/7th October 1918, when his company made a successful attack on the village of Aubencheul-au-Bac. By personal reconnaissance, he succeeded in obtaining sufficient information to get his company through the enemy wire and to occupy the village and establish posts on the canal de la Sensee during the night."

2nd Lieutenant Gordon Ernest CRONK. 1/5th Battalion. Citation London Gazette 11.05.1917 page 4590.

"For conspicuous gallantry and devotion to duty during a night attack on the enemy's trenches he directed the organization and despatch of bombing parties on the enemy's trenches, and personally obtained touch with the company on the right."

2nd Lieutenant Frank Parker CROSSE. 1st Battalion (& 8th Bn). Citation London Gazette 26.11.1915 page 11534.

"For conspicuous gallantry in action. With another officer he carried out a daring patrol in daylight entering an enemy night post and obtaining most valuable information. Later, he led a successful raid and was again similarly successful."

Temporary Captain Hugh Ellis Davies CULLEN. 9th Battalion. London Gazette 01.01.1918 page 34.

No Citation. New Years Honour.

Temporary Lieutenant (Acting Captain) Herbert Ayres CUNDALL. 1st Battalion. Citation London Gazette 18.07.1917, page 7226.

"For conspicuous gallantry and devotion to duty during an attack, when although severely wounded he continued to lead his men on with great bravery until wounded a second time. He has on previous occasions done fine work."

Temporary Lieutenant Stuart Gordon CUXON. 1st Battalion. Citation London Gazette 16.09.1918 page 10939.

"For conspicuous gallantry and devotion to duty when in command of three platoons. He led them with great skill and determination, and played a leading part in overcoming the enemy's resistance. He shot one of the enemy dead with his revolver. Both before and during the operation his example infused his men with keenness and courage."

2nd Lieutenant Raymond Tom DANIELS. 2nd Battalion. Citation London Gazette 15.10.1918 page 12069.

"For conspicuous gallantry and devotion to duty while in command of a trench mortar battery. Four mortars of his battery were barraging during a raid by the infantry. Several minutes after zero a heavy bombardment of the area in which the mortars were in action commenced, many shells falling very close to the open positions of the mortars. It was largely due to the excellent example and forceful direction of this officer that the mortars kept up their rate of fire under exceedingly difficult conditions."

Captain George DAWES DSO. 2nd Battalion. London Gazette 14.01.1916 page 577 (For 01.01.1916).

No Citation. New Years Honour.

Lieutenant A. de HAMEL. 4th Battalion. London Gazette 14.01.1916 page 582 (For 01.01.1916).

No Citation. New Years Honour.

Captain Joseph Leslie DENT DSO. 2nd Battalion. Citation London Gazette 03.06.1916 page 5572. (Killed in Action 11.04.1917)

No Citation. King's Birthday Honour.

Temporary 2nd Lieutenant William Brewis DENT. 2nd Battalion Attached Machine Gun Corps. Citation London Gazette 17.09.1917, page 9567.

"For conspicuous gallantry and devotion to duty in handling his machine guns with the utmost dash and efficiency in support of an infantry attack. His own gun being put out of action, he went in search of an enemy gun, which he secured and got into action. His conduct was highly praised by the infantry whom he was supporting, and to whom he rendered most valuable support."

2nd Lieutenant L.T. DESPICHT. 4th Battalion Bedfordshire Regiment attached 2nd Battalion South Staffordshire Regiment. Citation London Gazette 10.03.1915 page 2461.

"For conspicuous gallantry at Givenchy on 20th February. 1915, when in command of the right storming party, he was almost buried by a German shell. After being extricated he was immediately shot, but crawled to the enemy's parapet, and there continued to conduct operations."

2nd Lieutenant William Anthony DICKENS. 1st Battalion. Citation London Gazette 25.11.1916 page 11535.

"For conspicuous gallantry in action. With another officer he carried out a daring patrol in daylight, entering an enemy night post and obtaining most valuable information. Later, he led a successful raid and captured two prisoners."

2nd Lieutenant Norman Reginald DICKSON. 6th Battalion. London Gazette 18.10.1917 page 10708. Citation London Gazette 07.03.1918 page 2912.

"For conspicuous gallantry and devotion to duty during a raid on the enemy's trenches. He commanded one of the parties in the raid, and showed the greatest spirit and determination throughout. Prior to the raid he carried out three patrols and obtained information which was of the greatest importance to the success of the operation."

Temporary Lieutenant James Eric DIXON. 8th Battalion. Citation. London Gazette 30.03.1916 page 3426.

"For conspicuous gallantry. When his trench had been very heavily shelled for two hours and he heard that the enemy were advancing on his right, he went over the parapet and crawled forward, under heavy fire to see if they were preparing for an attack on his own trench. He was badly wounded."

2nd Lieutenant William DRAYCOTT-WOOD. 2nd Battalion. London Gazette 23.06.1915 page 6123. Killed in Action 29th June 1915.

No Citation. King's Birthday Honour.

Lieutenant Cyril EASTOUGH. 3rd Battalion. Special Reserve. London Gazette 18.02.1918 page 2159. Citation London Gazette 18.07.1918 page 8458.

"For conspicuous gallantry and devotion to duty. He led his platoon to the attack and drove back the enemy. Though wounded, he continued the advance, established a bombing block, and reorganized his men. He showed great courage and determination."

Lieutenant Godfrey Lewis Trevor EATON. 3rd Battalion Attached 1st Battalion. London Gazette 03.06.1919. page 6941 (Italy).

No Citation. King's Birthday Honour.

Captain (Temporary Major) G. ELWELL. 6th Battalion. London Gazette 01.01.1919 page 25.

No citation. New Years Honour.

2nd Lieutenant Cyril Stuart EMBREY. 1/5th Battalion. Citation London Gazette 15.10.1918 page 12071. Killed in Action 12.10.1918. Attached 6th Battalion.

"For conspicuous gallantry and devotion to duty when on patrol. He located an enemy post consisting of one officer and seven men. With a party of five he rushed the post, captured two prisoners and killed one of the enemy. The remainder ran away. He displayed great initiative, coolness and dash."

Temp Lieutenant William Richard ENGLISH-MURPHY DSO. 1st Battalion. London Gazette 01.01.1917 page 33.

No Citation. New Years Honour.

Lieutenant Arthur Ford ENNALS. (Walsall) 5th Battalion Attached 9th Battalion Yorkshire Light Infantry. Citation London Gazette 02.12.1918 page 14238.

"For conspicuous gallantry and devotion to duty during an attack. On a dark night he successfully directed two battalions straight on to their objective. While doing so he was blown over by a shell, but held on. It was largely owing to his good work that the attacking force arrived at the objective which it had been ordered to capture. Throughout the operations he set a fine example to his men."

Lieutenant Charles Wilmot EVANS. London Gazette 23.06.1915 page 6123. Killed in Action (Captain) 01.07.1916.

No Citation. King's Birthday Honour.

2nd Lieutenant John Frederick Gwyn EVANS. 4th Battalion. Citation London Gazette 13.02.1917 page 1540-1.

"For conspicuous gallantry in action. When the attack was held up he formed a block, and by his great example to the men under him, although very short of bombs, checked an enemy counter attack."

2nd Lieutenant Harold Walter FORD. 6th Battalion Attached 7th Battalion, Attached HQ 53 Infantry Brigade. London Gazette 03.06.1919 page 6827.

No Citation. King's Birthday Honour.

Temporary Captain Howard FORREST. 7th Battalion. London Gazette 02.04.1919 page 4327. Citation London Gazette 10.12.1919 page 15333.

"On the night of 6th October 1918, near Fressies, information was received that the enemy had withdrawn from the railway.

He was ordered to send out a strong patrol at once to take up a position commanding the railway. This he succeeded in accomplishing under heavy fire. On the 9th October during the advance through Abancourt, he led his company with marked skill and dash and eventually took up a forward position under difficult circumstances."

Lieutenant (Acting Major) James Milroy FREW. 1/6th Battalion. Attached from 7th Battalion Royal Scots. Citation London Gazette 20.10.1916 page 10181.

"For conspicuous gallantry during a raid. He handled his portion of the raiding party with great skill and determination, showing initiative of a high order. The success of the raid was largely due to his good leading."

James Milroy FREW. Bar to MC. London Gazette 08.03.1919 page 3229. Citation London Gazette 04.10.1919 page 12242.

"For conspicuous gallantry and ability at Bellenglise on the 29th September, 1918. He was sent to ascertain the position of the attacking troops as a thick fog prevented anything being seen from the rear. Besides sending useful information back to battalion headquarters, he collected some men who had temporarily lost direction, and led them forward, and was thus able to push the enemy back and capture a body of 50. His action greatly encouraged the men round him. His work just previous to the attack was invaluable to his commanding officer."

Temporary Lieutenant James Francis GADD. 9th Battalion. London Gazette 04.06.1917 page 5479.

No Citation. King's Birthday Honour.

3/9737 Company Sergeant Major George GARDNER. 1st Battalion. Citation London Gazette 26.05.1917 page 5185.

"For conspicuous gallantry and devotion to duty in digging a line of posts in open ground swept by fire. He continually moved from post to post over fire swept ground in order to supervise the work of consolidation. He set a fine example of coolness and courage."

Lieutenant Frederick John GIBBS. Attached Royal Flying Corps. London Gazette 26.09.1917 page 9975. Citation 09.01.1918 page 607.

"For conspicuous gallantry in attacking enemy aircraft and engaging hostile troops from the ground. He has in all driven down five enemy machines which were destroyed, and another completely out of control. He has also attacked and silenced a hostile battery with machine gun fire, displaying on every occasion the same dash and determined offensive spirit."

Temporary Captain William GIBSON. 8th Battalion. Citation London Gazette 25.08.1916 page 8460.

"For conspicuous gallantry during the capture of an enemy position. Though wounded, he carried up a machine gun to an important position."

Lieutenant Robert Henry S. GILLENDER. Special Reserve attached 1/5th Battalion. London Gazette 08.03.1919 page 3240. Citation London Gazette 04.10.1919 page 12292.

"On September 29th, 1918, north of Bellenglise, he commanded the right front company. He was severely wounded on the west bank of the canal, but his splendid energy and powers of organizing, combined with his fearless leadership, stood his company to the good, and enabled them to carry out their task to the final objective."

Temporary 2nd Lieutenant Richard Wilson Arnall GLEED. 8th Battalion. London Gazette 26.11.1917 page 12319. Citation London Gazette 06.04.1918 page 4213.

"He led the front line of the attack with the utmost coolness and courage, and though blown up and wounded by a shell,

continued to direct his men. After having had his wound treated, he returned to the front line and remained with his men, though suffering severely, until they were relieved."

Captain Guy de Coursey GLOVER DSO. 2nd Battalion. London Gazette 15.02.1917 page 1596. See amendment 23.07.1917 page 7461.

No Citation. New Years Honour.

Captain William Charles GREEN. 1st Battalion. London Gazette 01.01.1918 page 37.

No Citation. New Years Honour.

Captain William Charles GREEN MC. Bar to MC. Citation London Gazette 24.09.1918, page 11282.

"For conspicuous gallantry and devotion to duty during an enemy attack. When the enemy had broken through on his left and his company suffered severe losses, he rallied the remainder of his men and held on for a considerable time. Having lost touch with troops on his right, he withdrew to a trench in the rear and again maintained touch with them. His numbers being greatly depleted, he attached himself to the troops on the right until wounded the following day."

Lieutenant John Hubert GRICE. 5th Battalion. Citation London Gazette 16.09.1918 page 10957.

"For conspicuous gallantry and devotion to duty. When the guns under his command ran short of ammunition and a hostile machine gun which had been silenced opened fire again, harassing the infantry, and he was wounded by a shell, he refused to leave, but organized a carrying party, he went through a heavy barrage to the nearest dump, returning with a large supply of ammunition, which eventually silenced the machine gun, and led to its capture with the crew."

Captain Charles Grice GRICE-HUTCHINSON. 7th Battalion. London Gazette 03.06.1916 page 5573.

No Citation. King's Birthday Honour.

2nd Lieutenant Richard Melville HALL. 2nd Battalion. Citation London Gazette 14.11.1916 page 11054.

"For conspicuous gallantry in action. He displayed great gallantry and devotion to duty in carrying orders under very heavy fire, and in conducting parties with stores."

Lieutenant (Temporary Captain) Charles Cecil HARLAND. 7th Battalion. London Gazette 01.01.1918 page 37.

No Citation. New Years Honour.

Captain Sidney HARPER. 2nd Battalion. London Gazette 01.01.1918 page 37.

No Citation. New Years Honour.

Lieutenant (Acting Captain) Gilbert Spencer HARRIS. 1/6th Battalion. London Gazette 08.03.1919 page 3241. Citation London Gazette 04.10.1919 page 12296.

"In the attack north of Sequehart on October 3, 1918, he displayed marked gallantry and initiative. In command of his company he overcame very strong opposition, and reached the final objective. Here his company was exposed to enfilade rifle and machine gun fire which he neutralized by skilful disposition of his men. He personally reconnoitred the enemy position, showing absolute disregard to personal danger."

Temporary 2nd Lieutenant John Thomas HARRISON. Attached 1st Battalion. London Gazette 01.01.1919 page 66 (Italy).

No Citation. New Years Honour.

Captain Stanley Sextus Barrymore HARRISON. Royal Army Medical Corps Attached 1/5th Battalion South Staffordshire Regiment. Citation London Gazette 11.05.1917 page 4591.

"For conspicuous gallantry and devotion to duty. He worked continuously for ten hours under very heavy fire and was responsible for saving many lives. He displayed great courage and determination throughout. He has on many previous occasions done fine work."

2nd Lieutenant Ladas Lewis HASSELL DSO. 2nd Battalion. Citation London Gazette 30.03.1916 page 3428. (Also shown 1st SSR Awards)

"For conspicuous gallantry and fine work with his bombers. The success of an attack was largely due to his bombers and to his own energy and very gallant leading. He displayed great personal bravery, and was eventually severely wounded going over the open to fetch reinforcements."

2nd Lieutenant Basil Dudley HATCHETT. 6th Battalion. Citation London Gazette 17.09.1917 page 9572.

"For conspicuous gallantry and devotion to duty when in command of two guns. Whilst directing the fire under heavy enemy barrage a shell burst near his bomb store in close proximity to his guns. Without hesitation he removed a live bomb which was at the point of exploding from the centre of at least 200 rounds and threw it away, when it at once exploded. By his prompt and very gallant action he saved the lives of the gun teams as well in all probability the whole of the rest of the ammunition."

2nd Lieutenant Hubert HAWKES. 1/5th Battalion. Citation London Gazette 18.11.1915 page 11452.

"For conspicuous gallantry and good work at Hollenzollern Redoubt on 13th October 1915, when he repelled a heavy bombing attack on "Big Willie" trench. He directed his own bombing party with great coolness and ability, and prevented the Germans from establishing themselves in our portion of "Big Willie."

2nd Lieutenant Harold Albert HAWKINS. 4th Battalion. Citation London Gazette 24.09.1918 page 11298.

"For conspicuous gallantry and devotion to duty during enemy attacks. He carried on his work with great coolness under the most trying conditions, and throughout the fighting gave a fine example of devotion to duty, and was of the greatest assistance to his commanding officer".

Quartermaster & Hon Lieutenant Arthur HAZLEGROVE DCM. 2nd Battalion. London Gazette 01.01.1917 page 35.

No Citation. New Years Honour.

Lieutenant Joseph HAZELWOOD DCM. 2nd Battalion. London Gazette 04.06.1917 page 5480.

No Citation. King's Birthday Honour.

2nd Lieutenant Charles Cuthbert HEDGES. Royal Berkshire Regiment attached 2/5th Battalion SSR. London Gazette 04.02.1918 page 1604. Citation London Gazette 05.07.1918 page 7910.

"For conspicuous bravery. On December 1st near FONTAINE-NOTRE-DAME, the enemy put down a heavy barrage on our front line and an attack appeared imminent as the enemy had been reported to be massing at LA FOLIE WOOD. All telephone wires were cut and it was essential that communication should be established between the front line and support

companies. 2 Lt C.C. Hedges who was in the support company volunteered to obtain information from the right flank company where the situation was obscure. He was heavily fired on by enemy machine guns on leaving the trench and was under observation and constant machine gun and shell fire until he reached the headquarters of the right flank company, a distance of 1600 yards. He obtained information of great value and returned under fire to battalion headquarters."

Temporary 2nd Lieutenant John HERRINGTON. 9th Battalion. London Gazette 01.01.1919 page 66.

No Citation. New Years Honour.

Temporary Captain Reginald Lockyer HIBBERDINE. 1st Battalion. London Gazette 03.06.1919 page 6941 (Italy).

No Citation. King's Birthday Honour.

Temporary Lieutenant Richard Douglas HIGGS. 7th Battalion. London Gazette 02.04.1919 page 4328. Citation London Gazette 10.12.1919 page 15342.

"On the night 10th/11th October, 1918, in command of a company he made an attack on Hem-Lenglet in connection with another battalion. The night was exceedingly dark and the ground to be covered to reach the preliminary forming up point was swept by enemy machine gun fire. In spite of these difficulties the operation was entirely successful. Throughout he led his company with great courage and skill."

Lieutenant Philip HIGHFIELD-JONES. 6th Battalion. Citation London Gazette 17.09.1917 page 9572.

"For conspicuous gallantry and devotion to duty. During an attack upon a village he was in command of a company of moppers-up. Two of the attacking companies having suffered heavily under machine gun fire, he took command of the remnants and with great gallantry and determination cleared the enemy out of the houses, which had been occupied, inflicting heavy casualties upon them, and capturing eight prisoners and three machine guns. He showed great initiative and resource in the way in which he handled a difficult situation."

Captain John Norman HILDICK-SMITH. 6th Battalion. London Gazette 01.01.1918 page 38 (Indian Army).

No Citation. New Years Honour.

2nd Lieutenant Cyril Tom HINDE. 3rd Battalion attached 2nd Battalion. London Gazette 18.02.1918 page 2160. Citation London Gazette 18.07.1918 page 8462.

"He led a bombing attack on a position which the enemy had captured, and drove them back. He led a bombing attack at night under very heavy machine gun fire, and continued to bomb the enemy until he was the only man left. He showed splendid courage and initiative."

8575 Company Sergeant Major George Alfred HOLLIS. 2nd Battalion. Citation London Gazette 26.05.1917 page 5185.

"He carried out three daring patrols in order to collect the remnants of his company and to clear up the situation. Later he rendered invaluable service reorganizing his company in the defensive positions."

Temp Captain Ruldolph HOLLOCOMBE. 6th Battalion. London Gazette 01.01.1918 page 38.

No Citation. New Years Honour.

Temporary 2nd Lieutenant Frank HOYLE. 7th Battalion. London Gazette 18.01.1918 page 957. Citation London Gazette 25.04.1918 page 5004.

"His platoon was on the left of the front line of the battalion advance, when opposition was met from a concrete dug out. He

rushed round the dug out and approached it from the rear and with the help of two N.C.O's was instrumental in killing or capturing the whole garrison of twenty men. Later in the advance, another concrete dug out was encountered, and he repeated his tactics, again killing or capturing the garrison of one officer and thirty men."

2nd Lieutenant Hubert Murray HUSSEY. 2nd Battalion. London Gazette 18.02.1918 page 2160. Citation London Gazette 18.07.1918 page 8463. Killed in Action 06.08.1918.

"For conspicuous gallantry and devotion to duty during an attack. He continually took messages to other companies and to isolated positions under heavy fire. He reconnoitred the position, and obtained most valuable information and organized the ammunition supply. His energy and fearlessness were an inspiring example to all ranks."

Captain Clive HUTCHINSON. 7th Battalion. (Formerly Linconshire Regiment). London Gazette 14.01.1916 page 583 (for 1.1.1916).

No Citation. New Years Honour.

2nd Lieutenant David Patrick Cuthbert IMRIE. 1st Battalion London Regiment Attached. London Gazette Citation 16.09.1918 page 10970.

"For conspicuous gallantry and devotion to duty. He was in charge of a platoon occupying a strong point, and after both flanks had been forced back he held on and inflicted very heavy casualties on the enemy at close range, thus delaying the enemy's advance and allowing troops, which had been withdrawn, to take up a new position. His tireless energy and cheerfulness deserve the highest praise."

Lieutenant (Acting Captain) Harold Alfred IVATT. 5th Battalion. London Gazette 03.06.1916 page 5574. Killed in Action 21.05.1918.

No Citation. King's Birthday Honour.

2nd Lieutenant Robert Crake JEPHCOTT. 6th Battalion. Citation London Gazette 25.08.1917 page 8811.

"For conspicuous gallantry and devotion to duty. He led his platoon through heavy shell fire to construct a strong point. He carried out the work allotted to him, in spite of his being wounded, and of having to work under direct observation of the enemy."

Captain Samuel George JOHNSON DSO. 2nd Battalion. London Gazette 18.02.1915 page 1694.

No Citation.

2nd Lieutenant Clifford JONES. 1/5th Battalion. London Gazette 08.03.1919 page 3242. Citation London Gazette 04.10.1919 page 12306.

"During operations on September 29, 1918, north of Bellenglise when his company commander was severely wounded, he took command of the company, which he led with great skill and courage, reaching the final objective after capturing eight machine guns and four field guns. It was greatly due to his example and energy that the northern portion of the village of Bellenglise was cleared of the enemy."

Lieutenant Michael Joseph KAVANAGH. 2nd Battalion. Citation London Gazette 14.11.1916 page 11057.

"For conspicuous gallantry during operations. Though knocked over and wounded by a shell, he took over command of a machine gun company two days later, and, though suffering from shock and in considerable pain, stuck to his command and did good work."

Temporary Lieutenant (Acting Captain) Luther James KELSEY. 4th Battalion. London Gazette 01.01.1918 page 39.

No Citation. New Years Honour.

Temporary Lieutenant (Acting Captain) Frederick Arthur KENDRICK DSO. 1st Battalion. London Gazette 26.11.1917 page 12319. Citation London Gazette 06.04.1918 page 4217.

"For conspicuous gallantry and devotion to duty when in command of his company, who were "mopping up". He had previously been wounded when reconnoitering the position, but remained with his company until relieved two days later."

Frederick Arthur KENDRICK DSO. Bar to MC. Citation London Gazette 16.09.1918 page 10894.

"For conspicuous gallantry and devotion to duty in leading a raiding party. He deployed his party so skillfully that in spite of a bright moon the raid was a complete surprise. He led the attack with great dash, himself inflicting several casualties on the enemy. It was largely owing to his skilful handling that the raid was completely successful and cost but few casualties."

Captain Arthur Forbes Gordon KILBY VC. 2nd Battalion. London Gazette 18.02.1915 page 1694. Killed in Action 25.09.1915.

No Citation.

Lieutenant Leonard James KNIGHT. 5th Battalion Attached 1/6th Battalion. London Gazette 03.06.1919 page 6830.

No Citation. King's Birthday Honour.

Captain Harold Dunmore LANE. R.A.M.C. Attached 6th Battalion. London Gazette 18.10.1917 page 10710. Citation London Gazette 07.03.1918 page 2922.

"For conspicuous gallantry and devotion to duty. During a daylight raid on the enemy's trenches he established his aid post in the front line trench, and worked there for many hours under heavy artillery fire. He attended to the seriously wounded cases in the open, and was instrumental in bringing in all the wounded from No Man's Land and getting them successfully away."

Lieutenant (Acting Captain) Roger James Iddison LANE. 1st Battalion. Attached 2/6th Battalion. Citation London Gazette 26.07.1918 page 8816.

"For conspicuous gallantry and devotion to duty in handling his reserve mortars. Three times during the day our forward lines were penetrated, but each time he took up a fresh position to cover our infantry, near an emergency dump of ammunition, and quickly got his mortars into action. His promptness and initiative enabled severe losses to be inflicted on the enemy."

Roger James Iddison LANE MC. Bar to MC. Citation London Gazette 16.09.1918 page 10894.

"For conspicuous gallantry and devotion to duty. The enemy had delivered a heavy attack which was broken up with heavy casualties by the fire of the mortars, which were most skilfully handled by this officer, who was in command. The enemy sought cover just out of range, but one of the mortars was advanced to the front line, and a heavy bombardment of the locality carried out, by which, after a machine gun had been silenced, our infantry were able to advance and capture eighteen prisoners and the machine-gun."

2nd Lieutenant (Temporary Captain) Frederick Oswald LANGLEY. 6th Battalion. London Gazette 03.06.1916 page 5575.

No Citation. King's Birthday Honour.

2nd Lieutenant George John Raymond LANSDELL. 1st Battalion. London Gazette 26.11.1917 page 12319 Citation London Gazette 06.04.1918 page 2418.

"For conspicuous gallantry and devotion to duty as Brigade Transport Officer. He led a very large convoy of pack mules across a shelled zone over two and a half miles in depth, and so established a forward dump some 300 yards in the rear of the front line."

Captain William Henry LASLETT. R.A.M.C. Attached 7th Battalion. London Gazette 01.01.1918 page 40.

No Citation. New Years Honour.

Temporary Lieutenant (Temp Captain) Charles Aikin LAWFORD. Attached 1st Battalion. London Gazette 03.06.1918 page 6469 (Italy).

No Citation. King's Birthday Honour.

Lieutenant (Acting Captain) John LECKIE. Attached Machine Gun Corps. London Gazette 03.06.1919 page 6468.

No Citation. King's Birthday Honour.

2nd Lieutenant Alec Wilfred LEE. 1st Battalion. London Gazette 03.06.1916 page 5575.

No Citation. King's Birthday Honour.

Lieutenant (Temporary Captain) Charles Roy LIMBERY. 1st Battalion. London Gazette 14.01.1916 page 584. (For 01.01.1916. For action 25.09.1915). Killed in Action 01.07.1916.

No Citation. New Years Honour.

Captain Cecil LISTER DSO. Northumberland Fusiliers Attached 1/6th Battalion. London Gazette 14.01.1916 page 579 (For 01.01.1916).

No Citation. New Years Honour.

2nd Lieutenant Walter Harry Richardson LLOYDS. 4th Battalion Attached 8th Battalion. Citation London Gazette 24.09.1918 page 11301.

"For conspicuous gallantry and devotion to duty while in command of a company. When the battalion was almost surrounded he formed a flank guard under intense machine gun fire in conjunction with a rear guard, and thus enabled the remainder of the battalion to withdraw in good order to a new position. Next day he maintained his position on a hill under close range field gun fire. He showed fine gallantry and leadership."

Captain Harry Leslie Bache LOVATT OBE. South Staffords later Royal Engineers. London Gazette 01.01.1918 page 40.

No Citation. New Years Honour.

Lieutenant (Temporary Captain) Arthur Stanley LOWE. 4th Battalion Attached 16th Battalion Tank Corps. London Gazette 08.03.1919, page 3243. Citation London Gazette 04.10.1919 page 12312.

"For gallantry and devotion to duty on 17th October, 1918, at Vaux-Andigny, when in command of a section of Tanks. He accompanied his Tanks into action, and personally assisted the infantry in capturing an enemy post. His section did fine work during the day and very materially assisted the infantry, which was in the main due to his courageous example and excellent leadership."

Lieutenant Percival Rodd LOWMAN. 1st Battalion Attached Machine Gun Corps. London Gazette 03.06.1918 page 6468.

No Citation King's Birthday Honour.

Temporary Lieutenant Joseph Randolph Morell MACKENZIE. Royal Army Medical Corps Attached 1st Battalion. Citation London Gazette 18.07.1917 page 7236.

"For conspicuous bravery and devotion on numerous occasions when attending wounded and leading stretcher bearer parties under every kind of heavy and continuous fire, and invariably exhibiting great skill, coolness and contempt of danger."

2nd Lieutenant Stewart Gordon MAITLAND. 2/6th Battalion. Citation London Gazette 26.07.1918 page 8822.

"For conspicuous gallantry and devotion to duty. His right flank being exposed, he went out with an N.C.O., to try and locate any of our troops on that flank . The N.C.O. was captured, but this officer followed up the enemy, shot one of them, and enabled the N.C.O. to escape. He afterwards took charge of the exposed flank, and reorganized the line three times after it had been broken. He eventually withdrew the party in good order. By his resource and tenacity the enemy, who were surrounding him on both flanks, were held up at this point for several hours."

2nd Lieutenant (Temporary Captain) Howard Vivian MANDER. 6th Battalion. London Gazette 14.01.1916 page 588 (For 01.01.1916).

No Citation. New Years Honour.

Captain George Herbert Hind MANFIELD. R.A.M.C. Attached 6th Battalion. Citation London Gazette 25.08.1916 page 8463.

"For conspicuous gallantry and devotion to duty in action. He worked day and night tending the wounded in our advanced positions under heavy fire, and carried many of them down the trench after all his bearers had been wounded."

Captain Charles Harwood MANGER. 8th Battalion. London Gazette 04.06.1917 page 5481.

No Citation. King's Birthday Honour.

Temporary Lieutenant Harry Conrad MARRIOTT. 9th Battalion Attached 1/6th Battalion. London Gazette 08.03.1919 page 3243. Citation London Gazette 04.10.1919 page 12314.

"In the attack on Bellenglise on September 29, 1918, he showed most conspicuous gallantry and good leadership in getting his platoon across the canal and attacking the enemy right through to the final objective. His cheerfulness under great difficulties inspired a similar spirit in his men."

2nd Lieutenant Oswald Henry MASON. 5th Battalion North Staffordshire Regiment attached. Citation London Gazette 16.09.1918 page 10984.

"For conspicuous gallantry and devotion to duty when in command of a company. He formed a screen through which part of another battalion was ordered to retire. His excellent dispositions enabled this to be done with complete success. When forced later to withdraw his men, he stayed behind with his one remaining Lewis gun, inflicting severe losses on the enemy until his company had reached its new position. He set a very fine example of courage and good leadership."

Temporary Captain Creagh Ivor MASSY. 7th Battalion. Citation London Gazette 16.08.1917 page 8735.

"For conspicuous gallantry and devotion to duty. He displayed the greatest coolness and fearlessness whilst in command of two

companies in an attack, leading his men over three lines of enemy trenches under heavy fire of every description. His conduct was most inspiring and set a splendid example to all ranks, as has been the case throughout every operation in which he has been engaged."

Temporary 2nd Lieutenant Leslie Beauchamp MAUNSELL. Citation London Gazette 14.11.1916 page 11060.

"For conspicuous gallantry in action. After his machine gun teams had suffered severe casualties, he led them and attacked an enemy bombing party, shooting two of the enemy with his revolver. He displayed great courage and coolness. He was severely wounded."

2nd Lieutenant Sidney McGOWAN. Kings Own Scottish Border Regiment. Attached 6th Battalion SSR. Citation London Gazette 20.10.1916 page 10187.

"For conspicuous gallantry during a raid. He handled his portion of the raiding party with great skill and determination, and contributed largely to the success of the operation."

2nd Lieutenant (Acting Lieutenant) George Osborne MERCER. 3rd Battalion Attached Trench Mortar Battery. Citation London Gazette 16.08.1917 page 8376.

"He fought his battery with the greatest skill and courage during a bombardment and in the heavy attack which followed. His coolness under heavy shell fire in organizing and maintaining ammunition supply was most marked. He also rallied a large party of infantry, and attended to wounded under intense shell fire with the utmost contempt of personal danger."

Captain Edward James Hugh MEYNELL. 1/5th Battalion. London Gazette 08.03.1919 page 3244. Citation London Gazette 04.10.1919 page 12318. Died of Wounds 04.10.1918.

"On the 28th September 1918, north of Bellenglise his company was in support of another which was being forced back, and he organized a counterattack of three platoons, which was led by himself. His courage and determined leadership prevented the other company from being cut off, and the remnants of his platoon and the ammunition they carried made possible a very gallant stand. His company lost 40 per cent in this fight. Next day he commanded the remnants of the two companies excellently, gaining his objective."

Temporary Lieutenant Albert Basil MILLER DSO. 1/5th Battalion Attached. Citation London Gazette 16.09.1918 page 10989.

"With his company he formed a screen, through which another battalion withdrew in perfect order and without a casualty, while he gave battle and held the enemy up. He withdrew his company, but remained himself, firing a Lewis gun, until all his men had taken up their new position. The success of the operation was largely due to his skill and courage."

Captain Frederick Thomas MONK. Scottish Rifles attached 6th Battalion. London Gazette 01.01.1917 page 38.

No Citation. New Years Honour.

Lieutenant Francis Arthur MORGAN. 5th Battalion Attached 1/6th Battalion. London Gazette 08.03.1919 page 3244. Citation London Gazette 04.10.1919 page 12320.

"For marked gallantry and determined leadership. In the attack on Bellenglise on September 29, 1918, when all the other officers in his company had been wounded in the first few minutes of the attack, he led his company on and captured his objective after overcoming all resistance in the village."

Lieutenant Charles Alfred MUSCAT. Malta Militia Attached 7th Battalion. Citation London Gazette 25.11.1916 page 11541.

"For conspicuous gallantry in action. He twice took command of his company and directed operations with great skill and determination at a very critical moment in the attack."

Temporary 2nd Lieutenant George Henry MURAS. 9th Battalion. Citation London Gazette 14.11.1916 page 11062.

"For conspicuous gallantry in action. He dug a new line of trench under very heavy fire, displaying great courage and determination. Later, although severely wounded, he remained on duty for three hours superintending his men."

Lieutenant Arthur J. MUSGROVE. 1/5th Battalion. London Gazette 08.03.1919 page 3244. Citation London Gazette 04.10.1919 page 12321.

"On the early morning of September 28th, 1918, north of Bellenglise, at a critical moment, when Captain Ball was short of small arms ammunition and bombs he took his platoon forward to support 'D' Company, and in spite of heavy machine gun fire and severe casualties he got his men into a position to render support and renew the supply of ammunition. His personal example achieved this."

Captain Robert Francis Brydges NAYLOR DSO. 1st Battalion. London Gazette 14.01.1916 page 580 (For 01.01.1916).

No Citation. New Years Honour.

Captain Frederick Cecil NICHOLS. Royal Army Medical Corps Attached 4th Battalion. Citation London Gazette 26.07.1918 page 8829.

"For conspicuous gallantry and devotion to duty. When the front line was forced back he maintained his dressing station in the newly formed front line until he had attended to every case, in spite of a heavy bombardment. Throughout the four days fighting he displayed untiring energy and great personal courage."

Captain Reginald D'Oyly OLDHAM. Hertfordshire Regiment Attached 4th Battalion. Citation London Gazette 26.07.1918 page 8830.

"For conspicuous gallantry and devotion to duty. He went forward with a Lewis gun under heavy fire, took up a commanding position and inflicted severe losses on the enemy, remaining there until all his ammunition was expended. He showed great initiative throughout the action, and was severely wounded."

13079 Company Sergeant Major Edward OLIVER. 1st Battalion. London Gazette 03.06.1918 page 6469.

No Citation. King's Birthday Honour.

Lieutenant (Temporary Captain) Tom OWEN. Attached Royal Air Force. Citation London Gazette 26.07.1918 page 8831.

"For conspicuous gallantry and devotion to duty. He has carried out many successful low reconnaissance's, bringing back good reports. When on artillery patrol he succeeded in completely disorganizing the traffic on a main road, getting direct hits on troops and transport by artillery. On this occasion it is estimated that forty lorries were destroyed. He also attacked enemy troops and transport with bombs and machine guns with success."

2nd Lieutenant (Acting Captain) Edgar Wells PAGE. 6th Battalion. Citation London Gazette 17.09.1917 page 9580.

"For conspicuous gallantry and devotion to duty when commanding the leading companies of an attack. Although wounded early in the attack he remained in command, setting a splendid example of coolness and courage under heavy artillery fire and inspiring all under him to consolidate the captured positions. On the following day, in spite of the pain of his wound, he pushed forward and occupied further trenches, where he remained established for thirty-six hours. His pluck and disregard of danger were deserving of the highest praise."

8689 Company Sergeant Major Frank PARR DCM. 1st Battalion. Citation London Gazette 27.07.1916 page 7443.

"For conspicuous gallantry and good work. At a critical moment he took command of a party and secured a strong point under heavy fire. He displayed great coolness and bravery under difficult conditions."

Captain Richard PERSSE DSO. 9th Battalion. Citation London Gazette 22.09.1916 page 9280.

"For conspicuous gallantry. When working in the front line trenches, he was knocked down and rendered unconscious, his subaltern being wounded. On recovering consciousness he dressed his subaltern's wounds and at once got the men back to work again. It was owing to his personal bravery that the task was completed under heavy fire."

Temporary Lieutenant Cecil Ernest PHILCOX. 1st Battalion. London Gazette 04.06.1917 page 5483. Died 24.05.1917.

No Citation. King's Birthday Honour.

Temporary Captain John Sydney PHILLIPS. 9th Battalion. London Gazette 03.06.1918 page 6496.

No Citation, Kings Birthday Honour.

Lieutenant Harry PIGGINS. 7th Battalion. Citation London Gazette 13.05.1918 page 5702 .

"For conspicuous gallantry and devotion to duty when in command of a fighting patrol of ten N.C.O.'s and men. He left eight of the party outside the enemy's wire and with two N.C.O.'s approached a post which they found to be occupied by five of the enemy. They at once attacked the enemy and killed them all. Leaving one N.C.O. to cover the advance he then made his way down a sap with the other N.C.O., after advancing some thirty yards they encountered and killed two of the enemy who were standing outside a small "pill box". At the sound of the firing three more of the enemy came out of the "pill box" and attacked them, these they also killed. He was then forced to withdraw owing to the approach of a party of about twenty of the enemy. He showed magnificent courage, initiative and determination throughout the enterprise and obtain much valuable information."

Harry PIGGINS MC. Bar to MC. Citation London Gazette 22.06.1918, page 7400.

"For conspicuous gallantry and devotion to duty. When in charge of a fighting patrol which was lying out in front of our wire in order to obtain identification, he was fired on by a strong enemy patrol on his way back to our lines. Immediately leading his men to the front line trench he opened fire with a machine gun, on the hostile patrol which was attacking the trench with bombs. He then climbed out of the trench accompanied by a few of his men, and advanced towards the hostile patrol, which finally retired, leaving one man dead and one wounded man in our hands. Throughout the whole operation he showed exceptional initiative, and by his courage and skilful handling of the situation he was instrumental in obtaining a prisoner and an identification at a time when it was of the utmost importance that one should be obtained."

Captain Harold POCHIN. 1/5th Battalion. London Gazette 04.06.1917 page 5483.

No Citation. King's Birthday Honour.

Temporary Lieutenant (Acting Captain) Eric Lessey POLLARD. Citation London Gazette 13.02.1917 page 1543.

"For conspicuous gallantry in action. He handled his men with marked courage and ability in the face of an overwhelming force of the enemy and under most difficult conditions."

Temporary 2nd Lieutenant George William POOLE. 2nd Battalion. Attached 1/5th Battalion. London Gazette 03.06.1919 page 6833.

No Citation. King's Birthday Honour.

Temporary Lieutenant Henry Arnold PORTER. 2nd Battalion. Citation London Gazette 13.02.1917 page 1543.

"For conspicuous gallantry in action. He established a telephone line and sent back most valuable information. Later he reorganized a mixed force and dispersed an enemy attack. He was wounded."

2nd Lieutenant Ernest Charles POWELL. 5th Battalion. Attached 2nd Battalion. Citation London Gazette 11.01.1919 page 639.

"For conspicuous gallantry and devotion to duty. This officer was sent with his platoon from the support company to reinforce the front line. By careful handling he cleared a wood of snipers, and then filled a gap, getting into touch with neighbouring troops on a flank. Later, when he saw the enemy attempting to blow up a bridge, he frustrated the attempt by capturing eight of them."

Captain Alexander John Loft PRITCHARD. 2nd Battalion. London Gazette 18.02.1918 page 2161. Citation London Gazette 18.07.1918 page 8470.

"For conspicuous gallantry and devotion to duty during an enemy attack. He had repeated bombing attacks, and succeeded in driving the enemy back 200 yards. He then established a block, and held it for twenty-four hours under heavy fire and against several attacks by the enemy. He also took command of scattered men of other units, and organized the defence with the greatest determination and energy."

2nd Lieutenant Robert RANKIN MM. 2nd Battalion. Citation London Gazette 26.07.1917 page 7637.

"For conspicuous gallantry and devotion to duty in rallying and collecting scattered details of various units, after our attacks had been repulsed with heavy loss, and reforming them into a defensive line for the remainder of the day. His courage and initiative contributed largely towards ensuring the safety of our line."

Temporary Captain Philip Hugh RAWSON. Royal Army Medical Corps Attached. Citation London Gazette 26.01.1917 page 1020.

"For conspicuous gallantry in action. On several occasions he rescued wounded men under very heavy fire. He set a fine example of courage and coolness throughout."

Lieutenant (Acting Captain) John Spence REID. 2/5th Battalion. London Gazette 01.01.1918 page 44.

No Citation. New Years Honour.

2nd Lieutenant Charles Humphrys RICKETTS. 2nd Battalion. London Gazette 15.02.1919 page 2379. Citation London Gazette 30.07.1919 page 9768.

"Near Flesquieres, on the night of September 27, 1918, he finding his platoon held up by machine gun fire, rushed forward alone, firing his revolver on the hostile post. He shot dead the No 1 of the team, which disorganized the enemy. He then called up his platoon and rushed the post, taking one prisoner, the remainder of the enemy being killed while running away. He showed great gallantry and determination."

6460 Company Sergeant Major Arthur RILEY. 1st Battalion. Citation London Gazette 18.07.1917, page 7252.

"For conspicuous gallantry on numberless occasions in bringing up rations to the battalion under heavy shell fire, thereby greatly contributing to the success of the operations."

Temporary 2nd Lieutenant Harold ROBERTS. 6th Battalion. Attached 9th Battalion. London Gazette 01.01.1918 page 45. Died of Wounds 27.10.1918.

No Citation. New Years Honour.

Temporary 2nd Lieutenant Fred ROBINSON. 1st Battalion. Citation London Gazette 18.07.1917 page 7243.

"For conspicuous gallantry in lengthy operations, when he led his company with great coolness and courage through heavy machine gun and rifle fire, to its final objective, consolidating the position in spite of great difficulties and heavy casualties. Later, although twice buried by heavy shells on his way back, he made a clear report on the situation."

2nd Lieutenant Samuel RUBERY. 1/5th Battalion. Citation London Gazette 11.05.1917 page 4592.

"For conspicuous gallantry and devotion to duty, during a night attack on the enemy's trenches he gallantly led a bombing party into the heart of the enemy's defences. He was severely wounded. He has on many previous occasions done fine work."

Temporary Lieutenant (Acting Captain) John Albert RUSSELL. 2nd Bn Attached 2nd Battalion Gloucester Regiment. Citation London Gazette 11.01.1919, page 642 (Salonika).

"For conspicuous gallantry during an attack and later during consolidation of the captured position under very heavy shell fire. Although badly wounded early in the attack he refused to have his wounds dressed till thirteen hours later. Inspired by his pluck and devotion to duty, his company wired and dug their position before daylight next morning."

2nd Lieutenant James SALT. 1st Battalion. Citation London Gazette 02.12.1918 page 14261 (Italy).

"For conspicuous gallantry and good leadership in a raid. With five of his platoon, who had got through the wire, he charged some twenty of the enemy, killing or wounding them, and enabling his platoon to follow. He then went out and bombed several dugouts, personally capturing an officer and five men. His courage and determination were most marked, and though wounded, he successfully saw two casualties cleared before withdrawing."

2nd Lieutenant (Temporary Lieutenant) Geoffrey Beville Reinharot SCHON. 1st Battalion & Royal Flying Corps. Citation. London Gazette 04.11.1915 page 10894. Died of Wounds 19.10.1917.

"For conspicuous gallantry from September 25 to 30, 1915, when in command of the machine gun detachment. He worked his detachment forward on the morning of September 25, and held onto the forward position when other troops had fallen back. He also took charge of the regimental bombers from 26 to 30, and displayed the greatest bravery and coolness in using both them and his machine guns. He inflicted heavy loss on the enemy."

Temporary 2nd Lieutenant Charles Anderson SCOTT. Citation London Gazette 18.07.1917 page 7244.

"For conspicuous gallantry and devotion to duty. He performed most valuable service as signals officer. He laid and maintained the lines under heavy fire, though wounded in the leg he carried on until he was ordered to be carried to the rear."

Temporary Lieutenant Thomas Harvey SEARLS. 1st Battalion. Citation London Gazette 16.09.1918 page 11012.

"For conspicuous gallantry and devotion to duty when in command of a platoon. He successfully completed an enveloping movement, with the result that none of the enemy garrison escaped death or capture. He showed conspicuous courage in hand to hand fighting, and personally inflicted several casualties on the enemy. He captured several prisoners single handed."

2nd Lieutenant James Alexander SHEDDON. Scottish Rifles Attached 6th Battalion SSR. Citation London Gazette 11.12.1916 page 12107-8.

"For conspicuous gallantry in action. He led a wire reconnaissance patrol with great courage and skill. On two occasions

he sent back for artillery support himself remaining in "No Mans Land", Finally, he rushed the enemy trenches and captured a sentry point."

Temporary 2nd Lieutenant George Alfred Charles SHEFFIELD. Attached 1st Battalion. London Gazette 26.11.1917 page 12321. Citation London Gazette 06.04.1918 page 4227. Killed in Action 26.10.1917.

"For conspicuous gallantry and devotion to duty as intelligence officer during an attack. He was knocked over and badly bruised by a shell just before zero hour. A relief was sent up for him, but he stuck to his work, and continued for two days more to send in valuable reports."

Lieutenant (Acting Captain) Frank Pitchford SILVERS. 6th Battalion. London Gazette 01.01.1918 page 46. Died of Wounds 27.05.1918.

No Citation. New Years Honour.

Lieutenant Francis Hugh SLINGSBY. 3rd Battalion Special Reserve Attached 2nd Battalion. Citation London Gazette 02.12.1918 page 14263.

"For conspicuous gallantry and initiative during an attack. He lent his company commander the greatest assistance, and by skilful handling of his platoon Lewis guns he prevented the withdrawal of an enemy battery, besides causing considerable casualties to men and horses. His fearlessness and devotion to duty were most marked."

Temporary 2nd Lieutenant Charles Newbald SMITH. 7th Battalion. Citation London Gazette 17.09.1917 page 9583.

"For conspicuous gallantry and devotion to duty in bringing up rations and water to his battalion under heavy barrage fire. He went forward alone over a fire swept area and reported to Headquarters, and it was through his determined and admirable control of men and animals under fire and over unknown country that the urgently needed rations were received. He repeated this act of gallantry on the following night."

2nd Lieutenant Gerald Howard SMITH. 6th Battalion. London Gazette 14.01.1916 page 589 (For 01.01.1916). Killed in Action 29.03.1916.

No Citation. New Years Honour.

Lieutenant Leslie Coleman SMITH. Attached Linconshire Regiment. Citation London Gazette 18.06.1917 page 5999.

"For conspicuous gallantry and devotion to duty. He led his platoon with great skill and gallantry under heavy fire. It was due to his initiative and courage that, that part of the village was taken with such small loss to us."

2nd Lieutenant (Temporary Captain) Joseph SNAPE DSO. 1st Battalion. Citation London Gazette 27.06.1916 page 7441.

"For conspicuous gallantry and good leadership during a successful assault on an enemy position."

Lieutenant (Acting Major) John Stanley SNOWBALL. 6th Battalion Seconded to 1st Battalion Machine Gun Corps. Citation London Gazette 04.10.1919 page 12335.

"For great gallantry and devotion to duty near La Vallce Mulatre on October 17, 1918, whilst commanding a machine gun company. He handled his company throughout the attack with great skill and rendered valuable assistance in the attack. On the afternoon of the 17th, when he received orders for a further attack, he went forward under very heavy shelling and machine gun fire and successfully reorganized his guns for the attack."

Captain James Calvert SPENCE. R.A.M.C. Attached 7th Battalion. Citation London Gazette 17.09.1917 page 9584.

"For conspicuous gallantry and devotion to duty in proceeding to a battery that was suffering heavily from intense enemy shell fire, and continued to search blown in dug outs and tend the wounded under heavy fire. He displayed exceptional coolness and gallantry on this occasion, and on many previous occasions he has carried out his duties with magnificent devotion."

Lieutenant (Acting Captain) John SPENCE-REID. 2/5th Battalion. London Gazette 01.01.1918 page 44.

No Citation. New Years Honour.

Lieutenant Robert Eric SPINNEY. 7th Battalion. Citation London Gazette 03.03.1917 page 2196. (Previously served in Intelligence Corps).

"For conspicuous gallantry in action. He made a personal reconnaissance of our enemy advanced post by himself. Later, accompanied by two bombers, he again visited the post and captured seven prisoners."

2nd Lieutenant (Acting Lieutenant) Frank Percival STEPHENS. 3rd Battalion. London Gazette 04.06.1917 page 5484.

No Citation. King's Birthday Honour.

Captain Lionel Fenton STEPHENSON. 8th Battalion. London Gazette 03.06.1918 page 6496.

No Citation. King's Birthday Honour.

Lieutenant Colonel John Ebenezar STEWART. 8th Battalion Border Regiment Attached 4th Battalion SSR. London Gazette 01.01.1917 page 41. Killed in Action 25.04.1918.

No Citation. King's Birthday Honour.

2nd Lieutenant Basil Read TAYLOR. 2nd Battalion. London Gazette 14.01.1916 page 589 (For 01.01.1916).

No Citation. New Years Honour.

Lieutenant (Acting Captain) Percy Randolph TEETON. 1/6th Battalion. London Gazette 08.03.1919 page 3247. Citation London Gazette 04.10.1919 page 12341. Died of Wounds 17.10.1918.

"At Bellenglise on September 29th, 1918, he showed great gallantry and leadership. He was one of the first to swim the canal and fix a line across. During the whole day his energy was untiring, and he inspired great courage and enthusiasm in the men of his company."

Lieutenant (Temporary Captain) Albert Garnett THOMAS. 1st Battalion Attached 5th Battalion Royal Sussex Regiment. London Gazette 01.01.1917 page 42.

No Citation. New Years Honour.

Albert Garnett THOMAS. Bar to MC (Acting Major) London Gazette 02.04.1919 page 4322 (Italy). Citation London Gazette 10.12.1919 page 15308.

"For conspicuous gallantry and devotion to duty during the advance into enemy Austria between November 1/3, 1918, particularly in pushing forward supplies and tools to the troops under the most difficult circumstances regardless of enemy shell and machine gun fire."

Lieutenant (Acting Captain) Harold THOMAS. 3rd Battalion. London Gazette 03.06.1919 page 6835.

No Citation. King's Birthday Honour.

Lieutenant (Acting Captain) William Frederick Pattern THOMAS. 1st Battalion. London Gazette 03.06.1918 page 6496.

No Citation. King's Birthday Honour.

2nd Lieutenant Herbert Donald THOMPSON. 1st Battalion. London Gazette 03.061918 page 6496.

No Citation. King's Birthday Honour.

Captain (Temporary Major) John Horace THURSFIELD. 6th Battalion. London Gazette 03.06.1916 page 5577.

No Citation. King's Birthday Honour.

2nd Lieutenant (Temporary Captain) William Henry TOSDEVINE. 7th Battalion. Citation London Gazette 17.09.1917 page 9585.

"For conspicuous gallantry and devotion to duty. Although he received his orders too late to take full advantage of the barrage, he led his company to the attack with the utmost skill and fearlessness, with the flanks exposed, and successfully gained his objective. It was due to his indomitable energy and great power of control that his own men, who were greatly fatigued and harassed by shell fire, were got forward and encouraged to consolidate the final objective."

William Henry TOSDEVINE. Bar to MC. London Gazette 17.12.1917 page 13181. Citation 23.04.1918 page 4858-9.

"For conspicuous gallantry and devotion to duty when in command of his company, which formed the front line during an attack. On reaching his objective, although slightly wounded, he personally organized the work and sent back valuable information to his commanding officer. The success of the operation was due largely to him."

Lieutenant J.S. TOWNSEND. 2nd Battalion. London Gazette 23.06.1915 page 6123.

No Citation. King's Birthday Honour.

2nd Lieutenant (Temporary Captain) Edward de TRAFFORD. 1st Battalion. Citation London Gazette 22.09.1916 page 9282.

"For conspicuous gallantry when leading his company during an advance to occupy a position. His bravery and example contributed greatly to repel the constant enemy counter attacks."

Temporary 2nd Lieutenant Oswald Archer TUNNICLIFFE. 10th Battalion North Staffordshire Regiment Attached 1st Battalion South Staffords Regiment. Citation London Gazette 27.07.16 page 7442.

"For conspicuous gallantry. When his Captain had become a casualty he took command and led his men forward. It was greatly due to his fine leading that an enemy position was captured."

Captain (Acting Major) Dudley Cyril TWISS. 1st Battalion. London Gazette 01.01.1918 page 48.

No Citation. New Years Honour.

Captain (Acting Major) George Albert WADE. 1/5th Battalion Attached 46th Battalion Machine Gun Corps. London Gazette 01.01.1918 page 48.

No Citation. New Years Honour.

George Albert WADE. Bar to MC. London Gazette 15.02.1919 page 2370. Citation 30.07.1919 page 9704.

"During the crossing of the St. Quinten Canal near Bellenglise, on September 29, and the further advance on October 3rd, he took up a forward position with his command close to our front trench line which was subjected to continuous shell fire. He saw to the formation of dumps, and to the prompt departure of the companies which were to go forward in support of the infantry attacking the canal defenses. The success of this part of the operation was greatly due to his forethought and untiring energy."

2nd Lieutenant George Shaw WALKER. 2/5th Battalion. London Gazette 18.02.1918 page 2162. Citation London Gazette 18.07.1918 page 8476.

"For conspicuous gallantry and devotion to duty. When all telephone wires were cut during a heavy bombardment and an enemy attack appeared imminent he went out under intense fire from his front line post to get in touch with the company on his right, realizing the urgent necessity of establishing communication. Though he was wounded as soon as he left his post, he succeeded in crawling to the other company at a critical time and obtained most valuable information. He set a splendid example of courage and contempt of danger."

Captain Thomas WALKER. Scottish Rifles Attached 6th Battalion. Citation London Gazette 11.12.1916 page 12108.

"For conspicuous gallantry in action. He led a daring raid with great courage and determination, killing seven and capturing two of the enemy. He has previously done fine work."

2nd Lieutenant Harold Robert WALLIS MM. 5th Battalion Attached 2nd Battalion. London Gazette 15.02.1919 page 2381. Citation London Gazette 30.07.1919 page 9783.

"During the operations between Canal due Nord and Canal de St. Quentin, near Noyelles, on September 27-28, 1918, he showed great contempt for danger. On many occasions he went forward to reconnoitre, and during the attack on Orival Wood took up a position in the open under machine gun fire. On the 27th-28th he took out a patrol, and materially assisted in obtaining touch and clearing up the situation."

2nd Lieutenant Sidney WALTERS. 3rd Battalion attached 1/6th Battalion. London Gazette 08.03.1919 page 3248. Citation London Gazette 04.10.1919 page 12345. Killed in Action 03.10.1918 or Died of Wounds 04.10.1918.

"For conspicuous courage in action on September 29, 1918, in operations near Bellenglise. With a few men he attacked an enemy machine gun which was holding up troops on his flank. He rushed the post and turned the gun on the retreating enemy. Throughout the operations he led his platoon, with great dash and coolness."

6824 Company Sergeant Major (Acting Regimental Sergeant Major) Frederick Arthur WARD. 2nd Battalion. London Gazette 03.06.1918 page 6472. Amendment London Gazette 24.09.1918 page 11321.

No Citation. King's Birthday Honour.

Temporary Quartermaster & Hon Lieutenant Charles Oliver WARDLE. 1st Battalion. London Gazette 26.11.1917 page 12321. Citation London Gazette 06.04.1918 page 4232.

"For conspicuous gallantry and devotion to duty in conducting the ration and water party to the front companies at night through deep mud and heavy artillery fire."

2nd Lieutenant (Temporary Lieutenant) Jesse WEST. 4th Battalion Special Reserve 2nd Battalion. London Gazette 04.06.1917 page 5485.

No Citation. King's Birthday Honour.

Jesse WEST. Bar to MC. Citation London Gazette 02.12.1918 page 14223

"For conspicuous gallantry in an attack. He handled his company splendidly to the final objective, and was instrumental in the capture of twenty machine guns and a large number of prisoners. He set a magnificent example of courage and fine leadership."

Temporary 2nd Lieutenant John WHARTON. 1st Battalion Attached 9th Battalion. London Gazette 01.01.1917 page 43.

No Citation. New Years Honour.

2nd Lieutenant (Temporary Lieutenant) Victor Rodney Stokes WHITE. 1st Battalion Attached Royal Flying Corps. Citation London Gazette 26.05.1917 page 5185.

"For conspicuous gallantry and devotion to duty when acting as forward observation officer. He constantly moved about in the open under very heavy fire and obtained valuable information."

Victor Rodney Stokes WHITE. Bar to M.C. London Gazette 26.11.1917 page 12317. Citation London Gazette 06.04.1918 page 4204.

"For conspicuous gallantry and devotion to duty. While acting as an observer on an offensive patrol he and his pilot shot down an enemy scout in flames. Later while on a reconnaissance with three other machines, he and his pilot engaged eight enemy aeroplanes and shot down and destroyed one of them. On another occasion they destroyed one of three hostile scouts and also a hostile two seater machine."

Lieutenant (Acting Captain) Arthur Percy WHITEHEAD. 3rd Battalion Special Reserve Attached 1/6th Battalion. London Gazette 08.03.1919 page 3248. Citation London Gazette 04.10.1919 page 12347.

"East of Bohain, on October 12, 1918, he was ordered to take his company to assist a company of another battalion which was being held up on the edge of a wood. He led his company through heavy machine gun and artillery fire, and succeeded in entering the wood. He was subjected to very heavy fire, hung onto the position as long as possible and when ordered to retire he got away all his wounded men and was himself the last to leave."

Temporary Lieutenant Dennis WHITTLE. 7th Battalion. London Gazette 17.12.1917 page 13184. Citation London Gazette 23.04.1918 page 4883.

"For conspicuous gallantry and devotion to duty as battalion intelligence officer. He twice visited the whole of the front line, in spite of heavy machine gun and snipers fire, and sent back information which was of great value to the commanding officer. On the second occasion, though severely wounded in two places, he insisted on being taken to headquarters to report."

2nd Lieutenant Bernard William Theodore WICKHAM. 8th Battalion. Citation London Gazette 26.09.1916 page 9432. Killed in Action 13.04.1917, or 14.04.1917 (9th Bn).

"For conspicuous gallantry in action. When his platoon had been wiring all night in "No Mans Land", the enemy made a bombing attack. Though the party was forced to pull back slightly for want of bombs, he held his ground, with two men, for more than an hour, until reinforcements arrived. He was wounded, but stuck to his command till the enemy's attacks were driven off."

The Rev Walter Charles WILKES. Army Chaplains Department Attached 7th Battalion South Staffordshire Regiment. Killed in Action 04.10.1917. Citation London Gazette 14.11.1916 page 11070.

"For conspicuous gallantry and devotion to duty. He tended the wounded for 48 hours under very heavy fire, displaying great courage and determination."

Temporary Captain Roger Llewellyn WILLIAMS DSO. Royal Army Medical Corps attached. Citation London Gazette 13.02.1917 page 1544.

"For conspicuous courage and devotion to duty. He displayed marked courage and determination in tending the wounded under very heavy fire. He has on many previous occasions done fine work."

2nd Lieutenant (Temporary Lieutenant & Acting Captain) David Butler WILSON. 4th Battalion Royal Scots Attached SSR. Citation London Gazette 16.08.1917 page 8387.

"For conspicuous gallantry and devotion to duty. He commanded a raid on the enemy trench, training and leading the raiding party with untiring energy and thorough attention to detail, thereby ensuring its complete success."

Lieutenant Hugh Winkworth WINSTANLEY. SSR (S.R.). London Gazette 12.12.1919 page 15446 (For 03.06.1919).

"For distinguished services in connection with Military Operation in the Balkans and with the British Army of the Black Sea, dated 3rd June 1919."

Captain (Temporary Major) William Allsop WISTANCE DSO. 1/5th Battalion. London Gazette 03.06.1916 page 5578. Killed in Action 25.04.1918.

No Citation. King's Birthday Honour.

Lieutenant Leonard WOLVERSON. 1st Battalion. London Gazette 26.11.1917 page 12322. Citation London Gazette 06.04.1918 page 4233.

"For conspicuous gallantry and devotion to duty when in command of his company in the front line during an attack. He gained the objective exactly according to orders, sending back clear and valuable information and consolidating the position until he was wounded."

Temporary Captain Edgar William WOOD. 8th Battalion. London Gazette 03.06.1916 page 5578.

No Citation. King's Birthday Honour.

Edgar William WOOD. Bar to MC. Citation London Gazette 09.09.1916 page 8873.

"For conspicuous gallantry and devotion to duty in action. He continued to command his company and direct operations after he had been severely wounded."

Lieutenant (Temp Captain) Alexander Lyttleton WOOD. 4th Battalion. London Gazette 01.01.1917 page 43.

No Citation. New Years Honour.

Alexander Lyttleton WOOD. Bar to MC London Gazette 26.09.1917 page 9972. Citation London Gazette 09.01.1918 page 580.

"For gallantry and devotion to duty in entering a cellar which had been destroyed by a shell and was full of gas, in order

to rescue a severely wounded gunner. This act of courage was done at the greatest possible personal risk, as he had to remove his gas mask in order to locate the wounded man, and the street outside was under heavy shell and gas bombardment."

Lieutenant (Acting Captain) John Patterson WOOD. 7th Battalion Scottish Rifles Attached 1/6th Battalion.

No Citation. King's Birthday Honour.

Temporary 2nd Lieutenant Thomas Newton WOOF. 1st Battalion. Citation London Gazette 18.07.1917 page 7250.

"For conspicuous gallantry in an advance of a small party through heavy machine gun and rifle fire to within sixty yards of an enemy trench. In spite of severe casualties he maintained his position for three days, repulsing attacks, and sending back valuable information."

Thomas Newton WOOF. Bar to MC Citation London Gazette 17.09.1917 page 9561.

"For conspicuous gallantry and devotion to duty when commanding a raiding party. He led them through heavy fire of every description, reaching the enemy's trench with only one man. He entered it, however although it was strongly held, and carried on a vigorous fight with bombs and revolver until forced to retire by superior numbers. He then took up a position in a shell hole within a few yards of the enemy parapet, and maintained himself there for half an hour, in spite of heavy bombing by the enemy, in hopes that fresh reinforcements would enable him to make another attack on the trench. He remained until the signal for a general retirement was given. Throughout the operation he showed exceptionally fine dash and utter contempt of danger."

2nd Lieutenant Charles Robert WOOLLEY MM. 2nd Battalion. Citation London Gazette 03.03.1917 page 2197.

"For conspicuous gallantry in action. He carried out a dangerous reconnaissance of the enemy's position. Later, he showed marked courage and skill in anticipating and repelling an enemy raiding attack as soon as it was launched."

2nd Lieutenant John James WOOLLEY. 4th Battalion. Citation London Gazette 16.09.1918 page 11037.

"For conspicuous gallantry and devotion to duty during an attack. When the right flank of the battalion was held up by enemy machine guns hidden in a farm, he rushed forward with a small party, surrounded the farm, and captured it, killing most of the garrison and taking eleven prisoners and two machine guns. His prompt action and great gallantry allowed the attack which would otherwise have been held up, to proceed according to the programme."

Lieutenant Albert Edmund WRIGHT. 7th Battalion. London Gazette 18.01.1918 page 959. Citation London Gazette 25.04.1918 page 5019.

"For conspicuous gallantry and devotion to duty as battalion signalling officer. He was continually inspecting the wires and superintending their repair under very heavy fire, and succeeded in maintaining communication by telephone with the front line."

Lieutenant (Acting Captain) Harold YEATMAN. 6th Battalion. London Gazette 03.06.1918 page 6472.

No Citation. King's Birthday Honour.

SELECTED PERSONAL DETAILS

Details of other recipients can be found on p.177 et seq.

Captain (Acting Major) Cecil Ernest Wells CHARRINGTON MC

Lieutenant A. de HAMEL MC

2nd Lieutenant William DRAYCOTT-WOOD MC

William Draycott-Wood was born in Birmingham and enlisted into the South Staffordshire Regiment on the 28th October 1897, at Worcester, aged 18 years 5 months. He is described as being 5 feet three and a half inches tall, weight 121 pounds, chest 34 inches, fresh complexion, blue eyes and brown hair, religion shown as Church of England and he was a saddle maker by trade. He had previously served in the 3rd Battalion Worcestershire Regiment.

He served in South Africa between 17th March 1900 and 11th August 1902 earning the Queens South Africa Medal, bars *Cape Colony* and *Orange Free State*, Kings South Africa medal bars *1901* and *1902*.

On the outbreak of war in 1914 he was posted to France on the 12th August and had risen to the rank of sergeant, promoted to Acting Company Sergeant Major on the 27th October 1914 in the 2nd Battalion. He then received a commission as a 2nd Lieutenant on the 4th January 1915. Details of his service after this date are confusing, as there appears to be a number of errors with the spelling of his name. In regimental records he appears as W. Draycott Wood. He received a Mention in Despatches (London Gazette, 22nd June 1915) and a Military Cross (London Gazette, 23rd June 1915 (No citation)).

He was killed in action on the 29th June 1915. It appears that he must have been reported missing at one stage as his sister wrote to the records office but they could not find any trace of him being reported as being a casualty. A telegram was sent to his sister Mrs Preece, informing her that he had been killed in action on the 29th June 1915.

William Draycott-Wood is buried in Cambrin Military Cemetery, Pas de Calais, France.

Lieutenant Frederick John GIBBS MC

2ⁿᵈ Lieutenant Harold Albert HAWKINS MC

Lieutenant Phillip HIGHFIELD-JONES MC

Lieutenant Michael Joseph KAVANAGH

Michael Joseph Kavanagh enlisted into the South Stafford in 1897 when aged 18 years, he saw service in the South African War 1899-1902. He was commissioned into the South Staffordshire Regiment on the 6th March, 1915 as a 2nd Lieutenant in the 2nd Battalion. On completion of his officer training he joined the battalion on the 22nd May 1915 and was made the Battalion Machine Gun Officer with the rank of Lieutenant, during this period he was wounded and sent to hospital, but he rejoined his unit whist still suffering from his wounds and shock. When back with his unit he was awarded the Military Cross for bravery in action. He was made acting Captain and sent home to fully recover from his wounds.

Michael Joseph Kavanagh was from Mount Street, Walsall and was deeply involved in community affairs. He was elected to the Town Council in 1931 as a representative of the Caldmore Ward standing as a Liberal. When the Second World War was declared he offered his services to the Home Guard and was the Platoon Commander of Number 21 Platoon, 27th Battalion. He was an accomplished shot and won a silver medal. In all he served for 31 years on the Walsall Town Council, and was the Mayor of Walsall six months after the end of WW2 and was elected to the aldermanic bench in 1948. He was keenly interested in charity work for the blind and with the Poppy Day Appeal. Due to ill health he had to retire from his council duties in 1962 and he died in February 1964.

Lieutenant Arthur J. MUSGROVE MC

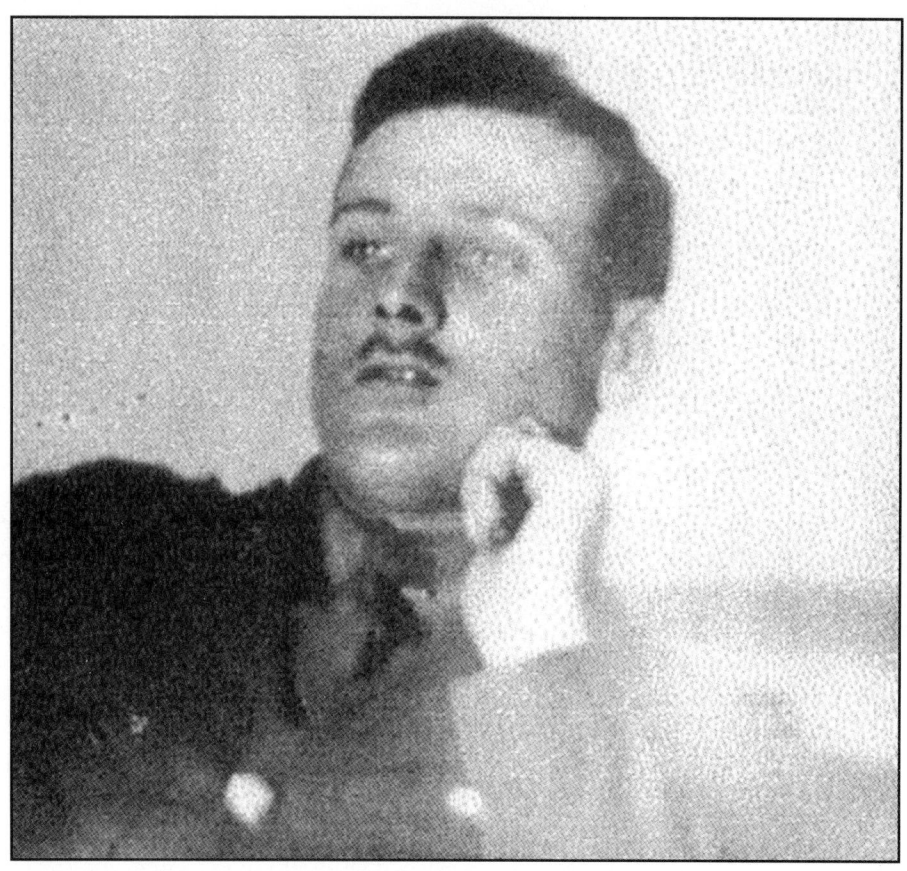

Temporary 2nd Lieutenant George William POOLE MC

George William Poole was born on the 18th February 1893, the son of George Poole and Hannah Mariah (Nee Nixon) of Wesley Street, Wood Lane, Bignal End, Stoke on Trent. He had three brothers Elijah, Bertram and Sydney, three sisters Louisa, Florence and Hannah. His father was a miner and later a colliery policeman. He was educated at Miles Green school before leaving to take up employment in the local mines.

During WW1 he volunteered for the army and served firstly in the Royal Lancastrian Regiment where he attained the rank of Corporal. Then to the 2nd South Staffords from where he was commissioned and served as a 2nd Lieutenant (Acting Captain), Officer Commanding B Company 27.8.1918, then in C Company 11.09.1918 before he moved to the 1/5th Battalion South Staffords who at the end of the war were serving as part of the Army of Occupation in Cologne, Germany. He was awarded the Military Cross in the King's Birthday Honour List, 3rd June 1919 whilst he was battalion Sports Officer.

During his service was twice wounded and was on active service on the Somme and at Mons.

On returning to civilian life he married Phyllis Maud (Nee Biddulph) in 1920, they had two children Sydney and Sheila Kathleen. He studied and qualified as a Member of the Institute of Mining Engineers in 1928. He was the manager of the Minnie Pit, the mine where many miners were killed in an explosion. Later he moved to Dawley, Shropshire where he was the manager of the Coalmoor Bassalt Quarry in Little Wenlock before moving to the Lilleshall Company as the estate and concrete works manager.

During WW2 he was a Major in the Home Guard, with the Kings Shropshire Light Infantry.

On retirement he moved to Treardurr Bay in Anglesey to be near his daughter. George William Poole died on the 12th May 1955 and is buried in Rhoscolyn.

Captain Ernest Charles POWELL MC

Captain Alexander John Loft PRITCHARD MC

Lieutenant (Acting Captain) William Frederick Pattern THOMAS MC

THE DISTINGUISHED CONDUCT MEDAL

IT was during the Crimean War that this award, for other ranks only, was instituted in December 1854. The medal is circular and made of silver, the ribbon is 32 mm wide, crimson with a dark blue central stripe. On the reverse side of the medal are the words

"FOR DISTINGUISHED CONDUCT IN THE FIELD"

14369 Corporal W. ADAMS. (Hanley). London Gazette 03.06.1918 page 6497, Citation London Gazette 21.10.1918 page 12323 (Italy).

"For conspicuous gallantry and devotion to duty and for excellent work for many months in active service. On one occasion his high courage and splendid example under heavy fire, were the greatest value in completing the difficult task of building a strong point in a captured area. He invariably displayed the greatest contempt of all danger."

9312 Private Charles ALLEN. 2nd Battalion. London Gazette 23.06.1915 page 6129. Citation London Gazette 30.06.1915 page 6358. Killed in Action 29.04.1916.

"For conspicuous gallantry and resource throughout the campaign as a scout, bomb thrower, guide. He has shown great courage and zeal, always ready to volunteer for any hazardous enterprise."

4456 Company Quartermaster Sergeant Thomas George ALLEN. 2nd Battalion. London Gazette 14.01.1916 page 594, Citation London Gazette 11.03.1916 page 2644. Killed in Action 29.04.1916 (Company Sergeant Major). Formerly 30702 West Yorkshire Regiment.

"For conspicuous gallantry, Company Quartermaster Allen and Lance Corporal Swinnerton crawled out along a tow path in spite of heavy fire and with utter disregard of danger rescued no fewer than two wounded officers and 10 men."

5437 Regimental Sergeant Major Richard BAKER. 1st Battalion. Citation London Gazette 17.12.1914 page 10780. Killed in Action 07.11.1914.

"Conspicuous bravery during evacuation of Kleine Zillerbeke, 31st October, during which he rallied his men under heavy fire."

4/8804 Private F. BALL. 2nd Battalion. Citation London Gazette 05.08.1915 page 7673.

"For conspicuous gallantry and resource on the 18th May 1915 at Rue de Bois. After the non commissioned officer and the remainder of the machine gun team had been killed or wounded, Private Ball, with the greatest coolness and courage succeeded, under a heavy shell fire, bringing his gun into action. He maintained his gun in an exposed position for two days on the left flank of a captured German trench under a heavy fire, and thus prevented the enemy repairing an important communication trench."

8392 Sergeant E.T. BALLINGER MM. (Lichfield). 1st Battalion. London Gazette 17.04.1919 page 5012. Citation London Gazette 25.02.1920 page 2280 (Italy).

"During the operations of 27th-29th October 1918, when crossing the Piave. His platoon, inspired by his dash and gallantry, was able to carry out every task assigned to them. Later, when the enemy held a forward trench position with machine guns he ran forward and dropped two bombs amongst the garrison, killing and wounding seven and taking the remainder prisoners. He then led his platoon in a bayonet charge, helping to capture the main position."

12053 Private R. BATEMAN. 1st Battalion. Citation London Gazette 11.05.1917 page 4595.

"For conspicuous gallantry and devotion to duty. He carried a message from his Company Commander to Battalion Headquarters, and then returned through an intense hostile barrage to inform his Company Commander that the message had been safely delivered. He set a magnificent example throughout the action, and repeatedly carried messages under intense fire."

8696 Sergeant J. BEARDS. 5th Battalion (TF). London Gazette 03.06.1916 page 5580, Citation London Gazette 21.06.1916 page 6137.

"For conspicuous gallantry at a critical time. He opened rapid fire on the enemy, who were counter attacking, and at the same time drove off their bombers. Although wounded in the head he stuck to his post all afternoon."

200908 Private (Acting Corporal) J. BENNETT. (Birmingham). 1st Battalion. London Gazette 17.04.1919 page 5012, Citation London Gazette 25.02.1920 page 2281 (Italy).

"During operations across the Piave, 27th-29th October 1918, he did excellent work in capturing a machine gun which was causing the advance much trouble. Later at point C. Peolotto, he was instrumental in knocking out a second machine gun, and led a determined bayonet charge in face of heavy fire, and although wounded, continued to lead his party. He afterwards saved a wounded comrade who lay in the open."

8479 Company Quartermaster Sergeant (Acting Company Sergeant Major) T. BILLS MM. (West Bromwich). 1st Battalion. Citation London Gazette 15.11.1918 page 13436.

"For conspicuous gallantry and devotion to duty during a raid. He rendered very valuable assistance to his Company Commander, who was one of the first into the enemy position. In spite of heavy machine gun fire he reorganised and led forward his men, inflicting considerable casualties to the enemy. Throughout he showed marked courage and initiative."

9513 Sergeant T. BIRCH. (Wednesfield). 1st Battalion. London Gazette 17.04.1919 page 5013, Citation London Gazette 25.02.1920 page 2280 (Italy).

"During operations 27th–29th October, 1918, he did excellent work. On the 28th he followed up the enemy and went forward into their territory. Coming into touch with a party of the enemy at Vazzola, he with two other ranks, attacked them and put them to flight, taking five prisoners. On the 29th he led his platoon, under heavy fire to his objective. At Cimetta he again led forward a strong patrol, and crawled forward, pushed back the enemy and enabled his company to dig in."

8569 Sergeant W. BIRCHALL MM. 1st Battalion. London Gazette 01.01.1917 page 48. Citation London Gazette 13.02.1917 page 1551.

"For conspicuous gallantry and devotion to duty. He has rendered valuable services as stretcher bearer sergeant, and has carried out his work under fire with great courage and determination."

8/13211 Acting Company Sergeant Major Henry Sydney BIRD. 8th Battalion. Citation London Gazette 30.03.1916 page 3432. Died of Wounds 8th July 1916.

"For conspicuous gallantry. When the enemy rushed an isolated trench he saved the situation by collecting bombs and superintending the erection of stops and barbed wire. During the whole operations he set a splendid example to his company."

12844 Private F. BLEWITT. (Oldbury). 1st Battalion. London Gazette 22.10.1917 page 10862, Citation 26.01.1918 pages 1291-2. (Also shown in 7th Battalion awards)

"For conspicuous gallantry and devotion to duty during an attack. He was sent forward with two men to get in touch with a company who's position had become obscure. He proceeded through a heavy barrage to a point where the fire was so intense that he decided to leave the men under cover and go forward alone. He succeeded in getting in touch with the company, but was severely wounded. Having obtained all the information he had been ordered to get although suffering severely from his wound, he made his way back to his company commander under heavy shell fire, delivered the message, and then collapsed. His pluck and devotion to duty were magnificent."

240187 Acting Sergeant J.W. BLYTHE. (Wolverhampton). 6th Battalion. Citation London Gazette 30.10.1918 page 12812.

"For conspicuous gallantry and devotion to duty in seizing an enemy post by daylight with one NCO and one private. Three prisoners were taken, but on the way back an enemy patrol of six was encountered, when the prisoners tried to escape they were immediately killed, Corporal Blythe then dispersed the patrol and brought back identification of the enemy who had been holding the line."

7834 Corporal (Acting Sergeant) J. BOLTON. (Blackhurst). 1st Battalion. Citation London Gazette 04.03.1918 page 2733.

"For conspicuous gallantry and devotion to duty when in charge of his platoon when his platoon commander had become a casualty, pressing home the attack in spite of heavy machine gun and rifle fire and bombing. He managed to work round the enemy, thus forcing them to retire, leaving behind many dead and a heavy machine gun. He held onto his position all day, although there were no troops on either flank. Eventually he was forced to withdraw his men to our original line, bur first destroyed the machine gun."

6650 Private C. BONNING. 1st Battalion. Citation London Gazette 05.08.1915 page 7675.

"For conspicuous gallantry between 16th and 18th May 1915, at Festubert. He displayed at all times the utmost coolness and courage in carrying in wounded under fire, and was himself wounded whilst attending to a wounded officer. In every action he has always exhibited the greatest devotion to duty."

39601 Acting Corporal A.E. BRUMMEL. (Bedford). 1/5th Battalion TF. London Gazette 12.03.1919 page 3381. Citation London Gazette 02.12.1919 page 14826.

"For conspicuous courage and good work. On the 29th September 1918, north of Bellenglise, when the enemy attacked and entered our outpost line on the west side of the St Quinten Canal, he showed conspicuous gallantry in beating them out of our trenches with a counter bombing attack, and later putting out of action an enemy light trench mortar before his company was finally driven back. On the 29th September he was the first of his company to cross the canal and take prisoners on the other side. Later, he was again first of his company to enter the second objective and captured 40 prisoners."

16173 Sergeant G.H. BULLOCK MM & Bar. (Brierly Hill). 2nd Battalion. Citation London Gazette 15.11.1918 page 13437.

"For conspicuous gallantry and initiative in the attack. He handled his section splendidly, and attacked a party of the enemy with a captured machine gun, and working round their flank, forced them to surrender. Using similar tactics, he captured a field gun also. His work throughout the day was magnificent."

4980 Company Sergeant Major (Acting Regimental Sergeant Major) A. BURGOYNE. 6th Battalion. London Gazette 01.01.1917 page 48, Citation London Gazette 13.02.1917 page 1552.

"For conspicuous gallantry and devotion to duty. He has on many occasions displayed great courage and initiative in organising a supply of bombs, ammunition etc. He has performed consistent good work throughout."

8362 Sergeant A. BUSBY. 2nd Battalion. London Gazette 23.06.1915 page 6130, Citation London Gazette 30.06.1915 page 6365.

"For conspicuous gallantry and ability throughout the campaign, particularly on the 20th February 1915, at Givenchy, in the attack on a German trench. As commander of a platoon, he has always shown great capacity as a leader, and been noted for his courage, enterprise and devotion to duty under fire."

8860 Company Quartermaster Sergeant (Acting Company Sergeant Major) Frank BYTHEWAY MC. (Walsall). 1st Battalion. London Gazette 23.06.1915 page 6130, Citation London Gazette 30.06.1915 page 6336. Killed in Action 14.07.1916.

"For conspicuous devotion to duty on the 29th October 1914, near Kruiseik during a counter attack, when he personally carried a machine gun in the firing line for three quarters of a mile and only ceased firing when his ammunition was exhausted, he then continued to carry the gun till the end of the attack."

8791 Private S. CADDICK. 2nd Battalion. Citation London Gazette 01.04.1915 page 3195.

"For gallant conduct on 20th February 1915, at Givenchy, when he went out of his trench at great risk, under heavy shell and rifle fire, and repaired a broken telephone wire."

8/13584 Company Sergeant Major R.W. CARTWRIGHT. 2nd Battalion. Citation London Gazette 16.08.1917 page 8401.

"For conspicuous gallantry and devotion to duty. During an attack upon enemy trenches he displayed great courage and

initiative at a critical moment in reorganising and directing leading waves, setting a magnificent example to all by his energy and total disregard of personal risk."

7589 Lance Corporal J. CASTLEFORD. 1st Battalion. London Gazette 18.02.1915 page 1702, Citation London Gazette 01.04.1915 page 3195.

"For gallant conduct, great coolness and ability. He has set a fine example to his comrades on all occasions, especially in dangerous situations."

9649 Private S. CATTELL. 3rd Battalion attached 1st Battalion. London Gazette 14.01.1916 page 597, Citation London Gazette 11.03.1916 page 2657.

"For conspicuous gallantry, he did fine work reconnoitering the enemy until he was severely wounded."

40762 Private H. CLAY. (Bradford). 1/5th Battalion. London Gazette 03.06.1919 page 6845, Citation London Gazette 11.03.1920 page 3025.

"In the attack near Givenchy on the 29th April 1918, he behaved with great gallantry. Since then, as company and battalion runner, he has taken part in every action of this brigade. In the battles of September & October he rendered valuable service, delivering many important messages under heavy fire."

1/9059 Sergeant J. CLEWS. (Walsall Wood). 8th Battalion. Citation London Gazette 04.03.1918 page 2735.

"For conspicuous gallantry and devotion to duty. He commanded his platoon in the attack when his officer was wounded and he led his men with great determination to their objective. When his Lewis Gun was put out of action by an enemy shell during the consolidation, he went back over the open in daylight and brought up another gun with eight drums of ammunition. Later he went out on patrol with another NCO, and together they killed two of the enemy. He set a splendid example of courage and resource throughout the whole action."

12521 Company Sergeant Major CLOWSLEY. (Jersey). 4th Battalion. Citation London Gazette 03.09.1918 page 10281.

"For conspicuous gallantry and devotion to duty. After the company had been badly cut up, and at a time when only one company officer was left, he rendered valuable assistance in the reorganisation and in withdrawing to a new line. During the whole of the operation he did excellent work, and his cheerfulness and untiring energy were an inspiration to all."

15455 Corporal W. COOPER. (Tipton). 9th (P) Battalion. London Gazette 03.06.1919 page 6942, Citation London Gazette 11.03.1920 page 3028 (Italy).

"During the period 15th September to 4th November 1918, he has shown great devotion to duty. His contempt of danger has at all times been a splendid example to his men. More especially during the operations on the Piave his efforts were untiring. During the period 6th November-2nd January 1919, he has proved himself an excellent disciplinarian."

6630 Lance Corporal H. COTTERILL. 2nd Battalion. London Gazette 23.06.1915 page 6131, Citation London Gazette 30.06.1915 page 6370.

"For conspicuous gallantry and resource on three occasions. 1. On the 9th January 1915, at Festubert, when holding with a party an advanced position, he was twice driven out by bombs and each time led the party back. 2. On the 12th January, when he stayed under a heavy fire dressing the wounds of a man whom he subsequently helped to carry back 3. On the 22nd January, near Rue de Bois, when his platoon sergeant being wounded in an isolated trench, he ran back under a heavy fire for medical aid and returned with it."

Lance Corporal H. COTTERILL. Bar to DCM. London Gazette 14.01.1916 page 614, Citation London Gazette 11.03.1916 page 2736.

"For conspicuous gallantry and devotion to duty on several occasions. Although shot through the right hand and wounded in the cheek, he insisted on going forward in the attack as he was the only NCO available with his platoon."

240087 Sergeant A. COX. (Wolverhampton). 6th Battalion. London Gazette 26.11.1917 page 12323, Citation London Gazette 06.02.1918 page 1761.

"For conspicuous gallantry and devotion to duty in reconnoitering the wire within 15 yards of the enemy posts. On the following day, accompanied by an officer, he cut the protective wire, and seeing the alarmed post about to escape fired his revolver, checked the enemy, and enabled the remainder of the party to account for the posts. One prisoner was taken by him."

17989 Private J.H. COX. (Walsall). 9th (P) Battalion. London Gazette 01.01.1919 page 67, Citation London Gazette 03.09.1919 page 11108 (Italy).

"During the period 26th February to 14th September 1918, he has shown great devotion to duty. On the 17th June, whilst at San Sisto, the camp came under heavy shell fire, and the men had to take shelter in deep dugouts. Two men were badly wounded and were unable to get to the saps. He showed great gallantry in dressing the wounded men and staying with them. After he had dressed them he got another man to bring a stretcher, and took the wounded men to the dressing station. The whole time the camp was being heavily shelled."

25745 Corporal (Acting Sergeant) J. CROWTHER. (Wolverhampton). 1st Battalion. London Gazette 26.11.1917 page 12323, Citation London Gazette 06.02.1918 pages 1761-2.

"For conspicuous gallantry and devotion to duty. In spite of very intense shelling, he set up a dressing station in a shell hole, and altogether bandaged and evacuated about fifty wounded. For three days he worked incessantly without any sleep, doing most of his work in the open under heavy shell fire."

241396 Sergeant A. CRUTCHLEY. (Wolverhampton). 1/6th Battalion. London Gazette 03.06.1919 page 6846, Citation London Gazette 11.03.1920 page 3030.

"During the attack on Bellenglise on 29th September 1918, he took command of a platoon at a critical stage of the advance, and led them to the final objective in the face of very heavy fire. His entire disregard of personal danger was a very fine example to his platoon."

8891 Corporal J. DALES MM. 1st Battalion. Citation London Gazette 25.11.1916 page 11555.

"For conspicuous gallantry in action. He held his post alone under intense fire, displayed great courage and determination. Later, he set fire to a box of smoke bombs, thus screening the infantry who had been forced to temporarily vacate the position."

200254 Sergeant G.T. DAVIES (Hockley) 1/5th Battalion TF. London Gazette 01.01.1919 page 38, Citation London Gazette 03.09.1919 page 11110.

"During the period 25th February to 16th September 1918, his conduct in carrying out his duties as a scout was exemplary. During July and August, while in the Essars and Loisne sector, he showed great courage and determination in leading daylight and night patrols into the enemy's lines. On several occasions, on his own initiative he took out daylight patrols, gaining important and valuable information as to the enemy's positions etc., during the latter's retirement on that front."

201876 Sergeant A. DEAVILLE (Burslem) 1/5th Battalion T.F. London London Gazette 12.03.1919 page 3382. Citation 02.12.1919 page 14835.

"On the 29th September 1918, north of Bellenglise, during the storming of the St Quentin Canal, he displayed most conspicuous gallantry. Being amongst the first to reach the canal he at once swam across with a few men, and in spite of opposition and confusion due to fog he got a great number of men of all units over. Having got a sufficient party across he at once overcame the enemy on the east bank of the canal, which secured a free passage for the remainder of our men. Later he led his mixed parties to the "Brown Line", where he reorganised and consolidated. Throughout he showed fine courage and enthusiasm."

8403 Sergeant (Acting Company Sergeant Major) J. DEFLEY. 1st Battalion, Citation London Gazette 03.03.1917 page 2200.

"For conspicuous gallantry in action. With a few men of his company he reached a very advanced position and remained there throughout the day. Later, he voluntarily guided a patrol beyond the front line to bring in the wounded."

8/10539 Company Sergeant Major C.P.G. DEWSON. London Gazette 01.01.1917 page 48, Citation London Gazette 13.02.1917 page 1554.

"For conspicuous gallantry and devotion to duty. He has performed consistent good work throughout, and has at all times under fire set a splendid example of courage and determination."

11916 Private (Acting Sergeant) G. DODD. 9th Battalion. Citation London Gazette 22.09.1916 page 9291.

"For conspicuous gallantry during operations. When his company was acting as a working party, he rendered valuable services in rallying men and keeping them to their tasks under very difficult circumstances."

2561 Company Sergeant Major J. DUGGAN. 1/6th Battalion. London Gazette 14.01.1916 page 599, Citation London Gazette 11.03.1916 page 2667.

"For conspicuous gallantry. When the parapet was blown in and three men buried, he rescued them at great personal risk under heavy shellfire. In the evening he superintended the rebuilding of the breach, although the enemy had trained rifles on it. He set a fine example to his men."

13002 Sergeant John EADES MM & Bar. MID. (Ocker Hill). 1st Battalion. London Gazette 26.11.1917 page 12324, Citation London Gazette 06.02.1918 page 1763.

"For conspicuous gallantry and devotion to duty in the attack. He led his platoon with complete disregard of danger, and helped to reorganise his company under heavy shell fire when the objective was captured. He did excellent work in the consolidation, and led forward a patrol at a time when information was badly needed and brought back a valuable report. He set a splendid example of courage and initiative."

242302 Lance Corporal William George EATWELL. 2/6th Battalion. London Gazette 03.06.1918 page 6478, Citation London Gazette 21.10.1918 page 12338. Killed in Action 14.07.1916.

"For conspicuous gallantry and devotion to duty while acting as runner. He succeeded in taking messages to and from the line through heavy enemy barrages, and thus kept up communication with the companies under very grave difficulties. His work was excellent."

3/8954 Private A.C. EDWARDS. 2nd Battalion. Citation London Gazette 05.08.1915 page 7686.

"For conspicuous gallantry on the 16th May 1915, near to Rue de Bois, when he bound up three severely wounded men, who had become entangled in the wire near the first line of German trenches, under a very heavy shell fire, he succeeded in releasing them. He assisted two of them to cover of the trench, and showed the greatest gallantry and devotion to duty throughout the action."

9600 Private Harold EDWARDS. 1st Battalion. Citation London Gazette 16.11.1915 page 11418.

"For conspicuous gallantry and devotion to duty on the 26th September 1915, near Hulluch, Private Edwards, acting as stretcher bearer, while dressing a wounded man under heavy fire during the attack on the German trenches, was severely wounded, and although several men offered to help him in his work, he refused to allow this, or to be attended himself. Having finished his work, he walked over, in full view of the enemy and attended another wounded man, when he was struck by another bullet, and fell wounded a second time. He gave a fine exhibition of the highest courage and disregard of personal danger."

12162 Private T.E. ELLIS. Citation London Gazette 16.08.1917 page 8403.

"For conspicuous gallantry and devotion to duty. When conducting a working party they came under sudden and unexpected shell fire. He showed the greatest courage and initiative in conducting them to their task in the front line, making several journeys backwards and forwards in order to do so. His coolness and energy enabled a valuable night's work to be successfully carried out."

240105 Company Sergeant Major G.E. EVANS. (Wolverhampton). 6th Battalion. London Gazette 03.06.1918 page 6478, Citation London Gazette 21.10.1918 page 12339.

"For conspicuous gallantry and devotion to duty. This warrant officer has done exceptionally good work in the field for nearly three years. Both in and out of the line he is always to be relied on, and sets a good example to NCOs and men of his company."

200895 Sergeant J.A. EVANS. (Blackheath). 1/5th Battalion. Citation London Gazette 03.09.1918 page 10292.

"For conspicuous gallantry and devotion to duty. When the platoon commander was killed, he led seven attacks, and eventually, after cutting a gap through the wire, led a strong storming party through and captured the post, killing twenty and taking eleven prisoners and a machine gun. He then rallied his men and reorganised the line."

11528 Sergeant W.E. EVANS. (Near Wolverhampton). 2nd Battalion. Citation London Gazette 30.01.1920 page 1220.

"For gallantry and distinguished services in the field, which have been brought to notice in accordance with the terms of Army Order 193 of 1919. To be dated 5th May 1919 unless otherwise stated."

241174 Corporal N.S. EVERITT. (Wolverhampton). 1/6th Battalion TF. London Gazette 03.06.1919 page 6848, Citation London Gazette 11.03.1920 page 3038.

"Near Bellenglise on 29th September 1918, he took command of his platoon at a critical stage in the attack, and led them to the final objective. With his Lewis Gun he successfully engaged an enemy machine gun, and himself killed or captured a large number of the enemy."

42137 Private (Lance Corporal) S. EXTON. (Grantham). 1/6th Battalion TF. London Gazette 03.06.1919 page 6848, Citation London Gazette 11.03.1920 page 3038.

"For gallantry near Bellenglise on the 29th September 1918. He entered a tunnel and encountered some 400 of the enemy. He caused the whole party to surrender, and marched them out and handed them over. In the attack near Sequehart, on the 3rd October 1918, he did excellent work while in charge of a Lewis Gun section."

8840 Private C. FARMER. 1st Battalion. Citation London Gazette 05.08.1915 page 7687.

"For conspicuous gallantry on the 16th May 1915 at Festubert, when in charge of a machine gun team in a most exposed position. Most of the team were killed or wounded, but he remained working his gun with extra men, although on one occasion he was blown into the trench from his position on the bridge by a shell."

200271 Sergeant A.H. FERGUSON. (Brierly Hill). 1/5th Battalion TF. London Gazette 12.03.1919 page 3383, Citation 02.12.1919 page 14839.

"During the storming of the St Quentin Canal north of Bellenglise on the 29th September 1918, he showed fine courage and determination, rapidly overcoming all opposition on the west side of the canal. He took forward his own section and a party of other men lost from different units. With these he scaled the east bank of the canal, chasing the enemy down dugouts and clearing these generally. In this manner, with fifteen men or so, he took ninety-eight prisoners and two machine guns. He did splendid work."

17684 Lance Corporal John FISHER. 7th Battalion, Citation London Gazette 04.03.1918 page 2738. Killed in Action France & Flanders (Corporal) 14.12.1917.

"For conspicuous gallantry and devotion to duty. During an attack he showed remarkable skill in handling his Lewis Gun, keeping it in action in spite of heavy shell fire, and inflicting severe casualties on the enemy. He successfully held up an enemy counter attack and although wounded, remained at his post until all danger of the position being lost was over. He set a magnificent example of courage and devotion to duty."

13043 Company Sergeant Major W. FISHER. (Tipton). London Gazette 03.06.1918 page 6497, Citation London Gazette 21.10.1918 page 12340.

"For conspicuous gallantry and devotion to duty during a long period of operations. On many occasions when billets have been shelled, he has shown great coolness, courage and initiative in getting the men to places of safety, and his prompt actions saved many casualties."

8152 Sergeant (Acting Company Sergeant Major) Alfred FLOWERS MSM. 1st Battalion. Citation London Gazette 18.07.1917 page 7264. Killed in Action France and Flanders 30.09.1917.

"For conspicuous gallantry and devotion. He continually moved about while an advanced position was being consolidated, in total disregard of heavy accurate sniping at close range, and owing to casualties finally assumed command, and maintained his position for three days."

7154 Private I.B. FLOWERS. 2nd Battalion. Citation London Gazette 05.08.1915 page 7688.

"For great gallantry and devotion to duty on the 17th May 1915, near Rue de Bois. While carrying a message from the firing line to the Commanding Officer he was badly wounded. He crawled along to where he saw the Commanding Officer and was hit again, but refused to be carried away until the message was taken from his pocket. On several occasions he had shown great coolness and bravery."

7577 Company Sergeant Major L. FORD. 1st Battalion. Citation London Gazette 16.11.1915 page 11419.

"For conspicuous gallantry from the 25th to 29th September 1915, near Hulluch. Although severely wounded in the head in the early part of the operation Company Sergeant Major Ford continued to advance and give encouragement to his men until he fell. His example and devotion to duty were of the highest possible value to all ranks. He had already been recommended for his gallant conduct at Festubert."

9633 Sergeant J.E. FREETH. 3rd Battalion attached 1st Battalion. London Gazette 14.01.1916 page 600, Citation London Gazette 11.03.1916 page 2673.

"For conspicuous good work in the trenches. He reconnoitred the advanced saps and wire along the enemy's front and was frequently fired at."

9404 Private E. GARRETT. (Cradley Heath). 2nd Battalion attached Machine Gun Corps. Citation London Gazette 28.03.1918 page 3856. (Was originally awarded MM but upgraded to DCM).

"For conspicuous gallantry and devotion to duty. He displayed the most magnificent courage and disregard for danger keeping his gun firing despite severe casualties amongst his team and the most intense shell fire. His energy, power of endurance and cheerfulness had the highest effect on the men all around him, and encouraged them to hold on at all costs."

13988 Corporal T. GIBSON. (West Bromwich). 9th Battalion. London Gazette 17.04.1919 page 5013, Citation London Gazette 25.02.19120 page 2285 (Italy).

"For conspicuous gallantry and devotion to duty during the bridging of the river Livenea at Sacile on the 31st October 1918. The enemy were holding the surrounding houses, and were maintaining a heavy machine gun and rifle fire upon the destroyed bridge. In spite of the intensity of the fire, and after two attempts, the bridge was finished and attacking infantry were able to advance."

241208 Sergeant Arthur Thomas GOODEY. (Clapham Common). 2/6th Battalion. London Gazette 01.01.1918 page 60, Citation London Gazette 17.04.1918 page 4664. Died of Wounds 05.02.1917.

"For conspicuous gallantry and devotion to duty. By his fearless courage and resource on wiring and covering parties, as well as on patrol, he has invariably set a splendid example to all his men."

8507 Lance Corporal J. GOUGH. 1st Battalion. London Gazette 18.02.1915 page 1703, Citation London Gazette 01.04.1915 page 3202.

"For gallantry under heavy fire. He has performed very good work during this campaign."

8/13628 Acting Quartermaster Sergeant Robert HANDY. (Cheslyn Hay). 8th Battalion. Citation London Gazette 18.07.1917 page 7265.

"For conspicuous gallantry and devotion to duty. He led his company with great daring under heavy fire. Later, he took command of another company and led them both to a second attack. Throughout he displayed the greatest skill and courage."

40124 Private R. HARLEY. 1st Battalion. Citation London Gazette 03.03.1917 page 2200.

"For conspicuous gallantry in action. He dug out by himself three wounded men who were stuck in mud and were being heavily shelled. Later, he rendered most valuable services during the consolidation of the position."

6098 Sergeant (Acting Company Sergeant Major) F. HARRISON. (Barton Under Needwood). 2nd Battalion. Citation London Gazette 28.03.1918 page 3858. (Was originally awarded the MM but upgraded to DCM).

"For conspicuous gallantry and devotion to duty. During the operations he acted with great coolness and courage under heavy fire, and during violent hostile attacks. His able assistance to his Company Commander in most trying circumstances helped greatly towards the repulse of these attacks, and his unfailing energy and marked ability were a splendid example to all ranks."

9939 Sergeant W.T. HARRISON. (Wednesford). 2nd Battalion. Citation London Gazette 28.03.1918 page 3858. (Was originally awarded the MM but upgraded to DCM).

"For conspicuous gallantry and devotion to duty. He repeatedly led counter attacks, repulsing the enemy attacks and successfully organising the defence of the line after his officer had become a casualty. Later, seeing a severely wounded man in the open being sniped at, he went out and brought him back safely to cover. He set a fine example of courage, enterprise and efficiency to his platoon."

8/13320 Corporal J.C. HARVEY. (Wednesford). London Gazette 04.06.1917 page 5489, Citation London Gazette 09.07.1917 page 6814.

"For conspicuous gallantry and devotion to duty. He behaved most gallantly attending wounded men all night whilst under heavy fire and set a fine example to all."

12628 Lance Corporal E. HATHEWAY. (Aldridge). 2nd Battalion. London Gazette 14.01.1916 page 602, Citation London Gazette 11.03.1916 page 2680.

"For conspicuous gallantry Lance Corporal Hatheway and Privates Tuckley and Knowles volunteered to crawl out to the enemy trenches for reconnaissance purposes. In spite of heavy and continuous fire he reached the trenches, observed the enemy and brought back an excellent report."

11265 Sergeant S. HAWKES. (Tipton). Citation London Gazette 30.10.1918 page 12823.

"For conspicuous gallantry and devotion to duty while commanding a platoon detailed to repair the wire in the front line. They came under heavy shell fire, but he got all through but two men, when suddenly enemy barrage was opened and other troops asking for assistance against the attacking enemy. After helping successfully repel the enemy attack, he went and repaired the front line wire. Throughout he set a splendid example to his men."

10343 Sergeant Thomas HAWKINS MM. 3rd Battalion attached 1st Battalion. London Gazette 03.06.1916 page 5582, Citation London Gazette 21.06.1916 page 6145.

"For conspicuous gallantry after the explosion of an enemy mine. Although blown into the air and much shaken, he rallied his platoon at once, and had it ready to meet any enemy attack."

2984 Company Quartermaster Sergeant A. HERBERTSON. 6th Battalion. London Gazette 04.06.1917 page 5489, Citation London Gazette 09.07.1917 page 6814.

"For conspicuous gallantry and devotion to duty. He has frequently behaved most gallantly in assisting wounded men under heavy fire in No Mans Land, and has done consistent good work throughout."

11509 Private B. HESSON. 2nd Battalion attached 170th Mining Company, Royal Engineers. Citation London Gazette 03.06.1915 page 5346.

"For conspicuous gallantry on the 25th and 26th April 1915, at Givenchy, in assisting to rescue officers and men from a deep mine full of poison gas. The courage and devotion to duty displayed were very pronounced, the risk of death through asphyxiation being very great."

26553 Private (Lance Corporal) H. HICKLIN MM. (Nottingham). 2nd Battalion. London Gazette 12.03.1919 page 3384, Citation London Gazette 02.12.1919 page 14849.

"For splendid courage and determination. Near Flesquieres on the night 27th/28th September, 1918, he on his own initiative, rushed forward under heavy machine gun fire, and single handed captured an enemy machine gun, putting the crew out of action. The capturing of this particular gun undoubtedly saved many lives of his company."

242478 Sergeant Thomas HIGGS. 2nd Battalion. Citation London Gazette 15.11.1918 page 13443. Killed in Action France & Flanders 29.09.1918.

"For conspicuous gallantry and good leadership during an attack. He handled his platoon splendidly, while engaging enemy machine guns, and was instrumental in the capture of several prisoners as well as dispersing a considerable force of the enemy who were collecting for a counter attack. He did very fine work."

200282 Sergeant C. HILL. (Walsall). 1/5th Battalion TF. London Gazette 12.03.1919 page 3384. Citation London Gazette 02.12.1919 page 14849.

"During an engagement east of Bohain, on the 11/12th October 1918, he showed marked courage and devotion to duty. On the morning of 12th October 1918, when leading his platoon to the attack, he had his rifle shot from his hand, and he himself was blown some distance by a shell. Nevertheless, he continued to direct his men, and when held up by enemy machine gun fire, he organized his platoon and did invaluable work in repulsing a local counter attack. Throughout the whole engagement he was a very fine example to his men."

8844 Private W. HILL. 4th Battalion attached 2nd Battalion. Citation London Gazette 03.06.1915 page 5346.

"For gallant conduct on the 10th March, 1915, near Givenchy, in going forward at night under heavy sniping fire whilst flare lights were being thrown up, digging out a wounded man who had been nearly buried and bringing him back into safety."

10632 Sergeant H. HOLDEN. (Wolverhampton). London Gazette 03.06.1918 page 6479, Citation London Gazette 21.10.1918 page 12348.

"For conspicuous gallantry and devotion to duty. This NCO has continually shown courage and resource as a platoon sergeant, cheering and encouraging the men during long periods of heavy shelling. On one occasion he remained with an officer who was mortally wounded close to the enemy's wire, being unable to move him and returned to the lines at nightfall. He has always set an example of pluck and determination."

240067 Sergeant T. HOLLOWAY. (Wednesbury). 1/6th Battalion attached 137th Trench Mortar Battery. London Gazette 01.01.1919 page 40, Citation London Gazette 03.09.1919 page 11127.

"For consistent gallantry and ability. He has served with the battery since its formation. He has at all times shown himself a reliable NCO, who has a sound knowledge of handling his guns and is cool regardless of danger when in action."

14720 Sergeant J. HOUSTON. (Clydebank). 7th Battalion. Citation London Gazette 04.03.1918 page 2740.

"For conspicuous gallantry and devotion to duty. When the platoon Commander was wounded in the attack he at once took command and led his men under heavy machine gun fire to the objective. He consolidated his position and reinforced the leading men of his company very skilfully at a critical moment when there was danger of loosing touch. Throughout the action he displayed exceptional skill and initiative in handling his men, and set a splendid example."

200540 Company Sergeant Major (Acting Regimental Sergeant Major) F. HOWSE. (Brierly Hill). 1/5th Battalion. London Gazette 03.06.1919 page 6850, Citation London Gazette 11.03.1920 page 3035.

"From the 28th September 1918, onwards and in particular on the 28th September near Bellenglise, and on Mannequin Hill on the 3rd October 1918, after his officers had become casualties, by his gallant leadership enabled the company to attain their objective."

6784 Acting Corporal J. HUNT. 2nd Battalion. London Gazette 23.06.1915 page 6133, Citation London Gazette 30.06.1915 page 6382.

"For conspicuous gallantry on the 10th March 1915, near Givenchy, when during an attack on the German position, he stood on the enemy's parapet throwing bombs into the trench and using his rifle remaining there for about 15 minutes under heavy fire until severely wounded. Subsequently he directed an attack of reinforcements from a shell hole."

8765 Sergeant J. IMM. 1st Battalion. Citation London Gazette 27.07.1916 page 7449.

"For conspicuous gallantry. When all the machine gunners had been wounded he went back and brought a gun into action single handed, and although wounded himself, kept up fire till all his ammunition was expended and reinforcement had arrived. He was the whole time under heavy fire."

11990 Company Sergeant Major Stephen JACKSON MM. 1st Battalion. Citation London Gazette 17.09.1917 page 9597. Killed in Action 26.10.1917.

"For conspicuous gallantry and devotion to duty during a raid. Although not taking part in it, he went out under a very heavy fire at a critical moment, having learnt that the raid was making very little progress owing to the considerable opposition. He reorganised the parties and led them forward, afterwards personally conducting stretcher bearers up to the enemy's line and clearing No Mans Land of wounded. His fearlessness and splendid initiative at a trying time proved invaluable to the success of the operation."

40483 Private A.H. JAMES. (Dudley). 1st Battalion. Citation London Gazette 03.09.1918 page 10311.

"For conspicuous gallantry and devotion to duty when the runner to the officer in charge of a raiding party. He carried several messages under fire over very exposed ground. Later, he took charge of a section and successfully cleared a dugout, inflicting many casualties on the enemy. He showed the greatest possible disregard for his own safety."

7352 Lance Corporal W. JOHNSON. 2nd Battalion. London Gazette 10.03.1915 page 2462, Citation London Gazette 01.4.1915 page 3206.

"For conspicuous gallantry at Givenchy on the 20th February 1915. After his officers had been wounded, he led the party of the right column with gallantry and skill in the attack into the German trench."

240729 Sergeant John KELLY. (Wolverhampton). 1/6th Battalion. London Gazette 22.10.1917 page 10865, Citation London Gazette 26.01.1918 page 1314. Killed in Action France & Flanders 30.12.1917.

"For conspicuous gallantry and devotion to duty during a raid on the enemy's trenches. He was in charge of a party which came upon a large dugout from which the enemy commenced to emerge. The first man was shot, and the remainder retired into the dugout and fired rifles through the entrance. He went alone to reconnoitre, and returning for help finally brought out four prisoners. He showed the greatest initiative and fearlessness throughout."

8988 Company Sergeant Major O.M. KING. (Camden Town NW). 2nd Battalion. Citation London Gazette 15.11.1918 page 13445.

"For conspicuous gallantry and devotion to duty during an attack and the subsequent reorganization. He set a fine example of courage and determination throughout, and was of the greatest assistance to his company commander."

202691 Corporal Fred KIRTON. 7th Battalion. Citation London Gazette 04.03.1918 page 2742. Killed in Action 01.09.1918. (Shown as 2/5th in War Diary).

"For conspicuous gallantry and devotion to duty. When several casualties were caused by enemy snipers he went out and located the position of the snipers. He returned and led his section against them with great skill and judgement, capturing three and killing one of the enemy. His courageous action was of the greatest service."

9740 Private R. KNOWLES. (Bloxwich). 3rd Battalion attached 2nd Battalion. London Gazette 14.01.1916 page 604, Citation London Gazette 11.03.1916 page 2690.

"For conspicuous gallantry, Lance Corporal Hatheway and Privates Tuckley and Knowles volunteered to crawl out to the enemy trenches and make a reconnaissance. In spite of heavy and continuous fire they reached the trenches, observed the enemy, and brought back an excellent report."

2682/240451 Private Edwin LANGFORD. 1/6th Battalion TF. London Gazette 23.06.1915 page 6134, Citation London Gazette 30.06.1915 page 6385. Killed in Action, France & Flanders 30.11.1917.

"For conspicuous courage and devotion to duty on 28th April 1915, near Kemmel, when he took his turn with a few others in entering a mine gallery to rescue comrades who had been overcome by gas. The rescuing party persevered till all had been saved."

8/12858 Private Samuel LEE. 8th Battalion. Citation London Gazette 22.09.1916 page 9296. Killed in Action France & Flanders 05.11.1916.

"For conspicuous gallantry after the capture of a trench. An officer had been wounded, and volunteers were called for to carry him back. Private Lee volunteered and succeeded in taking him safely through intense shell fire, returning himself afterwards to the trench."

10615 Corporal C.W. LEONARD. 1st Battalion. Citation London Gazette 20.10.1916 page 10204.

"For conspicuous gallantry in operations. He led a party to assist in consolidating an advanced position, under heavy shell fire, and later, patrolled in front of the line. He also carried back a wounded sergeant, under heavy shell fire."

9398 Corporal George Henry LESTER. 2nd Battalion. Citation London Gazette 03.03.1917 page 2201. Killed in Action France & Flanders 22.07.1917.

"For conspicuous gallantry in action. He handles his machine gun with great gallantry under intense fire. He set a splendid example of courage and devotion to duty throughout the operation."

15856 Private J.H. LEWIS. (Willenhall). 1/6th Battalion. London Gazette 12.03.1919 page 3386, Citation London Gazette 02.12.1919 page 14858.

"During the operations at Bellenglise on 29th September 1918, he displayed most conspicuous gallantry and coolness under heavy fire. During the whole time he was the first man in his platoon, on more than one occasion single handed killed or captured enemy posts. His conduct throughout was of the highest order."

8912 Sergeant (Acting Company Sergeant Major) T. LOCKETT MM. (Cheslyn Hay). 1st Battalion. Citation London Gazette 01.05.1918 page 5305.

"For conspicuous gallantry and devotion to duty. He crossed a river in front of our lines alone and secured a rope to the far bank, but while he was returning to fetch the remainder of his patrol the rope gave way, and he was carried away by the stream. Nevertheless, on the following night he again crossed the river and fixed a rope to the far bank, which enabled patrols to get across. He afterwards led patrols across the river with great skill on three occasions, and obtained valuable information. He set a magnificent example of determination and initiative."

7/9183 Sergeant W. LOCKLEY. (Wolverhampton). 8th Battalion. Citation London Gazette 04.03.1918 page 2734.

"For conspicuous gallantry and devotion to duty. He took command of his company in the attack when all the officers became casualties, and led his men with great dash and judgement. When the objective had been captured he cleared the

ground in front of the company of enemy snipers who were inflicting heavy casualties. He cleared three shell holes of snipers and rushed another single handed, putting both occupants out of action. He continued to command the company for two days with splendid skill and resource, and carried out a difficult relief successfully."

8/13686 Private J. LYNOCK. 8th Battalion. Citation London Gazette 30.03.1916 pages 3438-9.

"For conspicuous gallantry when carrying messages under heavy shell fire. Finding parties of bombers who had lost their way he took charge and guided them to the firing line. When the dressing station was blown in he displayed great coolness in receiving the wounded."

8068 Corporal (Acting Sergeant) William Charles MALKOWSKY. 2nd Battalion. London Gazette 01.01.1917 page 49, Citation London Gazette 13.02.1917 page 1560. Died of Wounds 22.07.1918.

"For conspicuous gallantry and devotion to duty. He has repeatedly displayed great courage and determination in tending and dressing wounded men under very heavy fire."

9472 Private W. MANFORD. 2nd Battalion. Citation London Gazette 05.08.1915 page 7698.

"For conspicuous gallantry on the 6th May 1915, at Rue de Bois. When the remainder of the machine gun team, had with one exception, been killed or wounded, Pte Manford went back twice under heavy shell fire to carry up machine gun equipment left by them, although he was himself wounded. He was wounded again on the third journey, but by his efforts he enabled the gun to be brought into action."

7866 Company Sergeant Major E. MARTIN. 1/5th Battalion. London Gazette 14.01.1916 page 605, Citation London Gazette 11.03.1916 page 2697.

"For conspicuous gallantry. When the dugouts of another battalion were being heavily shelled he volunteered to assist stretcher bearers in removing large numbers of wounded, and showed great coolness and courage."

5160 Company Sergeant Major I. MAXFIELD. 1st Battalion. London Gazette 18.02.1915 page 1704, Citation London Gazette 01.04.1915 page 3210.

For gallantry and ability on 29th and 30th October 1914, when he was wounded. Has been noted as a first class leader of men."

12774 Sergeant M. McEVOY. (Wednesbury). 7th Battalion. Citation London Gazette 04.03.1918 page 2743.

"For conspicuous gallantry and devotion to duty. He handled his platoon with the utmost skill and judgement in an attack. When his platoon was held up by fire from two emplacements, he crept forward with two others, rushed the emplacements, and succeeded in capturing them with fifty prisoners and two machine guns. He set a splendid example of courage and contempt of danger, and it was mainly due to his splendid work that the objective was captured with so few casualties."

241097 Sergeant J. MORRIS MM. (Bilston). 1/6th Battalion. TF. London Gazette 12.03.1919 page 3386, Citation London Gazette 02.12.1919 page 14866.

"During the operations at Bellenglise, on the 29th September 1918, for marked gallantry and skill under difficult conditions. He led his platoon in the assault in heavy fog, and was instrumental in killing and capturing a considerable number of the enemy. He showed great dash and promptness, and inspired the men he led with a splendid fighting spirit."

5505 Private A. MUTLOW. 2nd Battalion. Citation London Gazette 06.11.1914 page 9016.

"This man volunteered to go and inform the Wiltshire Regiment of the presence of the South Staffordshire Regiment on the 20th September. In order to do so he had to cross an open fire swept zone, where he ran considerable danger."

8/13804 Lance Corporal S. NEAL. 8th Battalion. Citation London Gazette 30.03.1916 page 3440.

"For conspicuous gallantry. He continued to throw bombs during two nights after being wounded, and refused to leave the trenches till his battalion had been relieved. Though only 19 years of age, this young NCO has set a splendid example to his men."

SS/24920 Company Quartermaster Sergeant (Acting Regimental Sergeant Major) W. S. NEALE. Attached London Regiment. Citation London Gazette 18.07.1917 page 7267.

"For conspicuous gallantry and devotion to duty. When his transport officer and others had been disabled by gas and HE shell fire he carried him to higher ground placed his respirator on, and returned to assist other casualties. On several occasions his coolness and fearlessness under fire have been the means of steadying the men and saving life as well."

14543 Private P. NOLAN MM. (Walsall). 9th Battalion. Citation London Gazette 22.09.1916 page 9298.

"For conspicuous gallantry during operations. When on a working party he was sent forward to reconnoitre the enemy's trench. On arrival there he found a sergeant of another regiment calling for bombers. He ran back, got permission to assist with three or four men as carriers did excellent work in the enemy's trenches, and returned with one of their machine guns."

Private P. NOLAN DCM. Bar to DCM. Citation London Gazette 17.09.1917 page 9593.

"For conspicuous gallantry and devotion to duty in voluntarily going a mile under shell fire to assist a platoon being shelled. He got them to a place of safety, and carried several casualties to the dressing station under heavy shell fire. His services have at all times been invaluable by reason of exceptional courage and resource, which have inspired all ranks with the greatest confidence in him."

200741 Sergeant J. NUTTING. (Rushall). London Gazette 03.06.1918 page 6481, Citation London Gazette 21.10.1918 page 12362.

"For conspicuous gallantry and devotion to duty. This non commissioned officer during two and a half years service in the field with his battalion has proved himself a fine fighter, especially on patrol and with raiding parties. On one occasion in a raid he led his platoon forward after the officer had been hit, reaching the objective, and when he withdrew brought back the wounded officer. He is always ready to volunteer for patrol work."

12557 Private F. PADMORE. London Gazette 01.01.1917 page 50, Citation London Gazette 13.02.1917 page 1562.

"For conspicuous gallantry in action. He carried out a daring reconnaissance under heavy fire. He has rendered very valuable services in several bombing attacks."

13503 Private C.J. PARKER. (Birmingham). 7th Battalion. London Gazette 01.01.1919 page 43, Citation London Gazette 03.09.1919 page 11147.

"For conspicuous devotion to duty and consistent gallantry during the past two years as brigade headquarters orderly. He is a pathfinder of the first order, and during the whole of his service he has shown a fine example to all other runners. He is most cool under fire, and has never failed to deliver messages no matter how adverse the conditions were."

8698 Company Quartermaster Frank PARR. 1st Battalion. London Gazette 14.01.1916 page 608, Citation London Gazette 11.03.1916 page 2709.

"For conspicuous gallantry, when he voluntarily carried rations across the open to the machine gun section under heavy fire."

8305 Private T. PARSONS. 2nd Battalion. Citation London Gazette 16.11.1915 page 11426.

"For conspicuous bravery and devotion to duty on the 25th September 1915, near Guinchy. During the assault on the embankment redoubts, two officers were wounded within a few yards of the German wire. Private Parsons, although wounded himself, crawled to these officers under a very heavy shell fire, and assisted them into a shell hole in the endeavour to give them some place of comparative safety."

1779 Lance Corporal W. PARTRIDGE. 7th Battalion. Citation London Gazette 14.11.1916 page 11099.

"For conspicuous gallantry in operations, when forming one of a patrol sent out to locate gaps in enemy wire. During the assault which followed he was the first man through a gap, rushed the enemy parapet, bombed them back. Although wounded, he refused to retire. His bravery and devotion offered a fine example to all ranks."

40652 Lance Corporal (Acting Corporal) S. PEAKE. (Wolverhampton). 1st Battalion. London Gazette 03.06.1919 page 6942, Citation London Gazette 11.03.1920 pages 3082-3 (Italy).

"He has invariably shown himself to be a most gallant and energetic soldier and a good leader of men. He did excellent work in August 1918, during a raid on Canove. When his Lewis Gun jammed he led his section forward armed with his revolver, entered a dugout and captured five prisoners. He again distinguished himself during the attack on St Michele di Piave on 27th October, 1918."

17772 Acting Sergeant A. PERRY. (Walsall). Citation London Gazette 21.10.1918 page 12364.

"For conspicuous gallantry and devotion to duty. This non commissioned officer was in charge of Stokes Guns which were assisting an artillery barrage for an attack. They were in a most exposed position, but he voluntarily remained with his guns for twenty four hours in the open, under intense artillery fire. He is always ready to volunteer for any dangerous work."

200124 Private H. PITCOCK. Citation London Gazette 16.08.1917 page 8408.

"For conspicuous gallantry and devotion to duty. He showed the greatest courage and promptness during a raid, especially distinguished himself in capturing a machine gun by hand to hand fighting, in which he killed an officer and several men. He afterwards organised and took command of a bombing party, showing total disregard of danger and setting a splendid example."

9495 Sergeant J.W. PITT. (Cannock). 1/5th Battalion TF. London Gazette 14.01.1916 page 608, Citation London Gazette 11.03.1916 page 2710.

"For conspicuous gallantry and devotion to duty when during a heavy bombardment of some hours he assisted his officer in rescuing buried men, and by his fine example of coolness and courage did much to encourage those round him. Again, on another occasion, he volunteered and did gallant work under fire with the stretcher bearers."

4270 Private G. PORTEOUS. 6th Battalion. (Later 4022 Acting Sergeant Worcester Regiment). London Gazette 24.01.1917 page 927, Citation London Gazette 03.03.1917 page 2203.

"For conspicuous gallantry and devotion to duty. He rescued several men under very heavy fire and continuously led attacks with great gallantry."

19039 Private R.C. POUNTNEY. 2nd Battalion. (Attached Machine Gun Company). Citation London Gazette 13.02.1917 page 1548.

"For conspicuous gallantry in action. He entered three dug outs that were full of the enemy, armed with only two bombs and a revolver, and drove the occupants out, when they at once surrendered. Later, he made a reconnaissance under very heavy fire."

25389 Private B. POVEY MM. (West Bromwich). 1/5th Battalion. London Gazette 12.03.1919 page 3387, Citation London Gazette 02.12.1919 page 14871.

"For marked gallantry and devotion to duty. In the operations on the St Quinten Canal, 28th/29th September 1918, north of Bellenglise, he did splendid work in tending the wounded. He worked without rest for forty-eight hours, fetching and dressing the wounded, and on three occasions went out in front of our lines and brought in badly wounded men on his back in front of intense machine gun fire."

4904 Company Sergeant Major (Acting Regimental Sergeant Major) G. PURCHASE. (Brownhills, Nr Walsall). 7th Battalion. London Gazette 01.01.1918 page 63, Citation London Gazette 17.04.1918 page 4681.

"For conspicuous gallantry and devotion to duty. He successfully organized the supply of rations and ammunition to the battalion, regardless of personal danger, though continually exposed to heavy enemy fire."

15270 Sergeant H. RENSHAW. 9th Battalion. Citation London Gazette 14.11.1916 page 11100.

"For conspicuous gallantry in action. He dug a trench under very heavy fire. Later, though wounded, he carried on his work with his platoon for three and a half hours, displayed great courage and determination."

11271 Corporal (Acting Sergeant) S. ROBINSON MM. (Heath Hayes). 1st Battalion. London Gazette 26.11.1917 page 12325, Citation London Gazette 06.02.1918 page 1770.

"For conspicuous gallantry and devotion to duty in charge of the battalion scouts, obtained valuable information regarding the progress of the attack. He captured single handed a "pill box" containing twelve of the enemy, which had been overlooked by the front line troops. He also bayoneted many snipers who had feigned death and had been passed over by the attacking troops."

2723 Lance Corporal F. ROGERS. 6th Battalion. Citation London Gazette 14.11.1916 page 11101.

"For conspicuous gallantry while in charge of a patrol which encountered two hostile patrols in succession. He attacked both patrols, causing them casualties and capturing three prisoners. He has previously been noted for gallant conduct."

12612 Sergeant T.H. ROGERS. Citation London Gazette 17.04.1917 page 3693.

"For conspicuous gallantry and devotion to duty. He rendered most valuable assistance to his platoon commander in the attack. Later, although severely wounded he continued to crawl from shell hole to shell hole urging his men to the attack."

7687 Sergeant H. ROLLINSON. (Bilston Staffs). 1st Battalion. London Gazette 01.01.1918 page 63, Citation London Gazette 17.04.1918 page 4683.

"For conspicuous gallantry and devotion to duty and consistent good work during a very long period. He has always taken part in many engagements and has always set a splendid example of courage and energy."

8/14687 Lance Corporal W. ROWLEY. 8th Battalion. Citation London Gazette 30.03.1916 page 3442.

"For conspicuous gallantry. On returning from a reconnaissance he found that one of his party was missing. He at once went out again, found the man badly wounded, and carried him back under direct machine gun fire. On other occasions he displayed great bravery."

8940 Sergeant R.G SAUNDERS. 3rd Battalion attached 1st Battalion. London Gazette 14.01.1916 page 610, Citation London Gazette 11.03.1916 page 2717.

"For conspicuous gallantry. He went out with a private in front of our wire at the front of the enemy trench and carried in a wounded man under heavy fire."

6849 Sergeant E. SHINE. 2nd Battalion. London Gazette 18.02.1915 page 1705, Citation London Gazette 01.04.1915 page 3218.

"For gallant conduct on 10th September 1914, at Villers-Cotterets, in assisting a wounded man across open ground for 800 yards, under heavy fire."

6871 Private W.A. SIMMONDS. 2nd Battalion. Citation London Gazette 17.12.1914 page 10789.

"For conspicuous gallantry on 7th October in locating the enemy's trenches by daring scouting at night, and subsequently rushing it with two sections, driving the enemy away."

18687 Sergeant E.B. SMITH. (Wednesford). Citation London Gazette 17.09.1917 page 9600.

"For conspicuous gallantry and devotion to duty when in command of a platoon. Coming under heavy shell fire he split it up into small parties personally conducted each out of the shelled area. When he returned and carried a wounded man to a dug out, afterwards proceeding to dig out three men who had been buried. He was successful in this, and his splendid gallantry under heavy shell fire cannot be too highly praised."

6520 Lance Corporal John SMITH. 2nd Battalion. London Gazette 01.01.1915 page 15, Citation London Gazette 16.01.1915 page 580. Killed in Action France & Flanders 10.03.1915.

"For gallant conduct on the 15th November, on Becelaere-Passchendale Road position, in taking an urgent message voluntarily over fire swept ground for 600 yards, there being absolutely no cover."

17555 Private P. SMITH. 7th Battalion. London Gazette 25.08.1917 page 8841.

"For conspicuous gallantry and devotion to duty in continually carrying messages between units under heavy fire of every description. His intelligent reports were of the greatest assistance to the success of operations, and one of his journies, seeing five of the enemy emerge from a dug out, he attacked and forced them to surrender, displaying great dash and presence of mind."

17838 Private W.E. SMITH. (Walsall). 7th Battalion. London Gazette 03.06.1919 page 6857, Citation London Gazette 11.03.1920 page 3096.

"During operations at Wytschaete and Poelcapple during June and September 1917, and when the battalion was in the Hulloch sector, until November 1918. During these operations he took up ration convoys, and frequently delivered ammunition under very heavy fire."

16795 Company Sergeant Major J. SMITHEMAN. (Tipton). 7th Battalion. Citation London Gazette 25.08.1917 page 8841.

"For conspicuous gallantry and devotion to duty in collecting stragglers of other units and bringing them into action under heavy machine gun fire. He afterwards helped to strengthen the left flank of another unit, displaying the greatest gallantry and coolness throughout the action and setting a splendid example to all ranks."

CSM J. SMITHEMAN DCM. Bar To DCM. Citation London Gazette 04.03.1919 page 2731

"For conspicuous gallantry and devotion to duty. He rendered valuable assistance to his commander throughout the attack and during consolidation. He took out a patrol and brought back valuable information, which contributed to the repulse of an enemy counter attack. He showed the greatest courage and initiative."

15061 Private J. SOUTHALL. (Dudley). 1st Battalion. London Gazette 01.01.1919 page 67, Citation London Gazette 03.09.1919 page 11160 (Italy).

"He has served continually with the battalion since 1914. He has acted as the company commander's runner during all the Somme battles, Croislles-Bullecourt, and has always done his work with the utmost contempt of danger, and with unfailing success. He has always proved himself an admirable example of reliability and gallantry, and has at all times set his comrades a magnificent example."

7866 Lance Corporal J.T. STANDLEY. 1st Battalion. London Gazette 18.02.1915 page 1705, Citation London Gazette 01.04.1915 page 3219.

"For gallantry under heavy fire. He performed very good work during the campaign."

200632 Company Sergeant Major J. STANTON. (Walsall). 2nd Battalion. Citation London Gazette 15.11.1918 page 13454.

"For conspicuous gallantry during an attack. With three other ranks he captured two enemy machine guns and turned them on the retreating enemy, inflicting severe casualties enabling the advance to continue. Although wounded, he remained with his company and assisted the reorganisation and consolidation. He set a very fine example of courage and devotion to duty."

5680 Private W. STOKES. 2nd Battalion. Citation London Gazette 05.08.1915 page 7713.

"For conspicuous gallantry on the 17th May 1915, near Rue de Bois. Private Stokes' attention was drawn to a wounded man lying in the open under heavy shell fire near a captured German trench. He volunteered, with another man to go out and carry him in. They both reached the wounded man, and finding the firing too heavy to return, lay down by him. Later endeavouring to take him back, they got hung up in some barbed wire, but Private Stokes remained with the wounded man. An officer seeing that he was unable to carry the man by himself ran out, got Private Stokes to lift the man on to his back and carried him in."

8/13740 Sergeant W.O.M. STREET. 8th Battalion. Citation London Gazette 15.03.1916 page 2894.

"For conspicuous gallantry when, in full moonlight and although frequently fired at, he made a good reconnaissance of the enemy's wire. He shows a total disregard for danger, and has an excellent influence on the men under him."

203373 Private T. SUTTON. (Walsall). 1/5th Battalion attached 137th Trench Mortar Battery. London Gazette 03.06.1919 page 6858, Citation London Gazette 11.03.1920 page 3099.

"He has on many occasions shown marked gallantry. During the attack upon Bellenglise, 29th September 1918, he single handed, captured 18 of the enemy, and personally secured one of the crossings on the canal, so that two mortars under his command could be hurried across."

8327 Lance Corporal Ernest F. SWINNERTON. 2nd Battalion. London Gazette 14.01.1916 page 611, Citation London Gazette 11.03.1916 page 2725.

"For conspicuous gallantry. Company Quartermaster Sergeant Allen and Corporal Swinnerton crawled out along the tow path in spite of heavy fire and with utter disregard of danger rescued no fewer than two wounded officers and ten men."

241989 Corporal A.E. TAYLOR. (Gravesend). 1/6th Battalion TF. London Gazette 12.03.1919 page 3389, Citation London Gazette 02.12.1919 page 14882.

"During the operations at Bellenglise, on 29th September 1918, he, after our final objective had been gained, saw four enemy officers escaping down a trench. He followed them through our barrage, killed two and captured two of them. Throughout the operation he showed marked gallantry and determination in attacking enemy posts."

9678 Lance Corporal G.W. TAYLOR. (Brownhills). 7th Battalion. Citation London Gazette 25.08.1917 page 8841.

"For conspicuous gallantry and devotion to duty in attending wounded under shell fire, during which the medical officer became a casualty. For several days he rendered most valuable assistance keeping admirable control of his men and successfully tending and evacuating all the wounded. His tireless devotion and courageous conduct have on every occasion proved invaluable to his battalion when in action."

240090 Company Sergeant Major T.R. TAYLOR MM. (Wolverhampton). 1/6th Battalion TF. London Gazette 12.03.1919 page 3389. Citation London Gazette 02.12.1919 page 14882.

"During the operations at Bellenglise, on 29th September 1918, he rendered invaluable assistance to the one remaining officer with the company in keeping his company together in the dense fog. He led several parties to clear dugouts and cellars occupied by the enemy. Throughout he showed magnificent coolness and fighting spirit a very fine example to all."

8/13954 Sergeant E. TERRY. (Appleton). London Gazette 03.06.1918 page 6483, Citation London Gazette 21.10.1918 page 12373.

"For conspicuous gallantry and devotion to duty as a patrol leader. He has obtained much valuable information, and carried out his duties in a very thorough manner. He inspires his men with the greatest utmost confidence at all times."

242520 Private G.H. THOMAS. (Hednesford). 1/6th Battalion TF. London Gazette 01.01.1919 page 45, Citation London Gazette 03.09.1919 page 11163.

"He has served with this battalion continuously for two years, and during the last few months has shown great initiative and daring on both day and by night. He has the qualities of a good leader, and is a fine example to his section."

42811 Private W. THOMPSON. (Richmond). 4th Battalion. Citation London Gazette 30.10.1918 page 12841.

"For conspicuous gallantry and devotion to duty for four day's heavy fighting. He was one of the Lewis Gun team, and on the first day the remainder of the team became casualties, and all the magazines were lost except the one on the gun. During each withdrawal he stayed behind with his gun, firing and unloading his own magazines himself, until everyone was clear. On the third day he took forward his gun, and by enfilade fire prevented the enemy for twenty-four hours from concentrating and organising an attack on his battalion. He showed fine courage and determination."

7408 Private S.E. TILL. 2nd Battalion. London Gazette 03.06.1916 page 5585, Citation London Gazette 21.06.1916 page 6156.

"For conspicuous gallantry. During operations he assisted a wounded officer to cover in a shell hole, and dressed his wounds and also those of a wounded private. He erected cover from flanking machine gun fire. When it was dark he went back and guided a rescue party. He was slightly wounded but remained at duty."

12005 Sergeant A. TITLEY. (Walsall). 4th Battalion. Citation London Gazette 03.09.1918 page 10353.

"For conspicuous gallantry and devotion to duty. On his own initiative he collected a body of stragglers and brought them forward to reinforce his company in the front line. Throughout five days severe fighting he showed great coolness, and by his fine example and courage greatly assisted an orderly retirement."

9686 Private Charles Henry TUCKLEY. (Walsall). 3rd Battalion attached 1st Battalion. London Gazette 14.01.1916 page 612, Citation London Gazette 11.03.1916 page 2728.

"For conspicuous gallantry, Lance Corporal Hatheway and Privates Tuckley and Knowles volunteered to crawl out to the enemy trenches and reconnoitre. In spite of heavy and continuous fire they reached the trenches, observed the enemy and brought back an excellent report."

201928 Private J. TUNSTALL. (Sutton). Citation London Gazette 28.03.1918 page 3878.

"For conspicuous gallantry and devotion to duty during an enemy counter attack in volunteering to take a message back to Bn Hd Qrs, 800 yards in broad daylight under intense shelling. When within 250 yards of their objective he and his companion were both wounded. His comrade died, but though seriously wounded in the leg he crawled the remainder of the distance and delivered his message before he collapsed."

13725 Corporal (Acting Sergeant) G.H. TWINBERROW MM & Bar. (Redditch). 1st Battalion. London Gazette 17.04.1919 page 5015, Citation London Gazette 25.02.1920 page 2297 (Italy).

"Throughout the operations 27th-29th October 1918, at Papadopoli. During the advance he frequently went forward to ascertain the position of enemy machine guns and brought back valuable information. On the 20th he pushed forward his scouts into Vayola and gained touch with the retreating enemy. On the 29th and 30th October he again went out, bringing back most useful information. Throughout he showed remarkable initiative and utter disregard of danger."

203284 Private L.T. VARNAM. (Appleby Magna). 1/5th Battalion TF. London Gazette 03.06.1919 page 6859, Citation London Gazette 11.03.1920 page 3105.

"He took part in the storming of the Scheldt Canal in September 1918. During the attacks he came across a large party of other troops, and led them forward and placed them in position. He did excellent work throughout. On the 3rd October with a few men, he rushed a machine gun pit, killing the garrison."

10521 Quartermaster Sergeant E. WALKER. 7th Battalion. London Gazette 03.06.1916 page 5585, Citation London Gazette 21.06.1916 page 6157.

"For consistent good work. He efficiently performed the duties of Quartermaster for a considerable time."

2475 Lance Corporal E. WARD. Citation London Gazette 19.08.1916 page 8244.

"For conspicuous gallantry when going up to and bringing in his captain, who was severely wounded on the enemy's parapet. He was in full view of a large party of the enemy, who threw bombs at him as he approached."

8/10879 Sergeant (Acting Company Sergeant Major) Hugh WARD. 8th Battalion. (Willenhall). London Gazette 26.11.1917 page 12325, Citation London Gazette 06.02.1918 page 1773.

"For conspicuous gallantry and devotion to duty. He led his company straight to the final objective with great coolness and disregard for danger, and organised the consolidation of the captured position, all the officers having become casualties. He personally captured twenty prisoners and continued to command the company with great courage and ability for two days."

10285 Corporal (Acting Sergeant) J. WAYMONT. 7th Battalion. London Gazette 03.06.1916 page 5585, Citation London Gazette 21.06.1916 page 6157.

"For conspicuous good work with patrols. He has always volunteered for risky enterprises."

9264 Corporal (Acting Sergeant) A. WHEATLEY MM. (Jersey, Channel Islands). 1st Battalion. London Gazette 26.11.1917 page 12325, Citation London Gazette 06.02.1918 page 1774.

"For conspicuous gallantry and devotion to duty. He attacked and captured a machine gun before it could be brought into action. He showed great energy in constructing a strong point on the threatened flank. He kept a Lewis Gun in his post, and killed many of the enemy who exposed themselves."

200436 Private (Acting Corporal) A.H. WILKINS. 1/5th Battalion. (Walsall). Citation London Gazette 03.09.1918 page 10361.

"For conspicuous gallantry and devotion to duty. He destroyed an enemy machine gun with a bomb and bayoneted two of the team. Then he reorganised his party, killed three more of the enemy himself and took several prisoners."

6622 Company Sergeant Major C. WITHERS. 1st Battalion. London Gazette 23.06.1915 page 6137, Citation London Gazette 30.06.1915 page 6409.

"For conspicuous energy and devotion to duty since November 1914, in the work of reorganising the battalion."

8322 Company Sergeant Major W. WRIGHT. 2nd Battalion. London Gazette 03.06.1916 page 5585, Citation London Gazette 21.06.1916 page 6158.

"For conspicuous and consistent good work. He is always ready to volunteer for dangerous enterprises. On one occasion he voluntarily joined a bombing party to deny a crater to the enemy and by his courage and good example helped save a critical situation."

200106 Corporal (Local Sergeant) William Thomas WRIGHT. (Birmingham). 1/6th Battalion. London Gazette 12.03.1919 page 3390. Citation London Gazette 02.12.1919 page 14889.

"In the attack north of Sequehart on the 3rd October 1918, when about 300 yards of our lines was being held up by an enemy machine gun, he on his own initiative made his way round the flank, which was covered by another enemy machine gun, and succeeded in getting up the post taking eighteen prisoners and capturing the machine gun. He showed conspicuous courage and did splendid work."

16274 Private (Acting Lance Corporal) George YATES. (Tipton). Citation London Gazette 15.11.1918 page 13457.

"For conspicuous gallantry during an attack. He was in charge of a Lewis Gun, and showed great initiative in pinning down enemy machine guns with fire while the rifle sections worked round their flanks. By this method the company rounded up twenty machine guns, which would have undoubtedly held up the attack. He rendered valuable services."

SELECTED PERSONAL DETAILS

Details of other recipients can be found on p.177 et seq.

Loos British Cemetery, Plot XVIII, Row B Grave 5

8569 Sgt W. BIRCHALL DCM MM
1st Bn South Staffords

8/13211 Acting Company Sergeant Major
Henry Sydney BIRD DCM
8th Bn South Staffords, DoW 8th July 1916

13002 Sgt John EADES DCM, MM & Bar
1st Bn South Staffords

John Eades was born in 1893 at Wednesbury and lived at 24 Leabrook Square with his parents. He was one of seven children, having four brothers and two sisters. When war was declared in 1914 he enlisted into the 1st Battalion South Staffordshire Regiment in September that same year and was posted to France on 27th January 1915.

He was soon promoted to Lance Corporal and not long after he received his first recognition for his actions in November 1916 when he received a Mention in Despatches (Oak Leaf). His next award was that of the Military Medal, this was for saving the lives of members of his unit who had been involved in a mining operation which being discovered by the Germans had infused gas into it. At risk to his own life he entered the mine and helped with the evacuation of the men overcome by the gas. Whilst he was on leave he received the medal and a silver watch from his former work mates at Bagnall's. He made a short speech and said he would be inspired to do greater deeds on return to his unit. On his return he was promoted to Corporal then Sergeant.

During the night 5th/6th August 1917 he was in the trenches at Bullecourt when the Germans attempted to raid the battalion front line, they were spotted and beaten off. For his part in this action he received a bar to his Military Medal.

On the 4th October 1917 the 1st South Staffords took part in the battle for Polygon Wood in Belgium. John Eades was in charge of a platoon of men and during the course of the battle he led his platoon and helped to capture and consolidate a position. He was subsequently awarded the Distinguished Conduct Medal.

It is quite remarkable that he saw active service with the Battalion throughout the war and served in France, Belgium and Italy and did not receive any major wounds. On his return to England he married Lillian Turner and had four children, three boys and one girl. He returned to his former occupation at Bagnall's until he was forced to retire with ill health. In 1957 he had an operation for lung cancer and had one of his lungs removed. It was as a result of this illness that he died on the 7th September 1958 aged 65.

John Eades was a very modest down to earth man according to his family members and enjoyed a drink at his local, the Boat Inn. Both he and his wife Lillian are buried at St Marks, Ocker Hill, Tipton. Lillian survived him until 21st January 1971.

9600 Private Harold EDWARDS DCM
1st Bn South Staffords

Harold Edwards came from Wolverhampton Street, Bilston and prior to the 1914-1918 was was employed at Messrs Sankey & Sons of Bilston.

He enlisted into the South Staffordshire Regiment and was posted to the 1st Battalion. It was while serving as a stretcher bearer, on the 25th September 1915 he was wounded himself but refused attention until he had dealt with the casualties.

He was awarded the Distinguished Conduct Medal and the French Croix de Guerre. Because of the severity of his injuries he was unfit for further active service.

After the war he married and had two children, Harold and Gwen. He took up market trading and purchased a pony and trap. After visiting various local markets he would stop at the Rose and Crown in Bilston for a few drinks. He had indifferent health but lived into his seventies.

8/13628 Acting CQMS Robert HANDY DCM

8/12858 Private Samuel LEE DCM

9398 Corporal G.H. LESTER DCM

9740 Private R KNOWLES DCM

SS/24920 CQMS (A/RSM) S.NEALE DCM. Attached London Regt

14543 Private P NOLAN DCM & Bar, MM

16795 CSM J. SMITHMAN DCM & Bar

9678 L/Cpl G.W. TAYLOR DCM
7th Bn South Staffords

9836 Pte C.H. TUCKLEY DCM
3rd Bn attached 1st Bn

THE MILITARY MEDAL

THE award of the Military Medal was announced in the Supplement to the *London Gazette* on Wednesday 5th April, 1916.

On the obverse of the medal is the Royal Effigy and on the reverse of the medal are the words "FOR BRAVERY IN THE FIELD", circled by a wreath surmounted by the Royal cipher and a crown. The ribbon is one inch and one quarter in width, and is coloured dark blue having in the centre three white and two crimson stripes alternating. When further acts or awards of the Military Medal are made a Bar is added to the medal already conferred.

No.	Rank	Name/Residence	Battalion	London Gazette	Page
10065	A/Sgt	E. ABELL	9th	03.06.1916	5586
32710	Pte	F.W. ABELL Leicester	7th	28.01.1918	1378
39886	Pte	A. ADAMS Chesterfield	4th	27.06.1918	7587
12803	Sgt	W. ALLCHURCH Stourbridge	1st	26.05.1917	5191
9047	Pte	B. ALLCOCK Bilston	2nd	17.06.1919	7675
15225	L/Cpl	T. ALLEN		09.12.1916	12041
42503	Pte	W.R. ALLEN Benwick	5th	17.06.1919	7675
40750	Pte	H. AMERY Farsley	2/5th	13.03.1918	3226
13352	A/Cpl	A.B. AMISON		09.12.1916	12041
11869	Pte	F. ANDREWS Wolverhampton	7th	19.11.1917	11961
16074	Cpl	D. APPLEBY	6th Coy MGC Now Sgt SSR	21.10.1916	10215
9132	Pte	J. ARBLASTER	7th	16.08.1917	8418
30787	Cpl	C. ARCHER Wednesbury	7th	17.06.1919	7675
200315	Pte	A. ARMS Bloxwich	2nd	17.06.1919	7675
10112	Sgt	W.J. ARNOLD Wolverhampton	7th	12.06.1918	7005
9011	A/Cpl	T. AUSTIN Darlaston	7th	28.01.1918	1379
8320	Cpl	C. BAGLEY	1st	12.03.1917	2482
4/9833	Pte	H. BAGNALL	7th	16.02.1917	1749
200317	L/Cpl	F.S. BAILEY Birmingham	1/5th	28.01.1918	1379

No.	Rank	Name/Residence	Battalion	London Gazette	Page
43251	Pte	F. BAINBRIDGE Nottingham	1st	04.02.1918	1609
14988	Pte	E. BAKER Darlaston		17.09.1917	9604
33255	Pte	J. BAKER	1st	18.07.1917	7275
5256	Pte	J.H. BAKER	6th	21.10.1916	10215
40004	Pte	W.L. BALDING Derslingham	1st	17.09.1917	9604
8932	Pte (L/Cpl)	E.T. BALLINGER	1st	01.09.1916	8653
40111	Pte	J.J. BARBER Smallthorne	1st	04.02.1918	1609
8963	Pte	J. BARLOW	2nd	16.02.1917	1749
200164	Pte	W. BARLOW Hockley	1/5th	14.05.1919	6033
7952	Pte	W. BARNES	5th	03.06.1916	5587
238036	Sgt	M. BARTHROPP Colchester	2nd Bar	21.08.1917 20.08.1919	8642 10556

(London Gazette Index for 21.08.1917 page 8642 shows M. Bartropp London Regt)

No.	Rank	Name/Residence	Battalion	London Gazette	Page
203711	Pte	W. BARRATT Spilsby	2nd	10.02.1919	2111
7173	Sgt	W.J. BARRATT		14.12.1916	12219
32509	Cpl	T.W. BARTLETT Blackburn	1st	29.08.1918	10114
16538	Pte	W. BARTON West Bromwich	6th	14.05.1919	6033
43536	Pte	S.J. BARTY Sutton	4th	29.08.1918	10114
12053	Pte	R. BATEMAN DCM	1st Bar	01.09.1916 12.03.1917	8654 2482
36030	Cpl	M.L. BATES Dudley		21.10.1918	12401

No.	Rank	Name/Residence	Battalion	London Gazette	Page
40130	Pte (A/Cpl)	S. BEASLEY Burslem	1st	29.03.1919 (Italy)	4131
9586	Pte	J.A. BEAVER	2nd	21.10.1916	10216
8862	A/CSM	W.A. BEECH	1st	01.09.1916	8654

William Arthur, Born Smethwick, Enlisted Birmingham, Killed in Action F & F 26.10.1917.
(Special Reserve Attached South Staffs Regt)

No.	Rank	Name/Residence	Battalion	London Gazette	Page
15593	Pte	W. BEESTON	7th	09.12.1916	12042
241953	Pte	O.W. BELLARS Peterborough	6th	14.05.1919	6033
16196	Pte	H.E. BELLFIELD	7th	19.11.1917	11962

Harry Ernest, Born Willenhall, Enlisted Wolverhampton. Killed in Action F & F 21.11.1917.

No.	Rank	Name/Residence	Battalion	London Gazette	Page
14087	Pte	H. BENNETT Kenilworth		21.10.1918	12401
4/9218	Pte	J. BENNETT		16.02.1917	1750
17149	Pte	J. BENTLEY	2nd	16.02.1917	1750

Born Walsall, Enlisted Darlaston, Resided Walsall. Died of Wounds F & F 25.03.1918.

No.	Rank	Name/Residence	Battalion	London Gazette	Page
240054	CSM	D. BETHEL Wolverhampton	6th	17.06.1919	7675
10308	Pte	E. BEVAN Wednesbury	7th	28.01.1918	1379
8479	Sgt (A/CQMS)	T. BILLS Great Bridge	1st	17.12.1917	13187
36961	Pte	R. BIRCH Walsall		27.06.1918	7587
241734	Pte	W. BIRCH Walsall	6th	17.06.1919	7675
8569	Sgt	W. BIRCHALL		14.12.1916	12219
9766	Pte	F. BIRD		14.12.1916	12219
8914	Cpl	J. BIRD Cannock	1/5th	14.05.1919	6033
19003	Pte	W. BIRD Bridgtown	7th	28.01.1918	1380

No.	Rank	Name/Residence	Battalion	London Gazette	Page
10089	Pte	R. BLUNT Sparkbrook	2nd	13.03.1918	3228
240827	Cpl	J.E. BLYTHE Wolverhampton	6th	21.10.1918	12402
12014	L/Cpl	C. BOARDMAN Hednesford	7th	28.01.1918	1380
200147	Sgt	H.S. BOND Birmingham	1/5th	29.08.1918	10115
10506	Pte	T. BOOKER		14.12.1916	12220
16331	Pte	E. BOOT	1st	26.05.1917	5191
240619	Sgt	A.J. BOWKER Wolverhampton	6th	17.06.1919	7675
32579	Pte (A/Cpl)	W. BOXALL Brentwood	1st	29.03.1919 (Italy)	4131
201140	Pte	G.E. BRACE Smethwick	1/5th	14.05.1919	6033
32511	Pte	A. BRADFORD	1st Bar	26.05.1917 17.12.1917	5191 13186

Born Oakthorpe, Leicestershire, Enlisted Mansfield Notts, Resided Kirby-in-Ashfield Notts, L/Cpl. Killed in Action F & F 26.10.1917. Formerly 12815 Leicestershire Regiment.

No.	Rank	Name/Residence	Battalion	London Gazette	Page
235356	Pte	S.W. BREWSTER Ipswich	2nd	11.02.1919	2111
8/10088	Sgt	G. BRICKNELL	8th	01.09.1916	8654

Born Hockley, Warwickshire, Enlisted Warwick, Resided Kenilworth. CSM. Killed in Action F & F 12.10.1917.

No.	Rank	Name/Residence	Battalion	London Gazette	Page
2484	Cpl	H.E. BRIDGWATER	6th	11.11.1916	10919
7388	L/Sgt	G.H. BRITTAIN	2nd	03.06.1916	5588
11468	L/Cpl	J.T. BROARDHURST	8th	17.04.1917	3697
9178	Pte	W. BROARDHURST	2nd	17.04.1917	3697
7106	Cpl	E. BROCKHURST Brownhills	1st	17.12.1917	13188

Edward Brockhurst was the son of Mr & Mrs James Brockhurst of Church Street, Brownhills, Staffordshire. James Brockhurst was formerly a soldier with 23 years service to his credit. Little is known about Edward Brockhurst's formative years prior to 1904 when he enlisted into the South Staffordshire Regiment. On completion of his basic training he joined the 1st Battalion who were stationed at Curragh Camp, Ireland. He served his time with the colours and was put on the reserve, returning to civilian life he married and became a miner.

On the outbreak of war he was recalled from the reserve and as the 1st Battalion were in South Africa he joined the 2nd Battalion. The battalion was sent to France from Southampton on the SS *Irawaddy* and landed at Havre on the 13th August 1914. After advancing to meet the Germans they were ordered to retreat in the direction of Harveng, this was the start of the retreat to Mons.

During the fighting at the end of October, early November around the area of Ypres, he was wounded having been shot through the hand and foot; he was evacuated to England for treatment. On recovering from his wounds he was posted to the 1st Battalion who had arrived from Africa.

He appears to have come through the battles of 1916 and most of 1917 without further injury; he was now promoted to Corporal. It was during the battle of Polygon Wood between the 3rd to 6th November 1917 that his actions were recognised by the award of the Military Medal.

It had been reported that he was missing presumed killed in action, this proved to be wrong.

He moved with the battalion to the Italian front and remained there until the armistice was signed on the 11th November 1918. Edward Brockhurst was a keen footballer and a member of the Brownhills Albion football team. He also played for the army and was captain of the team that won the army cup in France, he himself scoring the winning goal. His discharge came through in January 1919 when he returned to Brownhills. He had attained the rank of Sergeant

No.	Rank	Name/Residence	Battalion	London Gazette	Page
36708	Pte	A.B. BROMAGE Smethwick	4th	29.08.1918 Amendment London Gazette 11.12.1918	10115 14671.
2349	Cpl	F. BROOKES	6th	11.11.1916	10919
241416	Pte (L/Cpl)	W.A. BROTHERS Birmingham	6th	02.11.1917	11329
10654	Pte	E. BROTHERTON	7th	19.02.1917	1751
17108	Sgt	I. BROWN Moseley		19.11.1917	11963
9960	A/Cpl	W. BRUERTON Wolverhampton	7th	28.01.1918	1381
9804	Pte	W. BUCKERFIELD	7th	16.08.1917	8419
16173	Pte	G.H. BULLOCK DCM	2nd Bar	21.10.1916 19.02.1917	10216 1756
15630	Pte (A/LCpl)	S. BULLOCK Birmingham	1/5th	14.05.1919	6033
19225	Pte	A. BUNCE	1st Bar	10.08.1916 18.07.1917	7886 7274
7317	A/Sgt	G. BUNDY		14.09.1916	8998
201823	Cpl	H. BURGESS	1/5th	29.08.1918	10116

Born Walsall, Enlisted Walsall, Died of Wounds 03.10.1918 (originally 2/6th SSR).

No.	Rank	Name/Residence	Battalion	London Gazette	Page
14473	A/L/Cpl	P.W. BURGESS	6th	23.08.1916	8360
40046	Pte (L/Cpl)	R.E. BURTON Swinton	1st	29.08.1918	10116
8016	A/CSM	L.F. BURTON	1/5th	11.11.1916	10919
26912	Pte	C. BUTTERICK Doncaster	7th	19.11.1917	11963
19550	Pte	H. BYTHEWAY	1st	12.03.1917	2842
43554	Pte	A.E. CADWALLADER Leicester	1/5th	14.05.1919	6033
200159	Sgt	W. CAHILL Walsall	1/5th	14.05.1919	6033
11309	Sgt	V. CAINE	1st	28.09.1917	10023

Born Penkridge, Enlisted Wolverhampton, Resided Penkridge. Killed in Action F & F 26.10.1917.

No.	Rank	Name/Residence	Battalion	London Gazette	Page
7234	Pte	J. CAPEWELL Wednesbury	2nd	17.06.1919	7675
8160	Pte	F. CARLESS		11.11.1916	10919
23237	Pte	R. CARLESS Walsall	2nd	11.02.1919	2111
9484	Pte	B. CARTER Wednesbury	7th	12.06.1918	7006
12629	L/Cpl	G.H. CARTWRIGHT Bloxwich	7th	28.01.1918	1381
8/13584	Sgt	R.W. CARTWRIGHT	8th	01.09.1916	8654
9487	A/Cpl	E. CASH	1st	19.02.1917	1759

Born Walsall, Enlisted Lichfield, Resided Walsall, Killed in Action F & F 01.07.1916.

No.	Rank	Name/Residence	Battalion	London Gazette	Page
200969	Sgt	J. CHAMERLAIN Wadsley	1/5th	14.05.1919	6033
26239	Sgt	C.J. CHAPPELL Nottingham	7th	23.07.1919	9376
42588	Pte	G.J. CHARLTON Wheatley Hill	1/5th	14.05.1919	6033
10501	Cpl	E. CHATWIN	1st	19.02.1917	1759

Born Rushall, Enlisted Mansfield Notts, L/Sgt. Killed in Action 01.07.1916. Formerly 3966 Notts & Derby Regt.

No.	Rank	Name/Residence	Battalion	London Gazette	Page
60	Sgt	F. CHEADLE	6th	11.11.1916	10920
241249	Pte	J. CENEY West Bromwich	6th	14.05.1919	6033
24225	Pte	G.A. CLARKE	1st	28.01.1918	1382

George Arthur, Born Leicester, Enlisted Leicester. Died of Wounds F & F 19.10.1917, Formerly 27623 Leicestershire Regt.

No.	Rank	Name/Residence	Battalion	London Gazette	Page
240151	Pte	D. CLEMPSON Bilston	6th	14.05.1919	6033
9627	A/Sgt	A. CLEVERLEY	1st	12.03.1917	2483

Born Powick Worcs, Enlisted Lichfield, Resided Whitbourne Worcs. Sgt. Killed in Action F & F 12.05.1917.

No.	Rank	Name/Residence	Battalion	London Gazette	Page
2806	Sgt	W.J.S. CLINTON	6th	11.11.1916	10920
46805	Pte	S. CLOWES Leek	2nd	11.02.1919	2111
242075	Cpl	H.E. COE (E) Stafford	2/6th	16.07.1918	8314
22046	Pte	A. COLE Oakham	2nd	13.03.1918	3230
241831	L/Cpl	J. COLLINS Wolverhampton	6th Bar	28.01.1918 13.09.1918	1382 10759
41481	Pte	R.C. COMLEY Warmley	1st	04.02.1918	1610
40843	L/Cpl	J. COOK Cranbrook	1st	04.02.1918	1610
200820	Sgt	J.T. COOK		21.08.1917	8643
238015	Pte (A/Cpl)	J.T. COOK Birmingham	1st	29.03.1919 (Italy)	4131
42895	Pte	W.F. COOK L/Cpl Stantonbury	2nd	11.02.1919	2111
20489	Pte	L.G. COOPER Walsall	7th	12.06.1918	7007
42511	Cpl	J.R. COOPER Scarborough	2nd	11.02.1919	2111
23560	Cpl	E. COPPOCK Chorley	4th	29.08.1918	10117

No.	Rank	Name/Residence	Battalion	London Gazette	Page
8/10424	Sgt (A/CQMS)	J. COURTNEY		11.10.1916	9829
9834	Sgt	J. COWLES West Bromwich	7th	28.01.1918	1383
12075	Pte	W.H. COX Bilston	7th (Also shown as 2nd)	13.03.1918	3230
17778	Sgt	C.T. CRADDOCK	7th	28.01.1918	1383

Charles Thomas, Born Rushall, Enlisted Walsall, A/CSM .Killed in Action F & F 06.05.1918.

No.	Rank	Name/Residence	Battalion	London Gazette	Page
43599	Pte	L. CRAWFORD Tooting	1/5th	14.05.1919	6033
8909	Pte	W. CRAWFORD Aston	1st Bar	09.12.1916 17.12.1917	12043 13186
200841	CQMS	S. CRESWELL Walsall Wood	1/5th	14.05.1919	6033
14959	Pte	C.J. CULLIS		09.12.1916	12044
242506	Pte	H.R. CULLUM Grimsby	6th	14.01.1918	834
9287	L/Cpl	H.W. CUMMINGS Hearne Hill	7th	25.04.1918	5033
24195	Sgt	J.F. CURTIS Leicester	1st	29.03.1919 (Italy)	4131
41622	Pte	R. CURTIS Grantham	1st	29.08.1918	10118
6660	Pte	W. DAINTY Small Heath	7th	17.06.1919	7675
8891	L/Cpl	J. DALES DCM	2nd (Also shown as 1st Bn)	10.08.1916	7886
1056	CSM	J. DANGERFIELD	6th	11.11.1916	10921
9751	Pte	J.T. DANKS Camwell	2nd	11.02.1919	2111
8836	Pte	G.H. DAVIES		11.10.1916	9830
17273	Pte	T. DAVIES	7th	19.02.1917	1751

No.	Rank	Name/Residence	Battalion	London Gazette	Page
10027	Pte	W. DAVIES	1st	17.04.1917	3697
8/43036	Pte	C.H. DAVIS	8th	18.07.1917	7277

Cecil Harry, Born Wolverhampton, Enlisted Wolverhampton, L/Cpl. Died of Wounds F & F 13.10.1917, Formerly 47923 Royal Army Medical Corps.

No.	Rank	Name/Residence	Battalion	London Gazette	Page
8783	Pte	G. DAVIS	1st	26.05.1917	5192
8292	Cpl (A/Sgt)	J. DAVIS Wednesfield	1st	29.03.1919 (Italy)	4131
8403	Sgt	J. DEFLEY	1st	01.09.1916	8655
9445	Pte (L/Cpl)	H. DEGVILLE Walsall	2nd	17.06.1919	7675
10833	L/Sgt	D. DEIGHTON Birmingham	7th	19.11.1917	11964
16306	Cpl	G.S. DELANEY	2nd	17.04.1917	3697
8587	Drum	J.A. DEVMAR	2nd	14.09.1916	8999
7013	Pte	F. DIXON Wednesfield	6th	17.06.1919	7675
11916	Sgt	G. DODD DCM	9th	16.08.1917	8420
7750	Pte (A/LCpl)	H. DODSON		18.07.1917	7278
39868	Pte	H. DRABBLE Mansfield	4th	27.06.1918	7689
12013	Sgt	H.R. DRAPER		14.12.1916	12220
9338	A/Cpl	J. DYAS Hednesford	1st	12.03.1917	2483
13002	L/Cpl	J. EADES Tipton	1st Bar	14.12.1916 28.09.1917	12220 10020
8/13819	L/Cpl	A.H. EDWARDS	8th	03.06.1916	5590
19568	Pte	G.R. EDWARDS	7th	28.01.1918	1384

George Roland, Born Tenby Worcs, Enlisted Hednesford, Resided Cannock, Killed in Action F & F 19.11.1917.

No.	Rank	Name/Residence	Battalion	London Gazette	Page
260060	Sgt	F.H. EDWARDS MSM Brownhills	6th	17.06.1919	7675

No.	Rank	Name/Residence	Battalion	London Gazette	Page
20596	L/Cpl	G.W. EDWARDS Guildford	Att RNVR	07.10.1918	11827
12735	Pte	W. EDWARDS Wolverhampton		21.10.1918	12405
9817	A/Sgt	D. ELWELL Walsall	1st	04.02.1918	1611
3/10375	Cpl	W. EMERY		18.07.1917	7278
8/11795	Pte	C. EVANS		11.10.1916	9830
14075	Pte	D.E. EVANS	1st	04.02.1918	1611

David Elias, Born Treharris Glam, Enlisted Merthyr, Glam, Resided Treharris, Died of Wounds Italy 26.04.1918.

241205	Pte	J. EVANS	2/6th	13.03.1918	3232

Enlisted Wandsworth Surrey, Resided Felinfack Cardigan, Killed in Action F & F 21.03.1918.

12466	Sgt	N. EYESTONE Leamington Spa		19.11.1917	11965
200868	L/Cpl (A/Cpl)	F.H. FARMER West Bromwich	6th	21.10.1918	12406
7022	L/Sgt	A.E. FAULKES	1st	10.08.1916	7887
11963	Pte	E. FEARNLEY Mirfield	4th	27.06.1918	7590
10562	L/Cpl	A. FEAST	1st (Was N&D MM)	09.12.1916	12045
16176	Pte	A. FELLOWS		12.03.1917	2483
15941	Pte	W. FELLOWS Wolverhampton	1st	04.02.1918	1611
17338	Pte	T.H. FINCH Cannock	7th	23.07.1919	9376
7952	Sgt	H. FINLAN Wolverhampton	2nd	16.07.1918	8316
10020	Pte	J.W. FLAVELL	2/5th	04.02.1918	1611

James William. Born Bilston, Enlisted Wolverhampton, Resided Bilston, Killed in Action F & F 12.101.1918 1/5th Bn SSR.

No.	Rank	Name/Residence	Battalion	London Gazette	Page
200960	Sgt	G. FLEMMING	1/5th	11.11.1916	10922

Born Aldridge, Enlisted Walsall, Resided Rushall, Died of Wounds F & F 22.03.1917.

18374	Pte	L. FLETCHER	7th	19.02.1917	1751
9271	L/Cpl	W. FLETCHER	1st	14.09.1916	9000
			Shown in 2 SSR awards		
8327	Cpl	F. FORD	1st	12.03.1917	2483
15268	Sgt	H.E. FORD		23.08.1916	8361
13563	L/Cpl	W. FORSBURY Wednesbury		07.10.1918	11828
8/12898	L/Sgt	G.C. FOSTER Wednesbury	8th	04.02.1918	1611
203588	Pte	H. FOSTER Sheffield	4th	27.06.1918	7590
16129	Sgt	H.W. FOSTER	2nd	21.10.1916	10217
9625	Pte	F. FOUNDLING	2nd	21.10.1916	10217
201363	Cpl (L/Sgt)	W. FOWLER Hednesford	1/5th	14.05.1919	6033
39330	Pte	I.S. FOX	4th	27.06.1918	7590

Issac Sowter, Born Tansley Derbyshire, Enlisted Matlock. L/Cpl. Killed in Action F & F 10.04.1918. (Alfreton)

40917	Pte	T. FRANKUM Reading	1st	28.01.1918	1385
46512	L/Cpl	A.E. FURZE Bristol	1/5th	21.10.1918	12406
13167	Cpl	A. GARBETT Walsall	6th	17.06.1919	7675
9737	A/CSM	G. GARDNER	1st	09.12.1916	12045
240480	Sgt	T.G. GARNER	1/6th	13.11.1918	13398

Thomas Montegue, Born Tettenhall, Enlisted Wolverhampton, Resided Tettenhall, Sgt. Killed in Action F & F 21.08.1918.

18567	L/Cpl	J.R. GATES Hednesford		28.01.1918	1386

No.	Rank	Name/Residence	Battalion	London Gazette	Page
9738	Pte	J. GAVIN Landywood Walsall	1/5th Bar 2nd Bar Also shown as 2nd	17.04.1917 13.03.1918 16.07.1918	3697 3224 8307
30667	Cpl	S. GIBBONS Wolverhampton		12.06.1918	7008
7527	Sgt	A. GIBBS Birmingham	2nd	13.03.1918	3233
8759	A/Sgt	G. GIBBS		11.11.1916	10922
241259	Cpl	W.H. GILBERT Wolverhampton		21.10.1918	12406
8789	Pte	S. GILL Darlaston	1st	29.08.1918	10121
240569	Sgt	G.N. GILL Wolverhampton	6th	17.06.1919	7675
241990	Cpl (L/Sgt)	W.W. GLADDISH Northfleet	6th	17.06.1919	7675
9037	Pte	H. GLEESON	2nd	14.09.1916	9000
19892	Pte	J. GOODALL		17.04.1917	3697
15899	Sgt	L. GOUGH Tipton		19.11.1917	11966
40134	Sgt	J.E. GOULD Tunstall Hanley	1st Bar (Italy)	29.08.1918 23.09.1919	10122 4122
9535	A/Sgt	W.H. GRANT	2nd	17.04.1917	3697

Walter Harry, Born Handsworth, Enlisted Lichfield, Resided Handsworth, Died F & F 10.11.1918.

No.	Rank	Name/Residence	Battalion	London Gazette	Page
2919	Sgt	R.G. GREATREX		06.01.1917	345
8/43104	L/Cpl	E. GREEN		09.07.1917	6830
13266	L/Cpl	H. GREEN		16.08.1917	8421
16285	Pte	J. GREEN	2nd	03.06.1916	5591
241725	Pte	J.T. GREEN Heath Town	6th	21.10.1918	12407
493	Sgt	T. GREEN	1/6th	19.02.1917	1760

Thomas, Born Darlaston, Enlisted Darlaston, Died of Wounds F & F 03.07.1916.

No.	Rank	Name/Residence	Battalion	London Gazette	Page
8/12188	Sgt	H. GREW		18.07.1917	7279
16699	Pte	J.C. GRIFFITHS	2nd	06.01.1917	345

James Charles, Born Bilston, Enlisted Birmingham, Resided Smethwick. Killed in Action F & F 28.07.1916.

No.	Rank	Name/Residence	Battalion	London Gazette	Page
40062	Sgt	J. GROCOTT Burslem	1st Bar	18.07.1917 17.12.1917	7279 13186
8/12406	Cpl	L. GROCOTT		11.10.1916	9831
9721	Pte	J.E. GUEST	7th	21.12.1916	12443
16148	Pte	R. GUNTON	1st	26.05.1917	5192
3184	Cpl	E. HALE	6th	06.01.1917	345
15432	Pte	S. HALE Coseley	2nd	11.02.1919	2111
11512	Pte	T. HALL Att R.E. Wednesbury		28.01.1918	1387
8095	Sgt	W. HALLETT	9th	23.08.1916	8361

Born Wolverhampton, Enlisted Wolverhampton, Died of Wounds F & F 10.07.1917.

No.	Rank	Name/Residence	Battalion	London Gazette	Page
200569	Cpl (A/Sgt)	J.S. HALLING	1/5th	26.05.1917	5192 (Formerly 9115)
200176	Cpl	T. HALLUM	1/5th	26.05.1917	5192
8325	L/Cpl	N. HAMBLETON	2nd	14.09.1916	9001
203423	Sgt	T. HARDWICK Walsall	1/5th	13.09.1918	10766
28513	Sgt	F.J. HARE	4th	27.06.1918	7591

Frederick James, Born Derby, Enlisted Long Eaton, Resided Draycott. Killed in Action F & F 26.04.1918.

No.	Rank	Name/Residence	Battalion	London Gazette	Page
45901	Cpl	W.H. HARE	Now D.L.I.	29.08.1917	9001
15573	Pte	F. HARRIS	7th	16.08.1917	8421
200257	Pte	G.R. HARRIS		21.08.1917	8644
8/43117	Pte	J. HARRIS Longton		19.11.1917	11966
9569	Pte (L/Cpl)	A. HARRISON Wednesbury	1st	29.08.1918	10123

No.	Rank	Name/Residence	Battalion	London Gazette	Page
41633	Pte	C.V. HARRISON Hythe		29.08.1918	10123
15080	Sgt	E. HARRISON	9th	21.08.1917	8644

Edward, Born Droitwich, Worcs, Enlisted Birmingham, Resided Droitwich, Worcs, Killed in Action F & F 27.08.1917.

No.	Rank	Name/Residence	Battalion	London Gazette	Page
201807	Pte	J. HARRISON Pleck	1/5th	29.08.1918	10123
40175	Pte	T. HARRISON Bilston	7th	17.09.1917	9608
8769	Pte	D. HATELEY		11.11.1916	10923
11050	Sgt	C. HATHERELL Bromsgrove		02.11.1917	11334
8821	Pte	G. HATHERLEY (Att TMB.) Nottingham		17.12.1917	13190
32731	Pte	J. HATTON	7th	16.08.1917	8421
200920	Sgt	S. HATTON West Bromwich	2/5th	13.08.1918	3235

"For conspicuous bravery. On December 1st, 1917, near Fontain-Notre-Dame the enemy put down a heavy barrage on our front line and an attack appeared imminent. All telephone wires were cut and it was essential that communication should be established between the front and support companies.

This NCO was in the support company volunteered to proceed to the right flank company where the situation was obscure. He went out with an officer and they were heavily fired on by enemy machine gun fire on leaving their trench. They proceeded to the Headquarters of the right flank company and were under observation and constant shell and machine gun fire for a distance of 1600 yards. Having obtained information Sergeant Hatton returned under fire to Battalion Headquarters."

No.	Rank	Name/Residence	Battalion	London Gazette	Page
3/10343	Sgt (A/CSM)	T. HAWKINS	3rd (Att 1st Bn)	01.09.1916	8656
40931	Pte	H. HAYNES Bethnal Green E.	1st	29.08.1918	10123
11025	Pte	H. HAYNES West Bromwich	7th	29.01.1918	1388
10045	Pte	W.G. HAYWARD	2nd	17.04.1917	3698

William Glenfred, Born Wellington, Salop, Enlisted Wolverhampton, Killed in Action F & F 30.11.1917.

No.	Rank	Name/Residence	Battalion	London Gazette	Page
18591	A/Cpl	P.J.R. HENDLEY	7th	09.12.1916	12046

Percy James Ransford, Born West Bromwich, Enlisted Walsall, Resided Bloxwich. Killed in Action F & F 19.08.1917.

No.	Rank	Name/Residence	Battalion	London Gazette	Page
18642	L/Sgt	J. HERRINGTON	2nd	21.10.1916 (Now Lieut)	10218

No.	Rank	Name/Residence	Battalion	London Gazette	Page
9330	Sgt	J. HEYWOOD	2nd	14.09.1916	9001
10845	Pte	D. HICKEN Heath Hayes	1st	17.12.1917	13191
26553	Pte	H. HICKLIN DCM Nottingham	2nd Bar	13.03.1918 13.03.1919	3235 3413
10915	Pte	J.W. HICKMAN	7th	16.08.1917	8421
23040	Pte	H. HICKS Doncaster	2nd	16.07.1918	8319
37001	Pte	T.W. HIGGS Hednesford	2nd	11.02.1919	2111
200282	Sgt	C. HILL DCM Walsall	1/5th	14.05.1919	6033
9142	Pte (L/Cpl)	F. HILL Wolverhampton	2nd	11.02.1919	2111
6638	Pte	H.P. HILL Burton on Trent	1st	17.12.1917	13191
31615	Pte	J. HILL Worksop	6th	17.06.1919	7675
200282	Sgt	J. HILL Walsall	5th	14.05.1919	6063
13949	Pte	J. HINTON Heathtown	1st	24.01.1919 (Italy)	1224
20153	Pte	G.E. HOARE (E) Staffs	4th	27.06.1918	7591
9233	Pte	D. HOBIN Wolverhampton	1st	04.02.1918	1612
8/13627	Cpl	A. HOLDCROFT	8th	11.10.1916 Died 03.03.1920 Rugeley	9832
3450	Cpl	W. HOLLAND	6th	11.11.1916	10924
17435	CSM	S. HOLLOWAY Derby	6th	17.06.1919	7675
9289	Pte	J. HOLLYHEAD	2nd	14.09.1916	9001

No.	Rank	Name/Residence	Battalion	London Gazette	Page
240592	Drum	C. HOLMES Wolverhampton	6th	09.07.1917	6831
9293	Pte (L/Cpl)	J. HORAN	1st	12.03.1917	2483
203335	Pte	J. HUDSON Wootton	1/5th	13.09.1918	10767
200156	L/Cpl (Cpl)	H. HUGHES (Formerly 8087)	1/5th	26.05.1917	5193
9687	Pte	A. HUMPHREYS	2nd	14.09.1916	9001

Born Southwark Surrey, Enlisted London, Resided Walworth, Surrey. Killed in Action F & F 17.02.1917.

No.	Rank	Name/Residence	Battalion	London Gazette	Page
19245	Pte	S. HUMPHRIES Bridgnorth	1st	17.12.1917	13191
203421	Cpl	J. HUNTBACH		18.07.1918	7280
8048	Pte	G. HUNTER Walsall	2nd	13.03.1918	3236
13308	Sgt	H. HUTCHINSON Walsall	6th	17.06.1919	7675
201899	Pte	G.A. HYDE	1/5th	14.05.1919	6033

George Arthur, Born Smethwick, Enlisted Handsworth, Resided Smethwick. Killed in Action F & F 03.10.1918.

No.	Rank	Name/Residence	Battalion	London Gazette	Page
7933	Sgt	R. HYDE	2nd	14.09.1916	9001
1238	A/Sgt	A.E. ILLIDGE	6th	11.11.1916	10924
9043	Pte	G. JACKSON	1st	12.03.1917	2483
11990	Sgt	S. JACKSON DCM	1st	26.05.1917	5193

Stephen, A/CSM. Born Birmingham, Enlisted Birmingham, CSM. Killed in Action F & F 26.10.1917.

No.	Rank	Name/Residence	Battalion	London Gazette	Page
17154	Pte	W. JACKSON	2nd	21.10.1916	10218
8/14106	Pte	W. JARRATT		11.10.1916	9832
202389	Pte	H.J. JENNER	6th	14.05.1919	6033
7757	CSM	W. JEVONS Poplar	2nd	14.09.1916	9001
240154	Sgt	A.E. JOHNSON Woodsetton	6th	17.06.1919	7675
9800	Pte	B.W. JOHNSON	1st	26.05.1917	5193

No.	Rank	Name/Residence	Battalion	London Gazette	Page
15616	Pte	C.H. JOHNSON Bilston	9th	29.03.1919 (Italy)	4131
12971	Pte	T.S. JOHNSON	1st	12.03.1917	2483

Thomas Silvester, Born Dudley Worcs, Enlisted Wolverhampton, Resided Sedgley. Died of Wounds F & F 24.04.1918. Attached from 4th Special Reserve .

No.	Rank	Name/Residence	Battalion	London Gazette	Page
40038	Pte	W. JOHNSON	SSR (Late Linc Regt)	14.12.1916	12221
40735	Sgt	W. JOHNSON Rusholme		19.11.1917	11968
8571	Pte	A. JONES Walsall Wood	1st	30.01.1920 To be dated 05.05.1919	1222
240620	Sgt	B. JONES Sedgeley	6th	28.01.1918	1390
16087	Cpl	C. JONES	MGC (Late SSR)	19.02.1917	1753
200891	Pte	C. JONES	1/5th	14.05.1919	6033

Born Jersey, Enlisted Old Hill, Resided Halesowen. Killed in Action F & F 03.10.1918.

No.	Rank	Name/Residence	Battalion	London Gazette	Page
9168	Pte	C.V. JONES	1st	14.12.1916	12221
16087	Cpl	E. JONES	MGC (Late SSR)	19.02.1917	1753
240154	Sgt	A.E. JONES	6th	17.06.1919 (Duplicate of below) (shown as A..E in 6)	7675
240154	Sgt	E.A. JONES Bilston	2/6th Bar	14.05.1919 20.10.1919	6033 12872
1680	Cpl	F. JONES	6th Also in 1st Bn awards	11.11.1916	10925
7083	Pte	F. JONES	1st	14.12.1916	12221
242591	L/Cpl	H. JONES Wolverhampton	6th	17.09.1917	9609
240851	Pte	J. JONES	6th	09.07.1917	6831
242532	Pte	J.C. JONES Hednesford	6th	17.06.1919	7675

No.	Rank	Name/Residence	Battalion	London Gazette	Page
17516	Pte	L. JONES	2nd	19.02.1917	1753

Leonard, Born Nottingham, Enlisted Nottingham. L/Cpl. Killed in Action F & F 23.08.1917.

No.	Rank	Name/Residence	Battalion	London Gazette	Page
10082	Pte	S. JONES Wednesbury		02.11.1917	11336
38122	Pte	W. JONES Brierly Hill	7th	28.01.1918	1390
37251	Pte	A.V. JORDAN Groby		06.08.1918	9243
10258	Pte	A. JOYCE	1st	26.05.1917	5193
18421	Pte	A. JOYCE	1st	18.07.1918	7281

Born Nuneaton, Warwickshire, Enlisted Atherstone, Resided Nuneaton. L/Cpl. Died of Wounds Italy 11.08.1918.

No.	Rank	Name/Residence	Battalion	London Gazette	Page
19193	L/Cpl	R. JUDD	7th	21.12.1916	12444
8/14124	Cpl	J. KEATLEY		11.10.1916	9833
235319	Cpl	A.S. KEEBLE Wetheringsett	2nd	11.02.1919	2111
29800	Pte	C. KEELING Deepfield	7th	28.01.1918	1390
13159	Pte	W. Kellett	9th	14.09.1916	9002

Walter, Born Brighouse Yorks, Enlisted Accrington Lancs, Killed in Action F & F 31.07.1916.

No.	Rank	Name/Residence	Battalion	London Gazette	Page
200420	Cpl	J. KELLY	1/5th	26.05.1917	5193

Born Walsall, Enlisted Walsall. Sgt. Killed in Action F & F 04.05.1917. Formerly 8822.

No.	Rank	Name/Residence	Battalion	London Gazette	Page
8817	L/Cpl	R. KENDRICK Walsall	1st Bar (Italy)	04.02.1918 29.03.1919	1613 4122
9749	A/Cpl	J. KENNERLEY		10.08.1916	7888
23545	Sgt	P. KIDDLE Framlington	2nd	11.02.1919	2111
8/13887	Sgt	F. KING		11.10.1916	9833
41751	Pte (L/Cpl)	T. KIRTON Northampton	1st	29.03.1919 (Italy)	4131
16007	Pte	E.L. KNIGHT		16.08.1917	8422
241907	Pte	W. KNIGHT Codicote Welyn	2/6th	28.01.1918	1390

No.	Rank	Name/Residence	Battalion	London Gazette	Page
9003	Pte	J. LAKIN Atherstone	7th	28.01.1918	1390
9721	Pte	O.L. LAKIN	2nd	14.09.1916	9002
10008	Pte	W. LAMB		14.12.1916	12221
13694	Sgt	G. LANCASTER Birmingham		12.12.1917	13015
8222	Sgt	A.E. LANE	2nd Bar	06.01.1917 17.04.1917	346 3696
5601	Pte	E. LANE	6th	06.01.1917	346
16387	Sgt	R. LANE Satley	2nd	13.03.1918	3238
16444	Cpl	A.A.E. LAW Lowestoft	2nd	11.02.1919	2111
4/9413	Sgt	H. LAWTON	1st	17.04.1917	3698
9039	L/Sgt	F. LEA	2nd	21.10.1916	10219
8344	Pte	J. LEARY	3rd (Att 1st Bn)	03.06.1916	5593
240408	Cpl (A/Sgt)	W.E. LEASON Heath Town	6th	17.09.1917	9609
7570	CSM	J.T. LEEKE Birmingham	1st	29.03.1919 (Italy)	4131
8/13112	L/Cpl	H.E LESTER	8th	03.06.1916	5593

Harold Ernest, Born Tipton, Enlisted Wednesbury, Resided Tipton, Died of Wounds F & F 13.05.1917.

No.	Rank	Name/Residence	Battalion	London Gazette	Page
4/8773	Pte (L/Cpl)	A.N. LETTS	2nd Bar	14.09.1916 21.12.1916	9002 12449
7585	SGT	G. LEWIS		21.10.1916	10219
7458	CQMS	W.H. LICHFIELD	2nd	14.09.1916	9002

William Henry, Born Birmingham, Enlisted Lichfield, Resided Birmingham. CSM. Died of Wounds F & F 10.08.1916.

No.	Rank	Name/Residence	Battalion	London Gazette	Page
200373	Sgt	A. LINNELL	1/5th	17.04.1917	3698

Born Bloxwich, Enlisted Walsall, Resided Bloxwich, Killed in Action F & F 14.03.1917, Late 8706.

No.	Rank	Name/Residence	Battalion	London Gazette	Page
240601	Pte	R. LITTLE	6th	09.07.1917	6832

No.	Rank	Name/Residence	Battalion	London Gazette	Page
41194	Pte	W.J. LITTLE Wembley	9th	29.03.1919 (Italy)	4131
8424	Sgt	F. LLOYD	 Bar	11.11.1916 21.12.1916	10926 12449
17913	Pte	A. LOACH West Bromwich	7th	23.07.1919	9376
8912	Pte (A/Sgt)	T. LOCKETT Cheslyn Hay	1st	17.09.1917	9609
46990	Pte	A. LOCKWOOD Shepley	2nd	11.02.1919	2111
235351	Cpl	G.F. LONG Ipswich	2nd	11.02.1919	2111
19954	Sgt	J.H. LOUNDS Willenhall		21.10.1918	12410
204456	Pte	H. LOVATT Old Woking	7th	23.07.1919	9376
200942	L/Sgt	S. LOWE	1/5th	11.11.1916	10926

Samuel, Born Netherton, Worcs, Enlisted Old Hill, Resided Netherton, Worcs, Killed in Action F & F 28.06.1917. Formerly 9987.

No.	Rank	Name/Residence	Battalion	London Gazette	Page
9832	Pte	G. LUNN	1st	12.03.1917	2484
32500	L/Sgt (A/Sgt)	W. LYCETT Coalville	1st Bar (Italy)	29.08.1918 29.03.1919	10127 4122
40001	Cpl	T. LYNCH	1st	17.04.1917	3698
202090	Pte	H. MADELEY	2/5th	29.08.1917	9001

Herbert John, Enlisted Wednesbury. L/Cpl. Killed in Action F & F 21.03.1918. 2/6th Bn .

"For conspicuous bravery. On the night July 1-2, 1917 an officers patrol was attacked by a strong party of the enemy east of our front line at Beauchamp. We suffered some casualties but owing to the darkness and the long grass it was impossible to find the wounded and bodies of the killed.

L/Cpl Shaw and Pte Madeley volunteered to go out and search the ground although it was under the enemy's observation and fire. They succeeded in finding the bodies of the killed and of one man who was severely wounded, and at great personal risk under the enemy's fire carried in the wounded man and the bodies of the dead undoubtedly saving the life of the wounded man and preventing the enemy from obtaining identification."

No.	Rank	Name/Residence	Battalion	London Gazette	Page
200364	Sgt	T. MALEY Quarry Bank	1/5th	14.05.1919	6033
12698	L/Sgt	B. MALLINSON	2nd	14.09.1916	9002

No.	Rank	Name/Residence	Battalion	London Gazette	Page
235374	Sgt	G.H. MANN	2nd	11.02.1919	2111

George Henry, Born Chesterton, Cambridgeshire, Enlisted Cambridge. Died of Wounds F & F 01.10.1918, Formerly 1343 Cambridgeshire Regt.

No.	Rank	Name/Residence	Battalion	London Gazette	Page
40102	Pte	L.P. MANSELL Burton on Trent	1st	04.02.1918	1613
6893	L/Cpl	S. MANTLE	1st Bar	17.12.1917 29.08.1918	13192 10111
15285	Cpl	E. MARKHAM Boston	9th	29.03.1919 (Italy)	4131
43594	Pte	G. MARRIOTT Sutton	6th	14.05.1919	6033
18989	Pte	W.D. Martin Worcester	7th	19.11.1917	11969
240118	Pte	A. MASON Willenhall	6th	23.07.1919	9376
4/10019	Cpl	F. MASON Wolverhampton	1st Bar (Italy)	18.07.1917 29.03.1919	7282 4122
40054	Pte	H. MASON	1st	17.12.1917	13192

Born Tunstall, Enlisted Stoke on Trent, Resided Tunstall. Killed in Action F & F 26.10.1917, Formerly 9766 NSR Regt.

No.	Rank	Name/Residence	Battalion	London Gazette	Page
14878	Sgt	J. MASON		16.08.1917	8422
8177	Sgt	J. MASSEY		21.10.1916	10219
32635	Pte	F.B.T. MATTHEWS Oxford	1st	17.12.1917	13193
8786	Pte	J.C.F. MATTHEWS	2nd Bar	17.04.1917 17.06.1919	3698 7643
8/11621	Pte	T. MCHUGH	8th	18.07.1917	7282
32519	L/Cpl (A/Sgt)	C.W. MEE Coalville	1st	29.08.1918	10129
40036	Pte	J.A. MERCER	1st	26.05.1917	5194
45683	Pte	E.W. MILES Tamworth		13.11.1918	13399
200991	Pte (Now L/Cpl Late 84)	W. MILLWARD	1/5th	26.05.1917	5194

No.	Rank	Name/Residence	Battalion	London Gazette	Page
12531	Pte	W. MINER Wolverhampton	1st	17.12.1917	13193
24649	Pte	H. MOORE Wolverhampton		29.08.1918	10129
14229	Pte	T. MOORE Pelsall	8th	28.01.1918	1393
4/9698	Pte	F. MORGAN	8th	09.12.1916	12049
17166	L/Cpl	E.C. MORRIS		10.08.1916	7889
240197	Cpl (L/Sgt)	J. MORRIS Bilston	6th Bar	21.08.1917 02.11.1917	8645 11326
3697	Pte	J.T. MOSELEY	2/6th	28.07.1918	7772

Killed in Action 01.07.1916. (C.W.G.C. Shows 1/6th)

No.	Rank	Name/Residence	Battalion	London Gazette	Page
242031	Pte	R.L. MOUNTFORD Wolverhampton	6th	02.11.1917	11339
40567	Sgt	S.P. MOYER Peterborough	2nd	11.02.1919	2111
8/40495	Pte	W.E. MUGGLETON Leicester	8th	14.01.1918	840
46654	Pte	G.B.MURRAY Gordon	6th	14.05.1919	6033
40049	Sgt	W.H. MURRELL	1st	18.07.1917	7283
14323	Pte	J. NASH		16.08.1917	8423
7511	Bman	W. NEVILLE	1st	14.12.1916	12221
242604	Pte	F. NEWTON Walsall	6th	17.06.1919	7675
17576	Pte	G. NICKS	7th	16.08.1917	8423
14543	Pte	P. NOLAN DCM	9th Bar to DCM	23.08.1916	8363
42951	Pte	A.F. NORGATE Norwich	2nd	11.02.1919	2111
7606	Cpl	F. NORTH	1st	19.02.1917	1754

No.	Rank	Name/Residence	Battalion	London Gazette	Page
40624	Pte	A. NORTON Leicester		23.02.1918	2427
12888	L/Cpl	J.H. NORTON Brierly Hill	7th	25.04.1918	5035
12685	Sgt	T.H. O'CONNOR Walsall	7th	23.07.1919	9763
241938	Pte	J. OLDFIELD Tottenham	6th	17.09.1917	9610
13079	CSM	E. OLIVER MC Willenhall	1st	29.03.1919 (Italy)	4131
15926	Pte	A. OSBOURNE	1st	12.03.1917	2484
43260	L/Cpl	E.C. OVERTON Mansfield	1st	29.08.1918	10130
23521	Cpl	G.T. OVERTON Needham Market	2nd	11.02.1919	2711
15053	Pte	A. PALMER	9th	16.08.1917	8423
241942	L/Cpl	C.S. PALMER	6th	06.01.1917	347 (Formerly 5558)
42952	Pte	F. PARNELL Elsworth	2nd	11.02.1919	2111
9453	Sgt (A/CSM)	W.H. PARR Nottingham	7th	28.01.1918	1394
9639	Pte	E. PARSONS	1st	14.12.1916	12222
4/8996	Pte (L/Cpl)	H. PARTON Moseley	2nd Bar	19.02.1917 13.03.1918	1754 3224
11417	Cpl	E. PARTRIDGE Walsall	1st Bar	17.12.1917 04.02.1918	13193 1609
42771	Cpl	L.B. PEARCE Newcastle	4th	21.10.1918	12413
9815	Pte (L/Cpl)	H. PEARSALL Birmingham	2nd	13.03.1918	3241
8868	Pte	E. PEARSON Wolverhampton	2nd	16.07.1918	8325

No.	Rank	Name/Residence	Battalion	London Gazette	Page
202109	Pte	H. PEARSON Wolverhampton	2/5th	28.01.1918	1394

"For gallantry during the night 23-24 September 1917. He was leading a mule in the pack convoy along No 5 Track for the troops in the line. The enemy put down a heavy barrage on the track and Private Pearson was wounded, in spite of his wounds he remained with his mule and delivered the load at the appointed place and brought back the animal to the transport lines at Vlamertinghe."

No.	Rank	Name/Residence	Battalion	London Gazette	Page
241710	Pte	E.V. PEDLEY Walsall	6th	14.05.1919	6033
240460	Cpl	H. PENNELL Walsall	6th	17.06.1919	7675
4684	A/Sgt	W.H. Pennington	6th	21.10.1916	10220
40619	Pte	H.C.A. PERKINS Camberwell	7th	17.09.1917	9610
200786	Pte	B. PERRY	1/5th	21.08.1917	8645
16895	Sgt	G. PHILLIPS Bilston	1st	29.08.1918	10131
16813	Pte	J. PHILLIPS Wolverhampton	6th	14.05.1919	6033
200335	Cpl	E. PICKEN	1/5th Shown 1st Bn awards	18.07.1917	7283
9497	Cpl	T. PICKERILL	2nd Bar	18.07.1917 16.07.1918	7283 8308

Thomas, Born Upper Ettingshall, Enlisted Wolverhampton, Resided Upper Ettingshall. Sgt. Killed in Action F & F 23.08.1918.

No.	Rank	Name/Residence	Battalion	London Gazette	Page
13662	Pte	G. PILKINGTON		16.08.1917	8423
200577	L/Cpl (Cpl)	E. PITCOCK	1/5th	26.05.1917	5194 (Formerly 9128)
18100	Pte	J.T. PITT		19.02.1917	1754
200848	Pte	A. POOLE	1st	18.07.1917	7283
18734	L/Sgt	R. POOLE		19.02.1917	1754
240243	Sgt	W. POSTANCE	6th	11.11.1916	10929 (Formerly 2176)
242613	Pte	W.E. POTTER Leicester	6th	17.09.1917	9611

No.	Rank	Name/Residence	Battalion	London Gazette	Page
201070	Sgt	W. POULTON Long Itchington	2/5th	28.01.1918	1395

"For gallantry after the operations east of Weiltje on September 26th, 1917. This NCO displayed great courage and initiative in rallying and organising his men under very heavy shell fire. He led his men forward and reoccupied an important advanced post out of which our men had been temporarily driven by the very heavy enemy barrage. His actions in reoccupying and consolidating this post was of great importance and prevented the enemy from obtaining a hold in our line."

No.	Rank	Name/Residence	Battalion	London Gazette	Page
23589	Pte (A/Cpl)	B. POVEY DCM West Bromwich	1/5th	14.05.1919	6033
14844	Pte	B. Powell Wolverhampton	7th	17.09.1917	9611
46407	Pte	J. POWELL Nottingham	1st	29.08.1918	10132
39541	Pte	S. POWELL Walsall	1st	29.08.1918	10132

Private Samuel Powell aged 20 of 68 Green Lane, has been awarded the Military medal for gallantry in the field. He joined the South Staffords in 1917, and had served in Italy for ten months. He is a single man, and formerly worked at the Cyclops Ironworks, Pleck Road. Three brothers and a brother in law are serving abroad.

No.	Rank	Name/Residence	Battalion	London Gazette	Page
12927	Pte	A. POWNEY Wolverhampton	1st	17.12.1917	13194
200230	Cpl	A. PRICE	1/5th	23.02.1918	2428

Born Cannock, Enlisted Hednesford, Resided Cannock, Killed in Action F & F 28.04.1918.

Arthur Price was born in 1893, the son of Mr & Mrs J. Price of Hawthorn View, 97 Cannock Road, Blackfords, Cannock, Staffordshire.

He was a miner and employed at the Number 3 Pit, West Cannock Colliery. On the outbreak of war he like many thousands flocked to join the army. He enlisted into the 1/5th Battalion at Hednesford and on the 3rd March 1915, fully trained for the time and equipped for overseas service, they proceeded to France as part of 137th Brigade of the 46th North Midland Division.

He was involved in the battle of Loos when on the 13th October the brigade attacked a German strong point known as the Hohenzollern Redoubt. The unit made it into the redoubt but had to withdraw owing to a lack of bombs and mounting casualties. It was during this attack that he was wounded and sent back to England.

On recovery from his wounds he attended a Lewis Gun course between 3rd - 10th January 1917 and rejoined the battalion on the 26th February 1917, promotion to Lance Corporal followed on the 2nd March, 1917 and to Corporal on the 23rd July 1917.

In December 1917 he was awarded the Military Medal for the actions below;

On 12th November 1917, he successfully attacked a post near Hulloch and secured identification. He cut his way with his officer through the enemy wire and advanced all the remainder of the patrol and acted with great resolution in spite of heavy rifle fire and bombing. When the enemy trench was entered he greatly assisted his officer by his coolness and energy in driving out the garrison. The NCO has done exceedingly good work on previous patrols.

On 26th April 1918 a post called "A Keep" was lost to the enemy. Arthur Price had been in charge of a Lewis Gun team north west of the Keep and which was reported to have been knocked out by shell fire. It was confirmed on the 28th April that he had been killed. His body was recovered and laid to rest in Beuvry Communal Cemetery, Plot 3, Row D, Grave 25.

At 5pm 19th October , 1918 a presentation was made in Cannock Market Square of a gold watch to Arthur's father in recognition of his late son being awarded the Military Medal.

No.	Rank	Name/Residence	Battalion	London Gazette	Page
3/10196	L/Cpl	A. PRICE		19.02.1917	1754
9579	Pte	G. PRICE		01.09.1916	8675
16940	L/Sgt	R. PRICE Wolverhampton	7th	17.09.1917	9611
200883	Pte	A. PRIEST	1/5th	21.08.1917	8645
1480	Sgt	E. PRITCHARD	6th	19.02.1917	1754
5205	S/Drum	J. PRODERICK		14.12.1916	12222
13109	CQMS	G. PROSSER Penarth	6th	20.08.1919	10574
10952	Cpl (A/Sgt)	J. PUGH Bilston	7th	19.11.1917	11971
16013	Pte	G.H. QUEMBY Whitwick	9th	29.03.1919 (Italy)	4131
37225	A/Cpl	G.W. RACEY Wisbeech	7th Bar	28.01.1918 23.07.1919	1395 9343
20047	Sgt	J. RAFFERTY Wolverhampton	7th	28.01.1918	1396
7334	CSM	R. RANKIN		14.12.1916	12222
14428	Sgt	W. READ		16.08.1917	8424
18178	Cpl	J.N. REEVE Eastwood	7th	23.07.1919	9376
15270	Sgt	H. RENSHAW DCM	9th	23.08.1916	8363
43405	L/Cpl	W. RENWICK	2nd	21.10.1918	12414

William, Born Alnwick, Northumberland, Enlisted Wallsend on Tyne, Resided Willington Quay, Northumberland, Died France & Flanders 16.09.1918, Formerly 1877/267593 Northumberland Fusiliers.

No.	Rank	Name/Residence	Battalion	London Gazette	Page
10175	Sgt	W. RHODES Wolverhampton		21.10.1918	12414
240420	Pte	W. RICHARDSON Bilston	6th	14.05.1919	6033

No.	Rank	Name/Residence	Battalion	London Gazette	Page
28049	Pte	J. RIDGEWAY Hanley	1st	24.01.1919 (Italy)	1224
638	Pte	M. REIMANN	6th	11.11.1916	10929
26537	Pte (L/Cpl)	J.W. RILEY Gainsborough Grindley on The Hill	2nd Bar	11.02.1919 17.06.1919	2111 7643
18191	Pte (A/Cpl)	T. RITCHIE	2nd	14.09.1916	9004
201951	Pte	A. ROBBINS	1/5th	18.06.1917	6023

Born Leicester, Enlisted Leicester, Killed in Action F & F 28.06.1917.

No.	Rank	Name/Residence	Battalion	London Gazette	Page
9040	L/Cpl	W. ROBBINS	2nd	19.02.1917	1754
42862	Sgt	A.G. ROBERTS Fenton	6th	23.07.1919	9376
8187	L/Cpl	D. ROBERTS		11.11.1916	10929
32186	Pte	J. ROBINSON Tipton	2/5th	13.03.1918	3243

"For conspicuous gallantry. On December 1st 1917, the enemy put down a heavy barrage on our line of Fontaine-Notre-Dame and an attack appeared imminent as information had been received that the enemy were massing in La Folie Wood. All telephone wires were cut and the S.O.S. Signal was observed on the left of the battalion.

This man was a runner in the centre front line company volunteered to take a message to the company on the left flank. As the front line consisted of a series of posts, he was under observation during the whole of the journey but in spite of heavy shell and machine gun fire, he succeeded in delivering his message and returned with a reply.

His conduct on this and other occasions under fire has been most praiseworthy."

No.	Rank	Name/Residence	Battalion	London Gazette	Page
11271	Cpl (A/Sgt)	S. ROBINSON Heath Hayes		17.09.1917	9611
43504	Pte	F. ROSE Wantage	4th	29.08.1918	10133
19794	Cpl	J. ROTCHELL Penkridge	9th	29.03.1919 (Italy)	4131

John Edward Rotchell was born in September 1880 at West Bromwich, Staffordshire, the son of Mr & Mrs John Rotchell. Little is known about his life prior to April 23rd, 1902, when he enlisted into the Coldstream Guards in Birmingham. The details recorded are age 21 years 8 months, height 5′ 9″, weight 112 pounds, chest 36″ expanded 39″, complexion fresh, eyes Brown, hair Black and his religion Church of England. His three years were all spent on home service and he was transferred to the reserve on the 23rd April 1905. He returned to the Birmingham area and took up employment in the mines. On January 1st 1910 he married Miss Ellen MacNicholas, at St James's Church, Ashted, Birmingham. They had a son John Edward born five months later, and they were to have several other children. In 1912 the family moved to Penkridge where he took up employment with the Stafford Corporation Gasworks Department. The home address was at The Goods Station, Penkridge.

He enlisted in the South Staffordshire Regiment on the 9th August 1915 and was posted to the 9th Battalion who were the Pioneer Battalion of the 69th Brigade of the 23rd Division.

In 1916 he saw action in the Armentieres area, also the Somme, Ypres and Messines. The battalion was transferred to the Italian front in November 1917 where its main task was bridge building. During operations on the river Piave he was awarded the Military Medal. It was reported that for conspicuous bravery and gallantry on the 27th and 28th October, 1918 at the footbridge near Lovadina across the river Piave, this NCO by day and night under heavy fire and bombing, led parties across the Island of Costanza, and his pluck was most marked. The success of the landing was largely due to his determination and devotion to duty.

He also received a Mention in Despatches on the 6th January 1919. John Rotchell was wounded and gassed during his service, the exact dates are unknown, he also attained the rank of sergeant prior to his discharge on the 10th February 1919.

His employers prior to enlisting for the war recognised his brave deeds and on the 18th February 1919 he received a gold watch from Alderman T. Westhead at the Swan Hotel, Greengate Street, Stafford and a sum of money from Mr T. Pike, given by the Gasworks Committee.

John Rotchell was taken ill whilst having a drink in the Horse & Jockey public house, Penkridge, it is believed he suffered a stroke and died on the 27th August 1927. He was laid to rest in St Michael's churchyard, Penkridge.

No.	Rank	Name/Residence	Battalion	London Gazette	Page
8187	L/Cpl	T. ROTTON		11.11.1916	10929
7283	Sgt	E. ROWLEDGE	2nd	14.09.1916	9004
40033	Pte (L/Cpl)	J. ROWLEY Rotherham	1st	29.03.1919 (Italy)	4131
202980	Pte	R. ROYCE Peterborough		13.03.1918	3243
202483	Pte	G.C. RUGG Walthamstow	6th	14.05.1919	6033
16612	Pte (L/Cpl)	E. RUSSELL Darlaston	1st	04.02.1918	1615
31768	Pte	T.F. RUTTER North Shields	1st	17.12.1917	13194
8/43154	Cpl (Sgt)	E. SALES Mansfield	8th Bar	21.08.1917 04.02.1918	8646 1608
8505	Cpl	J. SADLER		10.08.1916	7890
40103	Pte	C.E. SALT Burton on Trent	1st	29.03.1919 (Italy)	4131
15765	L/Cpl	C. SALTER		16.08.1917	8424
15700	Pte	J.A. SCOTT		21.09.1916	9203
200817	L/Cpl	D.A. SCOTT		18.07.1917	7284

No.	Rank	Name/Residence	Battalion	London Gazette	Page
23570	Pte	R.P. SCOTT Baddingham	2nd	11.02.1919	2111
16539	Cpl	T.H. SCOWCROFT Bolton	E. Lancs Now SSR	13.09.1918	10773
30237	Pte	T. SCREEN Wolverhampton	2nd	13.03.1918	3243
41653	Pte	T. SCRIMGEOUR Rhydid Bridge of Earn		02.04.1918	4021
13341	Pte	J.T. SEDGELEY Birmingham	4th	21.10.1918	12415
30894	Pte	A. SELICK Wolverhampton	1st	29.08.1918	10134
242629	Pte	W.D. SHARMAN Great Yarmouth	6th	17.06.1919	7675
202193	L/Cpl	B.D. SHAW Ilkeston	2/5th	29.08.1917	9001

"For conspicuous bravery. On the night of July 1-2, 1917 an officers patrol was attacked by a strong party of the enemy east of our front line at Beauchamp. We suffered some casualties but owing to the darkness and to the long grass it was impossible to find the wounded and the bodies of those killed.

L/Cpl Shaw and Pte Madeley volunteered to go out and search the ground although it was under the enemy's observation and fire. They succeeded in finding the bodies of the killed and of one man severely wounded, and at great personal risk under the enemy's fire carried in the wounded man and the bodies of the dead undoubtedly saving the life of the wounded man and preventing the enemy from obtaining identification."

Brian Duncan Shaw was born on the 10th February 1898 and was educated at Ilkeston Secondary School. He became a student teacher. He married his first wife Elsie in 1916 and they had a son who died in 1917 aged four months. In February, 1916, he enlisted into the Sherwood Foresters (T.A.) on the advice of his elder brother Clarence Gordon Shaw who was serving as a Lieutenant in the 1st Battalion Lincolnshire Regiment, as he stated the replacement officers they were being sent knew nothing and were being killed within days.

Clarence was killed in action on the 1st July 1916. Brian Shaw was then transferred to the 2/5th Battalion South Staffordshire Regiment later that year. He had a natural ability with a rifle and was soon a designated marksman and acted as one of the regimental scouts in the sniper section. Because of the troubles in Ireland during Easter 1917 he was sent to Dublin. Later the unit was transferred to France. On 1st July 1917 a patrol was sent out by the 2/5th South Staffords but came across a much stronger German patrol and had taken casualties, one officer 2/Lieut Thornally and ten other ranks were missing. On the 2nd July L/Cpl Shaw and Pte Madeley volunteered to go back and attempt to locate those who were missing in broad daylight. They eventually found the patrol and the officer was dead and only Pte Wilson who was badly wounded was alive. For their actions on the patrol L/Cpl Shaw and Pte Madeley were both awarded the Military Medal and were presented with the medal ribbon by Brigadier General R.A. Currie DSO on the 20th July 1917.

Brian Shaw was granted leave and went home to Ilkeston and it was hoped that his father who was Mayor could have presented him with the Military Medal, however the medal did not arrive in time and he had to return to the front.

There were moments of humour even during the horrors of WW1, during one incident when the unit was ordered to attack the German's position one of the men carrying the rum ration was wounded by shrapnel, which also shattered the rum jar. Shaw said "This must never happen again, next time we'll take the rum before we attack".

He now applied for a commission, this was at first blocked by the commanding officer but eventually he was sent back to England and commissioned as a 2ndLieutenant in the 3rd battalion Lincolnshire Regiment. Service in Ireland followed before he was about to start training as a pilot in the Royal Air Force. On the 11th November 1918 the war ended and he eventually returned to civilian life and went to Nottingham University and obtained a degree in chemistry with Honour. He again joined the Officer Training Corps as a Lieutenant in the 5th Battalion Sherwood Foresters. Promoted Captain 23.2.1919 (employed OTC) major 16.5.1939, 2ic Battalion 1939.

On the outbreak of World War 2, he was sent to France as part of the B.E.F. And during the absence of the Commanding Officer he took charge of the unit. Whilst he and other senior officers of the battalion were out on a reconnaissance patrol they were cut off from the rest of the battalion and spent the next three months trying to avoid capture by the Germans. He was captured whilst attempting to get to the Spanish border on a pedal cycle and interned in Spangenburg Bei Kassal as prisoner No 15832. He put his chemistry skills to use and was in charge of the brewing stills and as a member of the escape committee to extract dyes for false documents. He was promoted Lieutenant Colonel whilst prisoner of war. Brian Shaw returned home and went back to University and continued his career as a scientist and with the OTC. His ability as a marksman was proven when he was awarded the Kings Medal at Bisley for the best shot in the Territorial Army in 1950, this was one of his many awards for shooting.

In all he lectured for 37 years at Nottingham University and because of his knowledge of explosives he lectured all over the world and was much in demand. He did not fully retire until he was aged 90. He gave evidence as an expert witness during the 111 day Angry Brigade trial at the Old Bailey in 1972. His second wife Alice died in 1998.

On The 23rd November 1998 Colonel Rene Dequen presented him with the Legion d'Honneur by the French government for his services during WW1. Brian Duncan Shaw died on the 7th November 1999 at the Silverwood Residential Nursing Home, aged 101 years. He was cremated at Bramcote Crematorium on 15th November 1999.

His group of medals consists of The Military Medal (GV), British War Medal, Victory Medal, 1939-45 Star, France & Germany Star, War Medal, Coronation Medal 1937, Coronation Medal 1953, Territorial Decoration, Kings Medal (best shot TA), Cadet Force Medal and the Legion D' Honneur. The medals were bequeathed to The Worcester & Sherwood Foresters Museum.

No.	Rank	Name/Residence	Battalion	London Gazette	Page
15638	Sgt	L. SHAW	9th	14.09.1916	9004
19820	Pte	W. SHAW Wolverhampton	2nd	11.02.1919	2111
201850	Pte	G. SHELDON West Bromwich	2/5th	28.01.1918	1397

"For conspicuous gallantry and devotion to duty when carrying messages on the night 24-25 September 1917. He twice carried messages between Gallipoli Farm and Bank Farm east of Weiljte although all traces of the tracks had been obliterated by the enemy barrage which was put down during the enemy counter attack on Hill 37. He was twice buried and although very exhausted he succeeded in reaching his destination with his messages. The importance of which had been impressed upon him."

No.	Rank	Name/Residence	Battalion	London Gazette	Page
242582	Cpl	R. SHELDON Birmingham	6th	17.09.1917	9612
11542	Pte	E. SHEPPARD	8th	01.09.1916	8658

Born Willenhall, Enlisted Wolverhampton, Resided Willenhall, Killed in Action F & F 12.10.1917.

No.	Rank	Name/Residence	Battalion	London Gazette	Page
13116	Pte	T. SILK	2nd	21.10.1916	10221
13854	L/Cpl	E. SIMCOX Oldbury	2/6th	28.01.1918	1397
25765	Pte	F. SIMNER	MGC Late	12.03.1917	2485
9385	Pte	H. SKIDMORE Birmingham	1st	17.12.1917	13195
30594	Pte	J. SKIDMORE Wolverhampton		21.10.1918	12415
241834	Pte	D.A. SLATER Dudley	1/6th	24.01.1919	1224
18687	Sgt	E.B. SMITH		16.08.1917	8424
241354	Pte (A/Cpl)	F.F. SMITH Wolverhampton	6th	14.05.1919	6033
22686	Sgt	G. SMITH Woodsetton	7th	23.07.1919	9376
7008	Pte (L/Cpl)	J. SMITH Birmingham	7th	28.01.1918	1398
235347	Sgt	J.W. SMITH Ipswich	2nd	11.02.1919	2111
17579	L/Cpl (A/Cpl)	R.E. SMITH	1st	26.05.1917	5195
235348	CSM	W. SMITH DCM Luston	2nd	17.06.1919	7675
10602	Sgt	W.H. SMITH	1st	14.12.1916	12222
15811	Pte	W.H. SMITH		19.11.1917	11972
7768	Pte	T. SNAPE	1st	19.02.1917	1760

Thomas, Born Millwall, Middlesex, Enlisted Birmingham, L/Cpl. Died of Wounds F & F 19.07.1916.

39191	L/Cpl	W. SPENCER	4th	29.08.1918	10135

William, Born Belpher, Derbyshire, Enlisted Derby, Resided Belpher. L/Cpl. Killed in Action F & F 27.05.1918.

21933	RQMS	E. STEPHENSON Tamworth	2nd	20.08.1919	10574
10125	Pte	D. STEVENS Wolverhampton	7th	23.07.1919	9376

No.	Rank	Name/Residence	Battalion	London Gazette	Page
14058	Pte	G. STEVENS Bilston		07.10.1918	11837
32957	Pte	G.F. STEVENSON Nottingham	1/5th	14.04.1919	6033
11300	Pte (L/Cpl)	C.E. STOKES Birmingham	1st	17.12.1917	13195
10672	Pte	W. STOKES Darlaston	7th	28.01.1918	1398
14620	Pte	S. STONE Walsall	1/5th	14.05.1919	6033
8281	L/Cpl	A. STYCHE	1/5th	11.11.1916 KiA 23.04.1917 7th Suffolks	10931
17803	Pte	T. SUTTON	7th	28.01.1918	1399

Thomas, Born Tipton, Enlisted Tipton, Killed in Action F & F 14.12.1917.

No.	Rank	Name/Residence	Battalion	London Gazette	Page
6917	Cpl (A/Sgt)	G. SWIFT St Helens, Lancs	1st	14.01.1918	843
240616	Cpl	G.H. TAME Wolverhampton	6th	17.06.1919	7675
36197	Pte	B. TATE Brierly Hill		29.08.1918	10136
19478	Pte	B. TAYLOR		12.03.1917	2485
4627	Pte	F. TAYLOR	6th	23.08.1916	8364
9928	Pte	G. TAYLOR		14.12.1916	12222
4/9345	Pte	H. TAYLOR	1st	01.09.1916	8658

Born Walsall, Enlisted Lichfield, Resided Walsall, Killed in Action France & Flanders 27.11.1916. Special Reserve.

No.	Rank	Name/Residence	Battalion	London Gazette	Page
10343	Pte	P.F. TAYLOR Wolverhampton		07.10.1918	11837
26263	L/Cpl	R. TAYLOR Chesterfield	7th	19.11.1917	11973
1614	CSM	T.R. TAYLOR DCM	6th	11.11.1916	10931
16398	Pte	S. THOMAS	2nd	21.10.1916	10221

No.	Rank	Name/Residence	Battalion	London Gazette	Page
17151	Pte	S. THOMAS Walsall	2nd	11.02.1919	2111
5/203277	L/Cpl	I. L. THOMPSON Birmingham	8th	14.01.1919	843
17851	Pte	J. THOMPSON		17.04.1917	3699

Joseph Thompson was born on the 10th January 1899 at 23 Court, 2 Hospital Street, Birmingham; he was the eldest of the two sons. He married shortly after the outbreak of WW1 on the 22nd August 1914. On the 1st March 1915 he enlisted into the South Staffordshire regiment and was posted to the 3rd battalion, later he was transferred to the 2nd battalion.

He landed in France on the 2nd October 1915 and served as a stretcher bearer on the Arras and Somme (Delville Wood) fronts. On the 17th April 1917 he was awarded the Military Medal by this time he was an acting corporal. Joseph Thompson was mortally wounded during a gas attack on his aid post at Douchy (Ayette) on the morning of 18th July, 1918 and as a result of his wounds died on the 26th July, 1918, aged 29 years. He left a widow May, they had a son but he was born and died in 1915. His home address was 109 Cheshire Road, Smethwick.

No.	Rank	Name/Residence	Battalion	London Gazette	Page
14110	Cpl	J.W. THOMPSON Stourbridge	9th	29.03.1919 (Italy)	4131
15783	L/Cpl	J. THORNTON		16.08.1917	8425
24209	Pte	W. TIMSON Leicester	1st	04.02.1918	1616
9419	Pte	E.S. TITLEY Walsall	1st	17.12.1917	13195
35826	Cpl	A. TOLLEY Heath Town	4th	27.06.1918	7597
38443	Pte	Z. TOLLEY Greets Green, Staffs	4th	27.06.1918	7597
10729	Pte	H. TREVELLION	1st	18.07.1917	7286
15792	Pte	C. TROTMAN		16.08.1917	8425
5993	Sgt	W. TRUBY	1st	10.08.1916	7890
10547	Pte	H. TRUMPER Wolverhampton	1st Bar	26.05.1917 17.12.1917	5195 13186
260101	Sgt	H. TURNER	6th	17.06.1919	7675
253314	Sgt	R.H. TURNER Leystone	2nd	11.02.1919	2111

No.	Rank	Name/Residence	Battalion	London Gazette	Page
200283	Pte	S. TURNER Walsall	5th	20.08.1919	10547
13725	Pte	G.H. TWINBERROW DCM Redditch	1st Bar	26.05.1917 17.12.1917	5195 13186
19517	Pte (L/Cpl)	G. UNDERHILL Brierly Hill	1st	17.12.1917	13196
5545	Pte	T. UNWIN	6th	21.10.1916	10222
235327	Pte	H.H. UPSOM Lowestoft	2nd	11.02.1919	2111
36695	Cpl	T.W. VAUGHAN Walsall	4th	27.06.1918	7597

Thomas William Vaughan was born in 1880, it is not known where he was educated, but he eventually took up employment at Kynochs, Witton. He was married had four children and lived at 1 Oxford Place, Pleck, Walsall.

In March, 1917 he enlisted into the 4th Battalion South Staffords and would have joined the unit who were stationed in Jersey. On the 10th October 1917 the Battalion landed in France at Havre as part of the 7th Infantry Brigade of the 25th Division.

It was during the German spring offensive of 1918 when the 4th South Staffords were in a position at Fremicourt and Beugnatre covering the withdrawal of troops from the 3rd Army. Many acts of gallantry were performed by men of the unit. Corporal Vaughan together with other non commissioned officers organised their men when the officers had become casualties. It was for these actions that he was awarded the Military Medal.

When the retreat had ended the battalion had covered 36 miles in 36 hours, a remarkable performance. Thomas Vaughan had been wounded three times in ten weeks; the last occasion he was seriously wounded in the back. He had attained the rank of Sergeant but it is not known if he returned to active service because of his wounds.

The 4th Battalion South Staffords was broken up due to the need for reinforcements for other units.

No.	Rank	Name/Residence	Battalion	London Gazette	Page
8807	Sgt	A.W. VIZOR	2nd	21.10.1916	10222
204417	Pte (L/Cpl)	A. WALKER Maidstone	1/5th	14.05.1919	6033
203285	Cpl	A.J. Walker Birmingham	1/5th	29.08.1918	10157
15896	Pte	G. WALKER Wolverhampton		17.09.1917	9613
10/11508	Pte (L/Cpl)	T. WALKER		09.12.1916	12053
17912	Cpl (A/Sgt)	F. WALMSLEY West Bromwich	7th	23.07.1919	9376

No.	Rank	Name/Residence	Battalion	London Gazette	Page
241967	Pte (L/Cpl)	W.R. WALMSLEY	6th	21.08.1917	8647
14223	A/Cpl	T. WALSH Wolverhampton	1st	04.02.1918	1616
200417	Pte	E. WANT Walsall	2nd	11.02.1919	2111
17682	Pte	H. WARD		19.02.1917	1756
9065	Pte	J. WARD		09.12.1916	12053
15313	Pte	J. WARD Wolverhampton	1st	17.12.1917	13196
12467	Sgt	S. WARD		16.08.1917	8425
11113	Pte	T. WARD West Bromwich	2nd	29.08.1918	10137
2129	Sgt	W.J. WASHINGTON	6th	06.01.1917	348
7329	Pte (L/Cpl)	J.D. WATSON	1st	12.03.1917	2485
41808	Pte	S.E WATSON Luton	1st	21.10.1918	12418
8267	Pte	H. WATTS	2nd	21.10.1916	10222
17987	Sgt	A.H. WEBB West Bromwich	1st	17.09.1917	9613
7851	CQMS (A/CSM)	F. WEBB Canada	1st	29.03.1919 (Italy)	4131
9285	Sgt	H.S. WEBB	1st	12.03.1917	2485

Henry Stephen, Born Blakenhall, Enlisted Wolverhampton. L/Cpl. Killed in Action F & F 04.10.1917.

No.	Rank	Name/Residence	Battalion	London Gazette	Page
11228	Pte	A.E. WELLS Birmingham	7th	28.01.1918	1401
16976	Pte	G. WESTON Birmingham	2nd	11.02.1919	2111
241425	Pte	F. WESTWOOD Sedgley	1/5th	14.05.1919	6033
9264	Pte	A. WHEATLEY	1st	14.12.1916	12222
8550	Pte	H. WHEATLEY	1st	11.11.1916	10932

No.	Rank	Name/Residence	Battalion	London Gazette	Page
12502	Sgt	A. WHILEY Brierly Hill		17.09.1917	9613
8341	Pte	A. WHITE	1st	11.11.1916	10932
9400	L/Cpl	B. WHITE Wolverhampton	7th	28.01.1918	1401
9615	Sgt	J.H. White		18.07.1917	7287
203256	Pte	W. WHITE		17.04.1917	3699 (Late 3369)
240976	Pte	F. WHITEHOUSE	6th	21.08.1917	8647
200060	Sgt	J. WHITTAKER	1/5th	26.05.1917	5195 (Formerly 7615)
9092	Cpl	R. WILKES Wednesbury	7th	23.07.1919	9376
6062	Sgt	T. WILKES	2nd	19.02.1917	1761

Thomas, Born Walsall, Enlisted Lichfield, Resided Walsall, Killed in Action F & F 29.07.1916.

No.	Rank	Name/Residence	Battalion	London Gazette	Page
7924	Sgt	A. WILKINS		09.12.1916	12054
16090	A/Cpl	A. WILKINSON Darlaston	7th	19.11.1917	11974
39234	Pte	G. WILKINSON Darlaston	6th	14.05.1919	6033
9152	Sgt	I.L. WILLIAMS	2nd	19.02.1917	1761

Issac Leonard, Born Wolverhampton, Enlisted Wolverhampton, Resided Swindon, Wilts, Killed in Action F & F 29.07.1916.

Issac Leonard Williams enlisted into the South Staffordshire Regiment during 1912; he was a resident of Dudley where his mother resided at High Street, Swindon, Dudley. He saw active service with the 2nd Battalion and was wounded the first time in June 1915. On the 29th July 1916 he was killed in Action, his Military Medal was gazetted on the 19th February 1917. At the time of his death he was 22 years of age. A report of his death appeared in the Express and Star on the 17th August 1916.

No.	Rank	Name/Residence	Battalion	London Gazette	Page
6443	A/Sgt	J. WILLIAMS		11.11.1916	10933
240234	Pte	J. WILLIAMS Wolverhampton	6th	14.05.1919	6033
40997	Pte	J.T. WILLIAMS Brenzett	2nd	11.02.1919	2111

No.	Rank	Name/Residence	Battalion	London Gazette	Page
242564	Pte	G. WILLETTS Walsall Brownhills	6th	14.05.1919	6033

"North of Sequehart. On October 3rd 1918 he spotted a Machine Gun firing on our troops, and at once got his Lewis Gun into action, wounding several of the team. Together with another man he then rushed the post, and captured it. During the whole time, he showed great bravery and initiative".

No.	Rank	Name/Residence	Battalion	London Gazette	Page
241403	Pte	F. WILSON Derby	6th	17.06.1919	7675
8549	Drum	E. WINCHESTER		21.10.1916	10222
8750	Pte	C. WINFIELD	1st	09.12.1916	12054
24093	Pte (L/Cpl)	H.E. WOOD Stourbridge	1st	17.12.1917	13196
9359	Pte	H.G. WOOD South Woodford	2nd	16.07.1918	8331
260140	Pte	W. WOOD Ipswich	6th	17.06.1919	7675
235359	Pte	C.E.V. WOODS Ely	2nd	11.02.1919	2111
8508	Sgt	C. WOOLLEY	2nd Bar	03.06.1916 21.12.1916	5598 12449
17642	Pte	J.H. WOOTON	7th	19.02.1917	1756
204421	Pte	W.H. WOOTTEN Newcastle	6th	14.05.1919	6033
8/40537	Pte	H. WOODWARD Bulwell	8th	04.02.1918	1617
8/13481	Sgt	W. WORKER Walsall	8th	14.01.1918	845
9688	L/Cpl	F. WORRALL	1st	09.12.1916 (Awarded 05.11.1916)	12054
11884	Sgt	H.E.T. WORRALL	1st	19.02.1917	1756
7927	A/Sgt	W.H. WORRALL Birmingham	1st	04.02.1918	1617
242310	Pte	A.J. WREN Lee	2/6th	29.08.1918	10139

No.	Rank	Name/Residence	Battalion	London Gazette	Page
16757	Sgt	C. WRIGHT	1st	12.03.1917	2485
12656	Cpl (A/Sgt)	H. WRIGHT	1st	18.07.1917	7287
15793	Pte	O. WRIGHT Polesworth		17.09.1917	9613
16566	L/Cpl	E. YATES	7th	16.08.1917	8426

Born Brownhills, Enlisted Walsall, Killed in Action F & F 20.12.1917.

No.	Rank	Name/Residence	Battalion	London Gazette	Page
18567	L/Cpl	J.R. YATES Hednesford	7th	30.07.1918	10780
	Originally Gazetted as	J.R.GATES		28.01.1918	1386
13787	Pte	W.C. YATES		21.09.1916	9204
			Bar	16.08.1917	8417
42563	Pte	G.W. YEARDLEY Sheffield	2nd	11.02.1919	2111
16290	Pte	T. YORK		12.03.1917	2485
14921	Sgt	A. YOUNG Wednesbury		19.11.1917	11974

SELECTED PERSONAL DETAILS

Details of other recipients can be found on p.177 et seq.

16074 Cpl D. APPLEBY MM

(Machine Gun Corps)

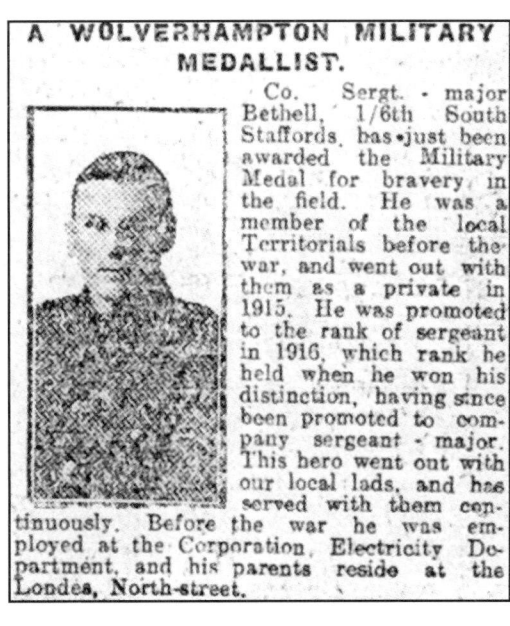

A WOLVERHAMPTON MILITARY MEDALLIST.

Co. Sergt. - major Bethell, 1/6th South Staffords, has just been awarded the Military Medal for bravery in the field. He was a member of the local Territorials before the war, and went out with them as a private in 1915. He was promoted to the rank of sergeant in 1916, which rank he held when he won his distinction, having since been promoted to company sergeant - major. This hero went out with our local lads, and has served with them continuously. Before the war he was employed at the Corporation Electricity Department, and his parents reside at the Londes, North-street.

20054 CSM D. BETHELL

WOLVERHAMPTON MILITARY
MEDALLIST. 2·10·18

Corpl. J. E. Blythe (South Staffords), whose home is at 18, Herbert-street, Wolverhampton, has been awarded the Military Medal. Prior to enlisting four years ago he was engaged at Stafford-road Works, and was an attendant at the Hippodrome. In July Blythe, with another corporal and a private, carried out a successful daylight patrol. On the two previous afternoons, by careful reconnaissance work, they had established the position of an enemy post, and although greatly hindered by German entanglements, they succeeded in forcing their way through. Approaching the post from the rear they effected its capture, and brought its occupants to the British lines, thereby securing important identifications.

Photo G. Whitfield.

240827 Cpl J. E. BLYTHE

7107 Sergeant E. J. BROCKHURST MM

Acting-Sergeant J. Collins (21), of Sutherland Place, Wolverhampton, formerly a drayman at the Old Wolverhampton Breweries, has been awarded a bar to his Military Medal. He joined the South Staffordshire Regiment three years ago, and secured his medal last September. The bar has been added for great bravery. He saw two wounded men on the other side of a canal to which he was, and although warned he was risking his life to cross the bridge, because of a destructive fire, he rushed to the aid of the men, and commenced to attend to their wounds. With assistance the two men, one of whom was wounded severely, were got away, but according to the record it was entirely due to Collins's great bravery and disregard for his own personal safety that their lives were saved. It was added that Collins, who was then a corporal, has on many occasions shown exceptional bravery in action.

241831 A/Sgt J. COLLINS MM &Bar

17778 A/CSM C.T. CRADDOCK

Pte J. GAVIN MM & 2 Bars

8/12188 Sgt H. GREW

8769 Pte D. HATELEY

3/10343 Sgt T. HAWKINS DCM MM

18591 Cpl P.R.J. HENDLEY

132

200420 Cpl John KELLY

200373 Sgt A. LINNELL

202090 Pte H. J. MADELEY

4/10019 Cpl F MASON MM & Bar

14229 Pte T. MOORE

3697 Pte J.T. MOSELEY
KiA 1st July 1916
Gommecourt Wood New Cemetery

200335 Cpl E. PICKEN

39541 Private Samuel POWELL MM

8136/200230 Corporal A. PRICE MM

19794 Sergeant J. Edward ROTCHELL MM

Photo in uniform B.D. SHAW MM

Photo at desk B.D. Shaw MM

Pte. Geo. Stevens, South Staffordshire Regiment, 5, Rose-street, Bradley, Bilston, has been awarded the Military Medal for bravery in the field. He joined the Army a month after the outbreak of war, and has been at the front over three years. He has been wounded four times altogether, the last occasion being in April this year, when he was badly hit in the arm. He is now stationed at Ripon.

14058 Pte G. STEVENS

10672 Pte W. STOKES

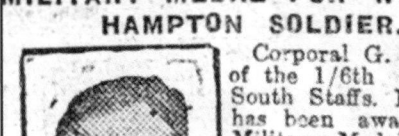

MILITARY MEDAL FOR WOLVER-HAMPTON SOLDIER.

Corporal G. H. Tame, of the 1/6th Battalion South Staffs. Regiment, has been awarded the Military Medal. During the operations north of St. Quentin he did invaluable work in bringing transport containing rations and small arms ammunition forward under heavy shell fire. Corporal Tame, whose home is at 47, Humber-road, Wolverhampton, has been in the Army four years. Prior to enlistment he was employed at Messrs. Butlers, Springfield Brewery.

240616 Cpl G.H. TAME

603824 Corporal Basil TATE MM

17851 Acting CPL J.Thompson MM

10547 Pte H. TRUMPER MM & Bar

36695 Sergeant T. W. Vaughan MM

15313 Private J. WARD MM

9152 Sgt Issac Leonard WILLIAMS MM

PRIESTFIELD SOLDIER'S BRAVERY

A Priestfield soldier, Lance-corporal J. Williams, South Staffs. Regt., has received the Military Medal for bravery and resource in action. The official accounts reads : " In an attack north of Sequehart on October 3, 1918, he took command of his platoon when his officers and seven n.c.o.s had all become casualties, and led his men forward to the final objective. On reaching this he did excellent work in pushing up posts and organising his platoon. His conduct throughout is deserving of the highest praise." This gallant young man, whose home is at 109, John-street, Priestfield, was formerly employed at Messrs. Smith's Tinplate Works, Ettingshall. He has been wounded and gassed twice. Prior to the war he served with the Territorials.

240234 Pte (L/Cpl) J WILLIAMS MM

THE MERITORIOUS SERVICE MEDAL

THE Army Meritorious Service Medal was instituted on the 19th December 1845. The ribbon was plain crimson until 1916; white edges were added in 1916-1917 and three white stripes since August 1917. In October 1916 when immediate awards for exceptional valuable and meritorious service were introduced this was in effect a second type of award as previously the recipient had to have 27 years service to become eligible. In January 1917 the award was extended for acts of gallantry not in the presence of the enemy.

No	Rank	Name	Battalion	London Gazette	Page	Remarks
6215	Sgt	W. ALSOP	2nd	18.01.1919	991	Falfield, Gloucester
18891	CQMS	W.H. ANDREWS		17.06.1918	7134	
12681	CQMS	W. ARMSTON		12.12.1919	15462	Lichfield (Depot)
8/13455	Sgt	Y. BAYLISS		17.06.1918	7136	Smethwick
202947	Sgt	C.A. BIRCHENOUGH	5th	03.06.1919	6888	Newcastle
200135	CQMS	H.E. BIRD	1/5th	18.01.1919	991	A/RQMS Brierly Hill
8545	RQMS	G. BLUNSON	4th	03.06.1919	6888	Wednesfield
14226	Sgt	E.V. BOX	9th	03.06.1919	6944	Penarth (Italy)

No	Rank	Name	Battalion	London Gazette	Page	Remarks
10811	CSM	E. BRAMNER	9th	03.06.1919	6944	Lincoln (Italy)
35101	RQMS	T.A. BULCOCK	1st (G) Bn	03.09.1920	8967	Settle
10650	CQMS	T. BURKE		03.06.1919	7015	New Ferry
10220	Cpl	J.J. CADDICK	7th	03.06.1919	6888	Hednesford
8438	Sgt	F.C. CHANDLER	2nd	03.06.1919	6888	Norwich
9308	Pte	J.T. CLEE	1st	30.01.1920	1226	Bilston
242193	Sgt	R. CLOWES	6th	18.01.1919	991	Leicester
200556	Sgt	J.E. DAVIES	1/5th	03.06.1919	6888	Sutton Coldfield
260060	Sgt	F.H. EDWARDS	6th	18.01.1919	991	Walsall
200003	CQMS	E. EVERTON	1/5th	18.01.1919	991	Walsall
7952	Sgt	H. FINLAN	2nd	17.06.1918	7145	Wolverhampton
8152	Sgt	A. FLOWERS DCM Killed in action 30.09.1917	1st Bn	31.11.1916	10934	
12279	Pte	A. FORD	7th	03.06.1919	6888	Witham
9732	Pte	G.H. FRANCIS	1st	01.01.1919	69	Smethwick (Italy)
200019	Sgt	W. GEE		17.06.1918	7147	A/CSM Walsall
200489	CQMS	C.C. GOUGH		17.06.1918	7148	Birmingham
200021	Sgt	A. GREGORY	2/5th	01.01.1918	70	A/CSM Wednesbury
200507	CSM	J. HARRISON		17.06.1918	7149	Burslem
7158	CQMS	C.H. HIAM	1st	03.06.1918	6499	Carlton (Italy)
200345	L/Cpl	W. HICKMAN		17.06.1918	7150	Wordsley
18638	Sgt	A. HIGGINSON	1/5th	28.10.1920	10389	A/CQMS Gt Harwood
9171	Sgt	J.C. HILL	2nd	17.06.1918	7150	Derby
204656	Sgt	A.W. HINTON	1st	03.09.1920	8967	1st (G) Bn Salisbury

No	Rank	Name	Battalion	London Gazette	Page	Remarks
8233	CQMS	P.H. HOGBEN	2nd	18.01.1919	991	Saltley
240022	CQMS	H. HORSEMAN	6th	18.01.1919	991	Wednesfield
202331	Sgt	L. JOHNSON	3rd	03.06.1919	7015	A/RQMS Birmingham
13741	Sgt	E. JONES		17.06.1918	7153	Penarth
7214	Sgt	W. KEY	2nd	18.01.1919	991	Smethwick
8988	CSM	O.M. KING DCM	2nd	03.06.1919	6888	Camden Town
9575	Sgt	M. LANE	1st	03.06.1919	6944	A/CQMS Willenhall (Italy)

8978/204392 Sergeant William Henry LATHAM MSM

No	Rank	Name	Battalion	London Gazette	Page	Remarks
200503	Sgt	W. H. LATHAM	1/5th	17.06.1918	7155	Birmingham
5991	CSM	J. LOCKLEY		18.01.1919	991	A/RSM Walsall
7917	Sgt	A. LORT	2nd	18.10.1916	10043	Acting CQMS
204680	Pte	H. MARSH	1st	03.09.1920	8967	A/Cpl 1st (G) Bn Swindon
242052	Pte	T.A. MARTIN	2/6th	17.06.1918	7157	Leicester
10078	CQMS	W.H. MASSEY		12.12.1919	15462	O.R. Sgt Bristol (Depot)
13422	CSM	J. McCARTHY	6th	03.06.1919	6888	Penarth

No	Rank	Name	Battalion	London Gazette	Page	Remarks
7417	Sgt	A. McCONVILL	1st	01.01.1919	69	Birmingham (Italy)
5858	Sgt	G. NICHOLLS		17.06.1918	7160	Birmingham
12888	L/Cpl	J.H. NORTON MM	7th	17.06.1918	7160	Brierly Hill, Staffs
240934	L/Cpl	G.C. PHILP	6th	17.06.1918	7162	A/Sgt Nottinghill
15967	Sgt	A.S. PLATTS		03.06.1918	6500	Barsby (Italy)
200564	CQMS	A PYETT	1/5th	18.01.1919	991	Four Oaks
1863	RSM	F.E.M. RICHARDSON	6th	22.02.1919	2695	Atherstone
6460	RQMS	A. RILEY MC	1st	03.06.1919	6944	Walsall (Italy)
15765	Cpl	C. SALTER	9th	01.01.1919	69	L/Sgt (Italy) Wolverhampton
204641	Pte	A.J. SCOTT	1st	03.09.1920	8967	1st (G) Bn Melksham
241444	L/Cpl	T. SCREEN	2/6th	17.06.1918	7166	Wolverhampton
8/13341	L/Cpl	J.T. SEDLEY		17.06.1918	7166	Birmingham
240485	Sgt	S.H. SHINTON	6th	01.01.1918	74	Wolverhampton
40080	Pte	J. SINAR	1st	03.06.1919	6944	West Bromwich (Italy)
202259	CQMS	E. SMITH	5th	03.06.1919	7015	Wolverhampton
10602	Sgt	W.H. SMITH	1st	03.06.1919	6888	West Bromwich
15069	CQMS	J. STEPHENS	9th	01.01.1919	69	Newtown North Wales (Italy)
17897	Sgt	G.W. STONE	7th	18.01.1919	991	Burton on Trent
5281	CQMS	A. TARBET	2nd	17.06.1918	7170	A/CSM LavenderHill S.W.
202331	Sgt	P.G. WADDHAMS	5th	03.06.1919	7015	A/CQMS Wolverhampton
240832	Sgt	J. WHITEHOUSE	6th	17.06.1918	7174	Wolverhampton
11444	Sgt	E. WHITEWORTH	9th	03.06.1919	6944	Birmingham (Italy)

MENTIONED IN DESPATCHES

THE Mentioned in Despatches Spray of Oak Leaves signified a mention in a despatch for a particular theatre of war; it was instituted during the First World War and continued to be awarded for active service up to August 10, 1920. It was worn on the Victory medal, unless the British War Medal was the only entitlement.

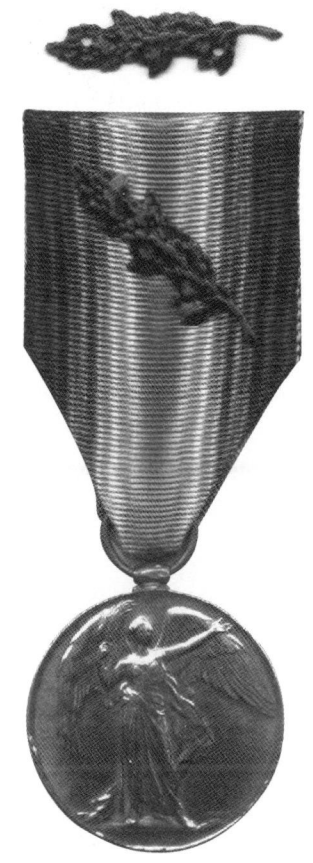

OFFICERS

Rank	Name	Battalion	London Gazette	Page	Remarks
Captain	C.B. ADAMS	1st	17.02.1915	1664	
Captain	T. ADDENBROOKE		22.05.1917	5036	Desp 15.5.17
Captain	C.E.R.G. ALBAN	2nd	18.12.1917	13229	L'pool Regt Att
Captain	C.E.R.G. ALBAN DSO	2nd	23.05.1918	6063	L'pool Regt Att
T/Captain	A.G. ALLEN MC		18.12.1917	13238	
2nd Lt	J.A. ARMSTRONG		18.12.1917	13238	Temp Lt
Lt	A.H. ASHCROFT	7th	13.07.1916	6949	

Rank	Name	Battalion	London Gazette	Page	Remarks
T/Captain	A.H. ASHCROFT	7th	04.01.1917	231	
T/Major	A.H. ASHCROFT	7th	28.12.1918	15153	
T/Lt	G.S. BAILEY	1st	30.05.1918	6334	
2 Lt	G.H. BALL	1/5th	22.05.1917	5036	Desp 15.5.17
Lt	G.H. BALL	1/5th	28.12.1918	15153	Act Captain
Captain	G.H. BALL DSO, MC.	1/5th	09.07.1919	8696	
Lt	J.A. BALLION	7th	24.05.1918	6096	T/ Captain
T/Major	W.A.J. BARKER DSO	8th	15.06.1916	5943	
Lt Col	W.A.J. BARKER DSO	8th	19.06.1916		
T/Lt Col	W.A.J. BARKER DSO	8th	04.01.1917	231	
T/Lt Col	W.A.J. BARKER DSO	8th	18.12.1917	13238	
Lieut	C.E.C. BARTLETT	1st	17.02.1915	1664	
2 Lt	C. BATES, DSO, MC	4th	28.12.1918	15153	
Captain	A.B. BEAUMAN, DSO	1st	15.06.1916	5918	
Captain	A.B. BEAUMAN, DSO	1st	22.05.1917	5036	Desp 15.5.17
Bt Maj	A.B. BEAUMAN DSO	1st	18.12.1917	13238	A/Lt Col
Captain	A.B. BEAUMAN, DSO	1st	06.01.1919	275	Bt Major T/Brig Gen (Staff) Italy
Captain	A.B. BEAUMAN, DSO	1st	05.06.1919	7201	Bt Lt Col T Brig Gen Staff
2nd Lt	E. BELL	1st	01.01.1916	44	Temp Lt
T Lt	G.W. BELLINGHAM		11.06.1918	6922	Salonika
Lt	J.F. BENOY	2nd	09.07.1919	8696	Act Captain
Captain	N.P. BIRLEY MC		11.12.1917	12909	
Captain	N.P. BIRLEY, DSO, MC		20.12.1918	14923	Staff
2nd Lt	W.J. BOND	1/5th	24.05.1918	6096	
Captain	S. BONNER	1st	17.02.1915	1664	
Major	S. BONNER DSO	1st	15.05.1917	5430	A Lt Col DoW 1.5.17 Haigs Desp 9.4.17
T/Lt	BOULNOIS	9th	05.06.1919	7207	Italy Staff
Lt	N.S. BOSTOCK, MC		20.12.1918	14923	Staff

Rank	Name	Battalion	London Gazette	Page	Remarks
Bt Lt Col	L.B. BOYD-MOSS	2nd	01.01.1916	44	
Bt Lt Col	L.B. BOYD-MOSS		15.06.1916	5918	Temp Brig Gen
Bt Lt Col	L.B. BOYD-MOSS CMG	2nd	04.01.1917	193	Temp Brig Gen
Bt Lt Col	L.B. BOYD-MOSS CMG	2nd	11.12.1917	12909	Temp Brig Gen (Staff)
Bt Lt Col	L.B. BOYD-MOSS CMG, DSO		20.05.1918	5944	Temp Brig Gen (Staff)
Bt Lt Col	L.B. BOYD-MOSS CMG, DSO		20.12.1918	14923	Temp Brig Gen (Staff)
QM Lt	S. BRADBURY	1st	01.01.1916	44	
Captain T/Major	E.C.P. BRIDGES	7th	28.01.1916	1201	(RoO)
Major	A.C. BUCKLE	1st	17.02.1915	1664	
T/Major	L.N.B. BULLOCK, DSO	9th	05.06.1919	7207	Staff Italy
T/Major	R.P. BURNETT MC	8th	18.12.1917	13238	
T/Major	R.P. BURNETT, MC	8th	28.12.1918	15153	Acting Lt Col 7 Bn R. Fus
T/Major	R.P. BURNETT, MC	8th	09.07.1919	8696	A Lt Col 7 Bn R. Fus
Major	W. BURNETT	1/5th	01.01.1916	44	
Captain	C.S. BURT	1st	30.05.1918	6334	Acting Lt
Captain	C.S. BURT, DSO	1st	06.01.1919	282	T/Lt Col Att 20 Bn Man R Italy
Major	S.S. BUTLER		05.11.1915	11001	Staff ANZAC
Major	S.S. BUTLER		04.01.1917	193	Staff
Major	S.S. BUTLER		15.05.1917	4745	Staff
Major	S.S. BUTLER, DSO		20.05.1918	5944	T Lt Col att Aust Corps
Major	S.S. BUTLER, DSO		05.07.1919	8488	Bt Lt Col T/Lt Col (Staff)
Lt	G. BYGRAVE, MC	3rd	06.01.1919	282	Att 1st Bn. Italy

George Bygrave was born on the 3rd November, 1890. His parent's address is given as 37 Stanley Road, Teddington, and his early school years were spent at Modern School, Bedford and Trafalgar School, Twickenham. He attended the University of London (Goldsmiths College) from 16th September 1914, and completed his first year passing all subjects. He was commissioned into the 3rd Battalion South Staffordshire Regiment and posted to the 1st Battalion on completion of his training.

The battalion was involved in some heavy fighting early in 1917 and it was during one attack that because of his actions he was awarded the Military Cross. The award was shown in the London Gazette of the 3rd March, 1917. In

August 1918 he was adjutant of the battalion and for his services in the Italian campaign he was awarded a Mention in Despatches, London Gazette 3rd January 1919. His medals are shown with a French Croix de Guerre but this does not show in the London Gazette which is not uncommon with foreign awards.

Sometime during his service he was married as is shown by the photograph, but details of his wife are unknown.

On leaving the army he took up a career as a teacher and was assistant master at Ponders End school from 12th June 1919. There is a memorial board at Trafalgar School, which lists nearly 400 names of Trafalgar staff and pupils who served during the 1914-18 war. The board had been renovated and was rehung in 1991.

Rank	Name	Battalion	London Gazette	Page	Remarks
Captain	D.W.A. CAMPBELL	4th	17.02.1915	1665	Att 1st N & D KiA 23.11.1914
T/Capt	J.J. CAMERON DSO, MC		24.05.1918	6096	Acting Lt Col
2nd Lt	A.M. CAMPBELL	2nd	18.12.1917	13238	(Spec Res)
2nd Lt	W.H. CARTER	7th	01.01.1916	44	
Lt	W.H. CARTER DSO, MC	7th	04.01.1917	231	
Capt A/Lt Col	W.H. CARTER DSO, MC		23.05.1918	6063	R War Regt
Lt	J.C. CHAYTOR	2nd	22.06.1915	5997	Temp Captain
Bt Major	J.C. CHAYTOR MC		15.06.1916	5919	Staff
Bt Major	J.C. CHAYTOR MC		15.05.1917	4746	Temp Lt Col
Bt Major	J.C. CHAYTOR MC		11.12.1917	12911	Temp Lt Col .
Captain	G.C.R. COLLERIDGE	8th	15.06.1916	5943	
Captain	G.C.R. COLLERIDGE	8th	19.06.1916		Adjutant
Major	W.J.J. COLLAS DSO	2nd	18.12.1917	13238	T/Lt Col
Major	W.J.J. COLLAS DSO	2nd	24.05.1918	6096	Temp Lt Col
Major	W.J.J. COLLAS DSO	2nd	09.07.1919	8696	T/Lt Col
Major	P.R.C. COMMINGS	1st	01.01.1916	3	Staff
Major	P.R.C. COMMINGS, DSO	1st	14.01.1917	194	Temp Lt Col
Major	P.R.C. COMMINGS, DSO	1st	15.05.1917	4746	Temp Lt Col
Major	P.R.C. COMMINGS, DSO	1st	20.12.1918	14925	Bt Lt Col
Captain	R.M. CRAIG		18.12.1917	13238	
2nd Lt	H.E.D. CULLEN		15.06.1916	5943	
2nd Lt	W.H. CURRY DSO	3rd	18.12.1917	13238	(Spec Res) KiA 25.10.17 Att 1st Bn
Captain	H.M.C.CURTIS, DSO	2/6th	28.12.1918	15153	Att from 2nd Bn NSR
Lt Col	C.S. DAVIDSON	2nd	09.12.1914	10544	
Lt Col	C.S. DAVIDSON	2nd	17.02.1915	1664	
Col	C.S. DAVIDSON CB	2nd	01.01.1916	44	T/ Brig Gen

Rank	Name	Battalion	London Gazette	Page	Remarks
2nd Lt	T.R.D. DAVIES	1/5th	09.07.1919	8696	Att 137th LTMB
2nd Lt	F. DAVIS, DSO	4th	28.12.1918	15153	
Captain	G. DAWES	2nd	31.05.1916	5426	For Cameroon's
Captain	G. DAWES	2nd	04.01.1917	231	Temp Lt Col
Captain	G. DAWES DSO, MC	2nd	24.05.1918	6096	Bt Maj Act Lt Col
Captain	G. DAWES, DSO, MC	2nd	28.12.1918	15153	Comd 21st Bn Lon Regt
Maj T/Lt Col	J.S.N.S. De JOUX		12.02.1918	1934	
Lt	J.L. DENT DSO	2nd	17.02.1915	1664	
Captain	J.L. DENT DSO	2nd	04.01.1917	194	KiA 11.4.17
Lt	L.T. DESPICHT	2nd	22.06.15	5993	Att from 4 Beds R
Lt	S.W.H.S. DOUGLAS-WILLAN	2nd	22.05.1917	5036	Desp 15.5.17 Killed 17.2.17
2nd Lt	W. DRAYCOTT-WOOD	2nd	22.06.1915	5997	KiA 29.6.15
T/Lt	W.B. DRYDEN	7th	22.05.1917	5036	Desp 15.5.17
Major	R. DUCKWORTH	1st	01.01.1916	44	
Major	R. DUCKWORTH	1st	11.12.1917	12912	Staff
Major	R. DUCKWORTH, DSO	1st	05.07.1919	8491	Staff
QM	W.C. DUFFIELD	1/5th	22.05.1917	5036	Hon Lt Desp 15.5.17
Captain	W.C. DUFFIELD	1/5th	09.07.1919	8696	Quartermaster
Captain	J.S.S. DUNLOP	1st	17.02.1915	1664	KiA 24.10.1914
2nd Lt	G. DUTTON	2nd	22.05.1917	5036	Desp 15.5.17
Lt	G. DUTTON	2nd	09.07.1919	8696	A/Captain
2nd Lt	G.F. ELLIOTT	8th	15.06.1916	5943	Temp Lt SR
Lt	G.F. ELLIOTT	8th	19.06.1916		KiA 31.8.16 4th Bn Att 8th
Lt	G.S. ELWELL	6th	15.06.1916	5919	Temp Captain
Captain	G. ELWELL	6th	11.12.1917	12912	Staff
T/Lt	W.R. ENGLISH-MURPHY, MC	1st	06.01.1919	282	Acting Lt Col. Italy

Rank	Name	Battalion	London Gazette	Page	Remarks
T/Lt	W.R. ENGLISH-MURPHY, DSO, MC		05.06.1919	7207	A/Lt Col Staff Italy
Lt	C.W. EVANS	1st	22.06.1915	5997	
Lt	G. EVANS	1/6th	09.07.1919	8696	KiA 03.10.1918
Lt	L.V. FITZPATRICK	1st	22.05.1917	5036	Desp 15.5.17 Spec Res
Lt	W.G. FLUKE DSO	2nd	04.01.1917	231	Temp Captain
T/Lt	F.L. FREEMAN	7th	18.12.1917	13238	
T/Captain	J.F. GADD, MC	9th	06.01.1919	282	Italy
Major	H.P. GAMON	5th	28.12.1918	15153	5th Bn NSR Attached
T/2 Lt	W.E. GIBBONS	1st	05.06.1919	7207	Staff Italy
2 Lt	R.B. GIBSON	2nd	01.01.1916	44	Temp Capt Spec Res
T/Major	W. GIBSON, DSO, MC	8th	28.12.1918	15153	Att 10th Bn WestY.R
Captain	G de C GLOVER		17.02.1915	1665	Att 2 N & D
Captain	G de.C. GLOVER, MC	2nd	15.05.1917	4747	
Captain	G de C GLOVER MC	2nd	11.12.1917	12913	Staff
Captain	G de C GLOVER, MC	2nd	20.05.1918	5946	Staff
Captain	G de C GLOVER, DSO,MC		20.12.1918	14927	Bt Maj or (Staff) 2nd Bn
Captain	G de C GLOVER, DSO, MC		05.07.1919	8492	Bt Major (Staff) 2nd Bn
Major	G.N. GOING		01.01.1916	44	Temp Lt Col (R of Off)
Lt T/Captain	F.H. GUNNER DSO	2nd	17.02.1915	1664	
Captain	F.H. GUNNER DSO	2nd	04.01.1917	196	Staff
Captain	C.H. GREEN		01.01.1916	44	
Captain	C.H. GREEN		06.08.1918	9227	Att Nigeria R. DoW 8.11.17
T/Lt	C.G. GRICE-HUTCHINSON	7th	13.07.1916	6949	
Captain	C.G. GRICE-HUTCHINSON, MC	7th	22.05.1917	5036	Desp 15.5.17
2nd Lt	G.B. HALL	9th	04.01.1917	231	Gloucester R. Attached

Rank	Name	Battalion	London Gazette	Page	Remarks
2 Lt	S. HALL		18.12.1917	13238	
Lt	A. de HAMEL	2nd	01.01.1916	44	Spec Reserve
Captain	H. HANFORD		22.05.1917	5036	Desp 15.5.17
2nd Lt	I. HARE		22.05.1917	5036	Desp 15.5.17
Lt	C.C. HARLAND, MC	7th	20.12.1918	14928	T/ Capt(Staff)
Lt	C.C. HARLAND, MC	7th	05.07.1919	8493	T/ Cap (Staff)
Captain	S. HARPER, MC	2nd	28.12.1918	15153	Acting Major
Lt	W. HARRIS	5th	09.07.1919	8696	Att 1st Bn MGC
Lt	L.L. HASSELL DSO, MC	1st	18.12.1917	13238	Act Captain
Lt	L.L. HASSELL, DSO, MC	1st	05.06.1919	7207	Italy
2nd Lt	H. HAWKES	1/5th	01.01.1916	44	Temp Lt
T/QM	J.E.HAWKES		18.12.1917	13238	Hon Lt
Captain	C.V.T. HAWKINS	5th	25.01.1917	944	KiA 26.9.17
QM/Capt	A. HAZLEGROVE, MC DCM	2nd	28.12.1918	15153	
Lt	J. HAZELWOOD	2nd	04.01.1917	231	
Captain	J. HAZELWOOD, MC,	2nd	28.12.1918	15153	DCM
Captain	J.R. HEMMING		24.05.1918	6096	
Lt	J.R. HEMPSEED		24.05.1918	6096	Act Capt
T/2nd Lt	J. HERRINGTON MC MM		30.05.1918	6334	9th Bn (Italy)
T 2nd Lt	J.D. HEWETSON John Dixon	10th	04.01.1917	231	DoW 30.5.18 Att 1st Bn
Lt	J.N. HILDICK-SMITH	6th	04.01.1917	231	Temp Captain
2nd Lt	C.R. HIND	2nd	01.01.1916	44	Spec Reserve KiA 30.5.16
2nd Lt	T.G. HOLDER		25.01.1917	944	Temp Lt
T/Capt	R. HOLLOCOMBE		18.12.1917	13238	
T/Lt	W.F.J. HORNE	9th	05.06.1919	7207	Italy
T/LT	W.F.J. HORNE	9th	06.01.1919	282	

Rank	Name	Battalion	London Gazette	Page	Remarks
LT	H. HUGHES	1st	09.07.1919	8696	A/ Captain Att L Corps
Lt	W.C. INGE		20.05.1918	5947	Temp Captain Staff
Captain	A.H.C. JAMES		22.06.1915	5978	Staff for 5.4.15
Major	A.H.C. JAMES MVO, DSO		11.12.1917	12915	Temp Lt Col (Staff)
Major	A.H.C. JAMES MVO, DSO		20.05.1918	5947	Temp Lt Col(Staff)
Fly Off	A. JERRARD VC		12.07.1920	7423	(prev 1/5th Bn) Omitted from 01.01.1919 14th Wing Italy
Major	E.de R. JERVIS	3rd	10.07.1919	8745	Att 48 PoW Labour C.
Lt Col	S.J. JERVIS	2nd	20.05.1918	5947	Staff
Captain	S.G. JOHNSON	2nd	17.02.1915	1664	
Captain	S.G. JOHNSON MC	2nd	06.07.1917	6768	Egypt
Captain	S.G. JOHNSON MC	2nd	18.12.1917	13238	Acting Major
Captain	S.G. JOHNSON	2nd	24.05.1918	6096	Acting Major
Major	B.A. JOHNSTONE OBE	1st G	11.06.1920	6454	Comd 1st (G) Bn SSR India Date 3.6.1919
2nd Lt	R.V. JONES	7th	28.12.1918	15153	Att 33 Bde
2nd Lt	R.W. JUKES		8.12.1917	13238	
T/Capt	E.O. KAY	2nd	18.12.1917	13238	
Lt	F.A. KENDRICK, DSO, MC	1st	05.06.1919	7207	A/Captain
Captain	A.F.G. KILBY VC	2nd	17.02.1915	1664	
Lt	W.L. LAMAISON	2/6th	30.12.1918	15198	Att from 16th Bn Lon Regt DoW 23.08.1918
2nd Lt	R.J.I. LANE	1st	18.12.1917	13238	A/Lt
Lt	G.J.R. LANSDALE MC	6th	06.01.1919	282	Att 1st Bn
Lt	J. LAMOND	1/5th	01.01.1916	31	Adj R Scots

Rank	Name	Battalion	London Gazette	Page	Remarks
Lt	J. LAMOND MC	1/5th	27.12.1918	15122	2 Bn R. Scots att.
Capt	W.H. LASSLETT MB	7th	13.07.1916	6951	RAMC Att
Captain	F.W.B. LAW	6th	15.06.1916	5943	Temp Lt Col
T/Lt	C.A. LAWFORD		18.12.1917	13238	
2nd Lt	A.W. LEE	1st	01.01.1916	44	
Lt	A.W. LEE MC	1st	18.12.1917	13238	A/Captain
Lt	A.W. LEE MC	1st	30.05.1918	6334	A/ Captain
A/Captain	A.W. LEE MC	1st	06.01.1919	282	Italy
Lt	A.W. LEE MC	1st	05.06.1919	7207	A/ Captain Italy
Captain	H. LEWIS		15.06.1916	5943	Att 37 Lan Ind A.
Lt	C.R. LIMBERY	1st	01.01.1916	44	Temp Captain KiA 1.07.1916
Captain	C. LISTER	1/6th	01.01.1916	44	
Captain	C. LISTER MC	1/6th	28.12.1918	15156	Att from Northants R.
Lt	R.H. LIVINGSTONE	4th	09.07.1919	8696	A/ Captain
2nd Lt	C.W. MACFIE	2nd	01.01.1916	44	Spec Reserve Killed 16.05.16 Att 2 Bn Bed
Lt	H.W. MacGEORGE	1st	01.01.1916	44	Temp Captain Killed 25.09.15
Lt	A.E. MACHIN	1/5th	09.07.1919	8696	A/Captain Walsall
Lt	J. MACKENZIE		24.05.1918	6096	
T/Captain	W. MACKENZIE, MD, FRCS		06.01.1919	286	9th Bn Att from RAMC.
Lt	H.L. MACKINTOSH	1st	22.06.1915	5997	Killed 05.03.15
T/Lt	R.M. MACTAVISH		24.05.1918	6096	
Lt	H.V. MANDER		01.01.1916	44	T/ Captain
Captain	C.H. MANGER MC		20.05.1918	5948	Staff

Rank	Name	Battalion	London Gazette	Page	Remarks
Captain	C.H. MANGER MC		20.12.1918	14930	T/ Major (Staff)
2nd Lt	H.J. MARLIN	3rd	04.01.1917	231	Specl Reserve KiA 2.04.17 Att1st Bn Linc
Lt	W.H. MARSHALL	5th	09.07.1919	8696	Att Int Corps
T/Lt	F. MASON	9th	06.01.1919	282	Italy
T/Lt	F. MASON	9th	05.06.1919	7208	Italy
T/2nd Lt	O.H. MASON, MC	4th	28.12.1918	15153	
QM	J. McGEVOR		24.05.1918	6096	Hon Captain
T/Lt	A.B. MILLER, DSO, MC	8th	28.12.1918	15153	Att 4th Bn
Major	R.W. MORGAN	2nd	01.01.1916	44	
Major	R.W. MORGAN DSO	2nd	04.01.1917	199 & 231	T/ Brig Gen (Staff)
Bt Lt Col	R.W. MORGAN DSO	2nd	15.05.1917	4750	Temp Brig Gen (Staff)
Bt Lt Col	R.W. MORGAN DSO	2nd	20.12.1918	14931	Temp Brig Gen (Staff)
Bt Lt Col	R.W. MORGAN CMG, DSO		05.07.1919	8497	Temp Brig Gen (Staff)
T/Captain	F.B. MORRIS	7th	28.12.1918	15153	Att XVII
Captain	R.J. MORRIS	1st	04.01.1917	231	Temp Major
Captain	R.J. MORRIS DSO	1st	18.12.1917	13238	Acting Lt Col
T 2nd Lt	H.C.S. MULOCK		15.05.1917	4754	R.F.C. T/Lieut
Captain	R.F.B. NAYLOR	1st	01.01.1916	44	
Captain	R.F.B. NAYLOR	1st	15.06.1916	5943	
Captain	R.F.B. NAYLOR	1st	28.02.1917	2093	MID 13.11.16 Pub 4.1.17
Captain	R.F.B. NAYLOR MC	1st	18.12.1917	13238	Acting Major
Captain	R.F.B. NAYLOR MC	1st	20.12.1918	14931	Acting Lt Col (Staff)
Captain	R.F.B. NAYLOR MC	1st	05.07.1919	8497	Acting Lt Col (Staff)
T/Lt	W.F.J. NORNE	9th	06.01.1919	282	Italy
2nd Lt	I.M.L. OLIVER	4th	28.12.1918	15153	
Lt Col	R.M. OVENS	1st	17.02.1915	1664	

Rank	Name	Battalion	London Gazette	Page	Remarks
Lt Col	R.M. OVENS CMG	1st	01.01.1916	44	
Captain	R. PERSEE		30.05.1918	6334	Temp Major
T/Lt	C.E. PHILCOX	1st	22.05.1917	5036	Desp 15.5.17 Died 24.05.17
T/Lt	J.S. PHILLIPS		22.05.1917	5036	Desp 15.5.17
2nd Lt	R.P. PHIPPS	2nd	04.01.1917	231	A/Captain KiA 13-15. 11.16 6th Att 2nd Bn
2nd Lt	R.C. PIPER	6th	04.01.1917	231	T/ Captain KiA 29.04.18
Captain	J.H. PORTER		18.12.1917	13238	Acting Lt Col
T/2Lt	J. POTTER DSO	1st	04.01.1917	231	DoW 24.7.16
2nd Lt	P.B.M. POWELL		04.01.1917	231	T/ Captain Spec Reserve
2nd Lt	R.S. PULLEN	1st	22.05.1917	5036	Desp 15.5.17 KiA 26.10.17
T/Major	R.G. RAPER		04.01.1917	231	Killed 2.07.16
T/Major	R.R. RAYMER	1/5th	01.01.1916	44	Temp Lt Col
T/Major	R.R. RAYMER	1/5th	15.06.1916	5943	Temp Lt Col
2nd Lt	J.S. REID		25.01.1917	945	Temp Lt
Major	P.C.L ROUTLEDGE	2nd	17.02.1915	1664	
Bt Lt Col	P.C.L. ROUTLEDGE	2nd	22.06.1915	5997	Killed
Bt Lt Col	P.C.L. ROUTLEDGE	2nd	01.01.1916	44	Killed 17.08.15
Captain	M.B. SAVAGE	2nd	09.12.1914	10544	
Captain	M.B. SAVAGE	2nd	17.02.1915	1664	
Major	M.B. SAVAGE DSO	2nd	04.01.1917	201	Staff
Major	M.B. SAVAGE DSO	2nd	11.12.1917	12920	Temp Lt Col (Staff)
Major	M.B. SAVAGE DSO	2nd	24.05.1918	6096	
Captain	F.S.N. SAVAGE-ARMSTRONG		22.06.1915	5997	1st Bn
2 Lt	B.J.H. SCOTT	2nd	17.02.1915	1664	KiA 23.10.14
Major	D.T. SECKHAM	7th	04.01.1917	231	Temp Lt Col

Rank	Name	Battalion	London Gazette	Page	Remarks
Lt Col	D.T. SECKHAM DSO	7th	18.12.1917	13238	Spec Res
Lt	J.S. SHARPE	2nd	17.02.1915	1664	
Captain	J.S. SHARPE	2nd	24.05.1918	6096	Acting Major
Captain	J. SHEPPARD	2/6th	25.01.1917	945	
Lt	R.M. SHEPPARD	2/6th	18.12.1917	13238	A/ Captain
Capt T/Maj	W.J.T. SHORTHOSE DSO	2nd	29.11.1920	11778	SSR & 6 Bn KAR Somaliland dated 15.05.1920.
2nd Lt	P.J. SLATER		15.06.1916	5943	Temp Lt
Lt	G.F. SMITH		20.12.1918	14938	Att from Staffs Yeo
2 Lt	G.H. SMITH		01.01.1916	44	Temp Lt
Lt	J. SNAPE MC	1st	30.05.1918	6334	Acting Major
Lt	J.S. SNOWBALL		24.05.1918	6096	A/ Captain att MGC
2 Lt	E.R. STANLEY		18.12.1917	13238	
T/Lt	E.R. STANLEY		24.05.1918	6096	A/ Captain
Lt	E.R. STANLEY		09.07.1919	8696	A /Captain
Lt	G. STARK	5th	06.01.1919	282	Att 9th Bn. Italy.
Captain	G.W.R. STACPOOLE	4th	28.12.1918	15153	T/Lt Col RoO (RP) DSO (S.A.)
Captain	L.F. STEPHENSON		15.06.1916	5923	
T/Lt Col	R. STEPHENSON DSO	9th	05.06.1919	7208	Italy
Lt Col	J.R. STUART-WORTLEY	2/6th	24.05.1918	6096	R o O
Major	B.H.W TAYLOR		21.06.1916	6181	Staff (Egypt)
Major	B.H.W. TAYLOR		25.09.1916	9339	Staff (Egypt)
Major	B.H.W. TAYLOR		12.01.1918	796	T/Lt Col Staff
Major	B.H.W. TAYLOR CBE		22.01.1919	1149	Bt Lt Col (T/LtCol. Egypt
Major	B.H.W.TAYLOR CBE		05.06.1919	7174	As above on Staff
2nd Lt	B.R. TAYLOR	2nd	01.01.1916	44	

Rank	Name	Battalion	London Gazette	Page	Remarks
Lt Col	H. TAYLOR		25.01.1917	945	
Lt	P.R. TEETON MC	6th	24.05.1918	6096	A/ Captain DoW 17.10.18
Lt	W. TEW	5th	09.07.1919	8696	A/ Captain
Lt	A.G. THOMAS, MC	2nd	06.01.1919	282	Att 5th Bn Sussex R. Italy
Captain	C.H. THOMAS	2nd	17.02.1915	1664	DoW 05.11.14
T/Lt	P.J. TIERNAN	9th	05.06.1919	7208	Italy
Lt	J.S. TOWNSEND	2nd	22.06.1915	5997	
Captain	J.S. TOWNSEND MC	5th	09.07.1919	8696	Act/Major Att 5th R Inn F.
2nd Lt	A.F.V.A. TREVARTHEN		15.06.1916	5943	Temp Lt SR, KiA 28.1.16
Captain	J.F. VALLENTIN VC	1st	17.02.1915	1664	KiA 07.11.14
T/2 Lt	A.P. WALKER		28.12.1918	15153	Att 4th Bn
Captain	E. WALKER DCM	7th	09.07.1919	8696	Temp QM
Major	H.E. WALSHE	1st	22.06.1915	5997	Att 1st Dorsets
T/2nd Lt	R.W. WARD		05.06.1919	7189	Att 1/4th Wilts R
QM	C.O. WARDLE		18.12.1917	13238	Hon Lt
Lt Col	T.F. WATERHOUSE		01.01.1916	44	
Lt Col	T.F. WATERHOUSE TD		27.02.1918	2586	TF Res
Captain	A. WHITE DSO	1/5th	09.07.1919	8694	A/Lt Col 4th E Surrey Regt att.
Qm Hon Capt	F.H. WHITE	1st	17.02.1915	1664	
2nd Lt	A.P. WHITEHEAD	2nd	04.01.1917	231	Spec Reserve
Lt	A.V. WHITEHEAD	4th	22.06.1915	5997	Att 2nd E Lan
Lt A/Captain	C.E.L. WHITEHOUSE	2/6th	24.05.1918	6096	
Lt	C.P. WHITEHOUSE		24.05.1918	6096	A/ Captain

Rank	Name	Battalion	London Gazette	Page	Remarks
Lt	J. DE T.A.C. WILLARD		09.07.1919	8696	A/ Captain
2nd Lt	D.M. WILLIAMS	2nd	01.01.1916	44	KiA 25.09.15 David Marmaduke
Major	G.A.S. WILLIAMS	4th	15.05.1917	4753	Spec Res
Major	G.A.S. WILLIAMS	4th	11.12.1917	12922	Staff
Major	G.A.S. WILLIAMS DSO	4th	30.05.1918	6329	Staff
Major	G.A.S. WILLIAMS DSO	4th	06.01.1919	277	Italy
T/Captain	R.L. WILLIAMS	2nd	30.12.1918	15208	Att from RAMC
QM	J. WILLNER		18.12.1917	13238	Hon Lt
T/2Lt	J.S. WILSON	8th	22.05.1917	5036	Desp 15.5.17 DoW 12.10.17
Captain	W.A. WISTANCE DSO, MC	1/5th	24.05.1918	6096	Acting Lt Col KiA 25.04.18 (Winstance)
Lt	A.L. WOOD		12.01.1920	497	T/ Captain
T/2nd Lt	M.W.T. WYON	2nd	24.05.1918	6096	A/ Captain
T/Lt	H.W. YOCKNEY		28.12.1918	15153	Att 1/5th Bn Man R.
Major	G.A. YOOL		18.12.1917	13238	Acting Lt Col
Major	G.A. YOOL		24.05.1918	6096	Acting Lt Col
Lt	L. YOUNG		22.05.1917	5036	Desp 15.5.17

NCO's / OTHER RANKS

No	Rank	Name	Battalion	London Gazette	Page	Remarks
18333	Cpl	W.J. ALLCHIN	7th	04.01.1917	231	Acting Sgt
6215	Sgt	W. ALSOP	2nd	24.05.1918	6096	
14478	Cpl	E. AMOR		22.05.1917	5036	Desp 15.5.17
240014	CSM	W. ASTON	2/6th	18.12.1917	13238	
6934	L/Cpl	H. BACHE	2nd	22.06.1915	5997	
17443	Pte	C. BAGNALL		04.01.1917	231	L/Cpl

Charles Bagnall is shown as having been awarded the Distinguished Conduct Medal, when in fact it was a Mention In Despatches, London Gazette dated 4th January 1917.

With details being passed to the newspapers it was not to uncommon for mistakes to be made in the transcription. He came from Walsall and he has no known grave but his name appears with the other officers and men of the South Staffordshire Regiment on the Arras Memorial, Pas de Calais, France. His photograph appeared in the Walsall Observer & South Staffordshire Chronicle.

No	Rank	Name	Battalion	London Gazette	Page	Remarks
8281	Cpl	A. BAKER	1st	17.02.1915	1664	
8/13641	L/Cpl	D. BAKER		01.01.1916	44	
4276	A/Cpl	J. BARRATT	2/6th	25.01.1917	946	Killed 29.04.1916
13265	Cpl	A. BATE	9th	06.01.1919	282	Italy
7322	Sgt	A. BELLERSON	2nd	22.05.1917	5036	Desp 15.5.17
9218	Pte	J. BENNETT		04.01.1917	231	
10308	Pte	E. BEVAN	7th	18.12.1917	13238	
200135	CQMS	H.E. BIRD	1/5th	22.05.1917	5036	Desp 15.5.17
8/13211	Sgt	H.S. BIRD		01.01.1916	44	
10577	Sgt	F. BLACK	9th	06.01.1919	282	Italy
6650	Pte	C. BONNING	1st	22.06.1915	5997	
10811	CSM	E. BRAMMER		30.05.1918	6334	
16489	Pte	J.W. BRIDGENS	7th	09.07.1919	8696	Act Corporal
7106	Sgt	E. BROCKHURST	1st	05.06.1919	7208	MM Italy
240319	Cpl	B. BROWN		22.05.1917	5036	Desp 15.5.17

No	Rank	Name	Battalion	London Gazette	Page	Remarks
8/14327	Sgt	H. BROWN		04.01.1917	231	
10609	CSM	T.G. BUTLER		22.05.1917	5036	Desp 15.5.17
7738	Cpl	H. CADWALLADER	1st	06.01.1919	282	A/Sgt Italy
9603	Pte	E.T. CARTLIDGE	4th	09.07.1919	8696	Act L/Cpl att 1/5th Bn
10501	Cpl	E CHATWIN	1st	01.01.1916	44	
242587	Pte	H.A. CHAVASSE	1/6th	09.07.1919	8696	Act L/Cpl
6596	Sgt	F. CLARKE	1st	01.01.1916	44	
240429	Cpl	G. CLARKE		18.12.1917	13238	
6983	CQMS	A. CLAY	1st	30.01.1920	1228	For Services whilst PoW
10988	Cpl	W. COLEMAN	7th	09.07.1919	8696	
41702	Pte	F.N. COOKE	1st	05.06.1919	7208	Italy Now 88487 22 Man R.
15299	Pte	G. COOPER	1st	01.01.1916	44	
8958	Pte	H. COOPER	1st	01.01.1916	44	
17989	Pte	J.H. COX, DCM	9th	05.06.1919	7208	Italy
6715	Pte	T. DEAKIN	2nd	22.06.1915	5997	
16306	Cpl	G.S. DELANEY	2nd	22.05.1917	5036	Desp 15.5.17
9047	CQMS	B.O. DOLEY	1st	04.01.1917	231	
3951	A/Cpl	D.V. DOWNES		25.01.1917	946	
203221	Cpl	A.C. DUDLEY	1/5th	09.07.1919	8696	Acting Sgt
8812	Cpl	W. DUNN	2nd	09.07.1919	8697	
13002	LCpl	J. EADES DCM MM	1st	04.01.1917	231	
240034	Sgt	J. EDGE		18.12.1917	13238	
8631	LCpl	W.T. EDWARDS		25.01.1917	946	Depot SSR Form Prov Bn

No	Rank	Name	Battalion	London Gazette	Page	Remarks
16075	CPL	W. EVANS		04.01.1917	231	
200003	RQMS	E. EVERTON	1/5th	09.07.1919	8697	
7072	L/Cpl	B.FITZPATRICK DCM	2nd	22.06.1915	5997	
240264	Pte	L. FLUKES	1/6th	09.07.1919	8697	
6911	Sgt	W.E.S. GASCOIGNE	2nd	09.12.1914	10544	
41091	Pte	G. GIDDENS	9th	06.01.1919	282	Italy
9037	Pte	H. GLEESON	2nd	15.06.1916	5943	
16285	Pte	J. GREEN	2nd	01.01.1916	44	
9742	RSM	T. GRIFFITHS	7th	22.05.1917	5036	Desp 15.5.17
18252	Cpl	F. HALL		30.05.1918	6334	
8325	L/Cpl	N. HAMBLETON	2nd	15.06.1916	5943	
3559	A/Sgt	C.H. HANDS		25.01.1917	946	
14344	Sgt	G. HARDING		30.05.1918	6334	
241651	Pte	S. HARPER	1/6th	09.07.1919	8697	
18377	Pte	T.E. HARTSHORNE	1/6th	09.07.1919	8697	
9763	Pte	W.H. HARVEY	3rd	05.06.1919	7208	Italy Att 1st Bn
1933	Sgt	S.H. HATTON		25.01.1917	946	
11256	Sgt	S. HAWKES		30.05.1918	6334	
12112	Sgt	J. HENNEY	9th	04.01.1917	231	Comm 2Lt 1/5th
7158	CQMS	C.H. HIAM	1st	22.05.1917	5036	For Desp 15.5.17
7158	CQMS	C.H. HIAM, MM	1st	05.06.1919	7208 Italy	Acting CSM, Italy
10915	Pte	J.W. HICKMAN	7th	22.05.1917	5036	Desp 15.5.17
200553	Cpl	J.W. HOLMES	1/5th	18.12.1917	13238	
13911	L/Cpl	W.A. HOMER	9th	05.06.1919	7208	Italy

No	Rank	Name	Battalion	London Gazette	Page	Remarks
241836	Sgt	S.G HOPKINS	1/6th	09.07.1919	8697	
8980	LCpl	C. HOWARD	2nd	15.06.1916	5943	
12298	CQMS	G. HUBBALL	2nd	09.07.1919	8697	
9930	Pte	B. JACKSON	7th	22.05.1917	5036	DoW 8.11.16 Wolverhampton Desp 15.5.17
14470	CQMS	T.T. JOHNSON	9th	04.01.1917	231	
14470	RQMS	T.T. JOHNSON	9th	30.05.1918	6334	
9853	Sgt	W.H. JORDON	1st	01.01.1916	44	
9749	Pte	J. KENNERLEY	2nd	22.06.1915	5997	
15995	CQMS	A.R. KNIGHT	9th	05.06.1919	7208	Acting CSM. Italy
13694	CSM	G. LANCASTER	9th	06.01.1919	282	Italy
9575	Sgt	M.LANE	1st	30.05.1918	6334	
7458	CSM	W.H. LICHFIELD	2nd	15.06.1916	5943	
6676	Pte	LITTLEWOOD	2nd	09.12.1914	10544	
5991	CSM	J. LOCKLEY		04.01.1917	231	Acting RSM
41053	Cpl	F. LYALL	1/5th	09.07.1919	8697	Acting Sgt
10019	Cpl	F. MASON MM	1st	30.05.1918	6334	
7417	Sgt	A. McCONVIL	1st	30.05.1918	6334	
10609	Pte	J. McHALE	1st	01.01.1916	44	
40582	Pte	C. McNEICE	2/6th	30.01.1920	1234	Att or Escaping Whilst PoW
43591	Pte	A. MEISCHKE	1/6th	09.07.1919	8697	Acting L/Cpl
8500	Pte	C. MILNER	1st	01.01.1916	44	
10410	LCpl	H. MONGER	1st	01.01.1916	44	
5005	Pte	A. MUTLOW	2nd	09.12.1914	10544	

No	Rank	Name	Battalion	London Gazette	Page	Remarks
7511	Bman	W. NEVILLE	1st	22.06.1915	5997	
7511	Bman	W. NEVILLE	1st	01.01.1916	44	
4137	A/Sgt	G.H. NORTON		25.01.1917	946	
12491	Sgt	W.H. PACE	1st	30.05.1918	6334	
19068	Cpl	W. PADMORE	7th	09.07.1919	8697	
241707	Sgt	J. PALMER	1/6th	28.12.1918	15153	
8689	CSM	F. PARR MC, DCM	1st	30.05.1918	6334	A/RSM
200050	Sgt	A. PEARCE	1/5th	28.12.1918	15153	Hednesford
9424	Pte	W. PEARSON	3rd	05.06.1919	7208	Att 91 TMB. Italy
241437	Pte	A.L. PERKS	2/6th	18.12.1917	13238	
242330	Pte	A.S. PERRY	2/6th	24.05.1918	6096	
7215	CQMS	W. PHILLIPS	2nd	09.07.1919	8697	
201537	Pte	T. PLATER	1/5th	09.07.1919	8697	
2176	Sgt	W. POSTANCE		15.06.1916	5943	
9158	Pte	W. PRICE	1st	01.01.1916	44	
32932	L/Cpl	W. PRICE	1/5th	09.07.1919	8697	Acting Cpl
16013	Pte	C.H. QUEMBY	9th	06.01.1919	282	Italy
7334	Sgt	R. RANKIN	1st	01.01.1916	44	
204248	L/Cpl	F.C. REEVES		05.06.1919	7248	A/Sgt Government Telegraph Dept Mespotamia
10175	Pte	W. RHODES		22.05.1917	5036	
6460	RQMS	A. RILEY	1st	22.05.1917	5036	Desp 15.5.17
6460	RQMS	A. RILEY MC	1st	30.05.1918	6334	
6460	RQMS	A. RILEY, MC	1st	06.01.1919	282	Italy
19794	Sgt	J. E. ROTCHELL MM	9th	06.01.1919	282	Italy
9320	Pte	J. RUSHBURY		04.01.1917	231	

No	Rank	Name	Battalion	London Gazette	Page	Remarks
10465	CQMS	J. SETTLE		22.05.1917	5036	A/CSM Desp 15.5.17
7770	Cpl	G. SHEPHERD	1st	01.01.1916	44	
201398	Pte	E. SIDDONS	1/5th	24.05.1918	6096	
8/13415	Sgt	F.W. SIMMS		18.12.1917	13238	
8185	Pte	A.F. SMITH	1st	05.06.1919	7208	Acting Cpl Italy
12489	Pte	B. SMITH	2nd	28.12.1918	15153	
16046	Cpl	C. SMITH		18.12.1917	13238	Acting L/Sgt
3171	Pte	G. SMITH		25.01.1917	946	
5881	CSM	J. SMITH	1/5th	11.05.1918	5666	For LG 18.2.17 Pg 13238 A/R.S.M.
5881	CSM	J. SMITH	1/5th	24.05.1918	6096	
10602	Sgt	W.H. SMITH	1st	15.06.1916	5943	
16795	Sgt	J. SMITHEMAN	7th	22.05.1917	5036	A/CSM Desp 15.5.17
4875	RSM	J. SNAPE	1st	01.01.1916	44	
200218	Sgt	A.W. STANWORTH		18.12.1917	13238	
9189	Pte	C.E. TANDY	4th	05.06.1919	7208	Act L/Cpl Att 1st Bn Italy
39532	Cpl	A. TAPAKO	1/5th	09.07.1919	8697	
200040	Sgt	W. TAPPER	1/5th	22.05.1917	5036	Desp 15.5.17
5281	CQMS	A. TARBET		04.01.1917	231	Acting SSM
15561	Pte	N. TAYLOR	9th	05.06.1919	7208	Italy
3356	L/Cpl	W.H. THOMAS		25.01.1917	946	
12388	Pte	R. THOMPSON	1st	05.06.1919	7208	Italy
8237	Sgt	F. THORNE	1st	01.01.1916	44	
200268	Sgt	W. TILL	1/5th	09.07.1919	8697	

No	Rank	Name	Battalion	London Gazette	Page	Remarks
15847	Pte	A.J. TIMMINS	9th	05.06.1919	7208	Hednesford Italy
8597	A/CSM	W.B. TIMMINS	1st	22.06.1915	5997	
8981	L/Cpl	F. TURNER	1st	01.01.1916	44	
4692	CSM	J.T. UPTON		15.06.1916	5943	
203284	Pte	T.L. VARMAN	1/5th	28.12.1918	15153	
9314	Cpl	W. VINCENT	1st	01.01.1916	44	

This is an example of not believing all you see in a newspaper. The photograph appeared in the Walsall Observer and South Staffordshire Chronicle. It shows Corporal Vincent as being awarded the DCM when in fact it was a Mention in Despatches dated 1st January 1916,

William Vincent was aged 33 years at the time of his death and was the husband of E. Leonard (Formerly Vincent) off 22 Cairns Street, Walsall.

He is buried in Bethune Town Cemetery, Pas de Calais, France.

No	Rank	Name	Battalion	London Gazette	Page	Remarks
8807	Sgt	A.W. VIZOR	2nd	22.06.1915	5997	
10521	CQMS	E. WALKER DCM	7th	13.07.1916	6949	
6824	RQMS	F.A. WARD	2nd	22.05.1917	5036	A/RSM Desp 15.5.17
6824	RSM	F.A. WARD MC	2nd	09.07.1919	8697	
240332	CSM	T. WATERS		22.05.1917	5036	Desp 15.5.17
7470	L/Cpl	H.H.B. WATKINS	2nd	09.12.1914	10544	
15223	Pte	J.R. WATSON	9th	05.06.1919	7208	Italy
10285	Cpl	J. WAYMONT	7th	13.07.1916	6949	Acting Sgt
10249	Pte	H. WAIN	1st	06.01.1919	282	Italy
7155	Pte	H. WESLEY	1st	06.01.1919	282	Italy
6003	Pte	J. WESTON		04.01.1917	231	LCpl
8550	Pte	H. WHEATLEY MM	1/5th	15.06.1916	5943	
11444	Sgt	E. WHITWORTH		30.05.1918	6334	
8939	A Sgt	A. WILCOX	1st	01.01.1916	44	
15027	Cpl	W.H. WILCOX	9th	06.01.1919	282	A/Sgt Italy

No/Rank		Name	Unit	Lon Gazette	Page	Remarks
240446	Sgt	A. WILKES		24.05.1918	6096	
6062	Sgt	T. WILKES	2nd	01.01.1916	44	
32523	Pte	F. WILLIAMS	9th	05.06.1919	7208	Italy
7403	Bman	J. WILLIAMS	1st	22.06.1915	5997	
7403	Cpl	J. WILLIAMS	1st	01.01.1916	44	
14349	CSM	J. WILLIAMS		30.05.1918	6334	
8549	Drum	E. WINCHESTER	1st	22.06.1915	5997	
8549	Drum	E. WINCHESTER	1st	01.01.1916	44	Also 2nd Bn awards
242397	Pte	E.F. WOOD	1/6th	09.07.1919	8697	
8112	Sgt	J. WRIGHT	1st	01.01.1916	44	
16866	Cpl	J. WRIGHT	9th	06.01.1919	282	Italy
16821	Pte	J. YATES	2nd	09.07.1919	8697	
18567	L/Cpl	J.R. YATES	7th	18.12.1917	13238	

SELECTED PERSONAL DETAILS

Details of other recipients can be found on p.177 et seq.

17433 Lance Corporal Charles BAGNALL

Captain George Bygrave MC

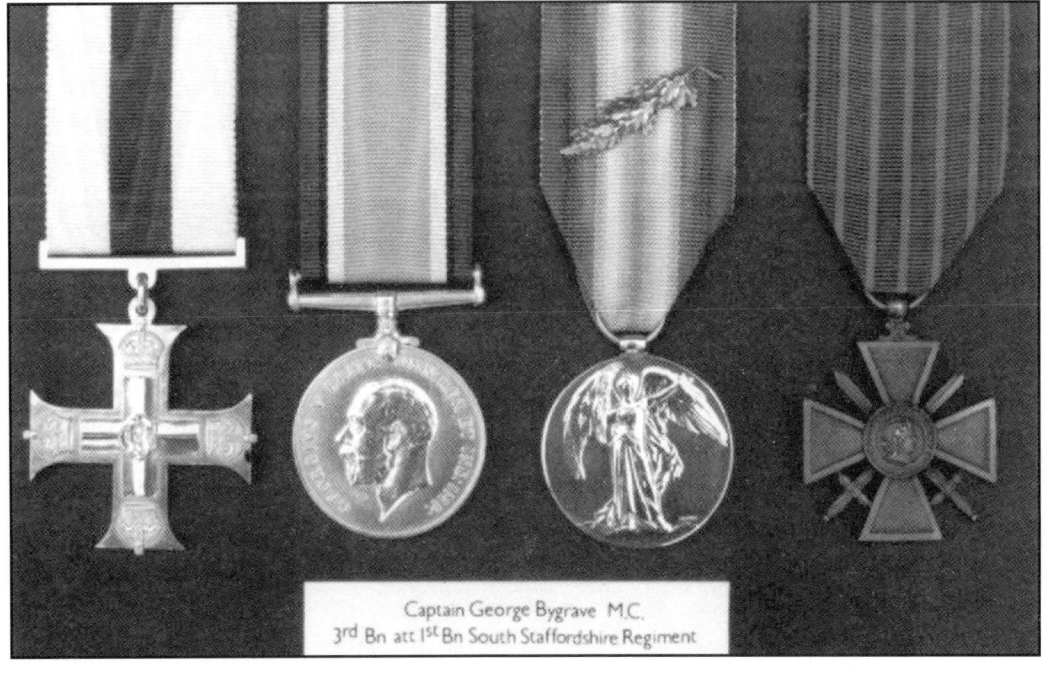

Captain George Bygrave M.C.
3rd Bn att 1st Bn South Staffordshire Regiment

Bygrave medal group

Lieutenant (Acting Captain) Stanhope W.H.S. DOUGLAS-WILLAN

7072 L/Cpl (Sgt) B. FITZPATRICK DCM

Captain QM Arthur HAZLEGROVE MC. DCM

9314 Corporal William Edwin VINCENT

FOREIGN AWARDS

THESE awards are those given by the Allied Governments to officers and men of the South Staffordshire Battalions for service during the Great War 1914-1918. The entries here are those shown in the London Gazette and the Regimental Records. Some that appear in the Battalion histories are not shown in the London Gazette. Where this has occurred there will obviously be no London Gazette date.

BELGIUM

No.	Rank	Name/Residence	Battalion	London Gazette	Page
Chevalier de l'Ordre de Leopold					
	Captain (Temp Major)	G.W.R. STACPOOLE DSO, OBE		14.02.1917	1593
Ordre de Leopold (Officer)					
	Brev Lt Col (T/Lt Col) CB	V.G.W. KELL (General Staff)		24.09.1917	9863
Croix de Guerre					
16831	Pte	J. BOWATER	7th	12.07.1918	8172
16831	Cpl	T. BOWLER Wordsley, Stourbridge		12.07.1918	8172
6957	Pte	G. H. BROMIGE Norwich	2nd	12.07.1918	8172
17108	Sgt	I. BROWN Moseley Village, Wolverhampton		12.07.1918	8172

No.	Rank	Name/Residence	Battalion	London Gazette	Page
	Brevet Major (T/Lt Col)	J. C. CHAYTOR DSO, MC	2nd	04.09.1919	11208
241765	Pte	F. DOWNS Long Sutton, Lincs	6th	12.07.1918	8174
7527	Sgt	A. GIBBS Barnsley	2nd	12.07.1918	8175
242176	Sgt	H. R. KING Bawdry, Yorks	2/6th	12.07.1918	8178
SS/2176	RSM	W. S. NEALE Lichfield, Attached London Regt	4th	12.07.1918	8181
8260	L/Cpl A/Cpl	J. SHERRARD Darlaston		12.07.1918	8183
13415	A/CSM	F.W. SIMMS Bourne Brook		12.07.1918	8183
16046	Cpl (L/Sgt)	C. SMITH Ibstock		12.07.1918	8183
	Lt (A/Major)Att H.A.C.	J. SNAPE DSO MC	1st	12.07.1918	8171
	Capt (Temp Major)	G.W.R STACKPOOLE DSO (RoO Late SSR)		11.03.1918	3097
200632	CSM	J. STANTON Walsall		12.07.1918	8184
26263	L/Cpl (A/Cpl)	R. TAYLOR MM Chesterfield,Derby	7th	12.07.1918	8184
7851	Sgt (A/CQMS)	F. WEBB Wolverhampton		12.07.1918	8185
200048	CSM	J. E. WYLDE Walsall	1/5th	12.07.1918	8186

Decoration Militaire

11916	Sgt	G. DODD Wolverhampton		24.09.1917	9863

EGYPT

Order of The Nile (3rd Class)

	Major & Brevet Lieut Colonel	B.H.W. TAYLOR CBE.		26.11.1919	14635.

No.	Rank	Name/Residence	Battalion	London Gazette	Page

FRANCE

Legion d' Honneur (Croix d'Officer)

	Lt Col	P.R.C COMMINGS CMG, DSO		14.07.1919	8957
	Major (T/Lt Col)	A.H.C JAMES MVO DSO		10.10.1918	11944
	Brev Lt Col (Temp Col)	V.G.W. KELL CB Retired Pay (RoO)		25.09.1917	9946
	Lt Col	L. BOYD-MOSS CMG, DSO		22.02.1916	2066
	Brevet Lt Col (T/Lt Col) B.H.W TAYLOR CBE			01.07.1920	7087

Legion d' Honneur (Croix de Chevalier)

	Lt	J. CHAYTOR	2nd	03.11.1914	8879
	Captain (Temp Major)	F.O. LANGLEY MC	6th	16.01.1920	701
	Captain	G.E.W. LEGG MVO (RoO)		21.08.1919	10607
	Captain (T/Maj)	C.H. MANGER MC		11.03.1919	3280
	Lt	R.F.B NAYLOR		03.11.1914	8880

Croix de Guerre

No.	Rank	Name/Residence	Battalion	London Gazette	Page
	Temp Lieut	S. BAKER	8th	01.05.1917	4156
	Temp Lt Col	W.J.A BARKER DSO	8th	14.07.1917	7094
	Captain (Temp Major)	C.E.C. BARTLETT MC (Att L North Lanc)		29.01.1919	1446
	Captain	H.S. BLOCKLEY	1st	17.08.1918	9655
4980	CSM (T/RSM)	A. BURGOYNE DCM (Walsall)	2nd (Att 1/6th)	21.07.1919	Page 9222
	Major	S.S. BUTLER	1st	24.02.1916	2068
	Lt	G. BYGRAVE	1st		
203864	Pte	F. DAVEY (Smethwick Nr Birmingham)	1/5th	21.07.1919	9222
	Brevet Major (A/Lt Col) G. DAWES DSO MC		2nd (Att 21st Lon R.)	29.01.1919	1446

No.	Rank	Name/Residence	Battalion	London Gazette	Page
9600	Pte	H. EDWARDS	1st	01.05.1917	4158
	Captain	W.C. GREEN MC	1st (Att E Yorks)	07.01.1919	313
8/13628	Sgt (A/CQMS)	R.HANDY	8th	14.07.1917	7096
	Lt Temp Major	C.C. HARLAND MC	7th	07.10.1919	12404
	Captain (Temp Major)	W.J.T SHORTHOUSE	2nd	31.08.1917	9109 (K.A.R.)
	Captain (Temp Major)	L.F. STEPHENSON MC	2nd	10.10.1918	11945
17151	Pte	S. THOMAS	2nd	01.05.1917	4160
	Lt Col	F.J. TRUMP	6th SSR	6th SSR War History (Awards)	

Medaille Militaire

385056	Farrier Sgt	J.S. KING North Road N	Labour C Formerly SSR	10.10.1918	11947
7866	CSM	E.MARTIN	1/5th SSR	24.02.1916	2073

La Medaille de la Reconnaissance Francaise
3rd Class "en Bronze"

	Lieut	H.E.MERRY MBE	6th SSR	08.03.1920	2870

Medaille d'Honneur Avec Glaives "en Bronze"

200056   Private William FELLOWS   1/5th SSR
London Gazette 17.03.1920
          Bloxwich
          Page 3406

HEDJAZ

Order of El Nahada (2nd Class)

	Brevet Lt Col. (Temp Colonel)	B.H.W. TAYLOR CBE.		09.04.1920	4227

ITALY

The Order of the Crown of Italy (Officer)

	Temp Major	A.H. ASHCROFT (Birkenhead)	7th	20.11.1918	14096

No.	Rank	Name/Residence	Battalion	London Gazette	Page
Silver Medal for Valour					
	Brevet Major (Temp Brig General)	A.B. BEAUMAN DSO	1st	07.01.1919	318
	A/CSM	T. BILLS DCM MM	1st	11.09.1918	
	Captain	G de C. GLOVER MC	2nd	26.05.1917	5201
	Captain	H.HANFORD	6th	26.05.1917	5201
40483	Pte	A. JAMES DCM Dudley	1st	07.01.1919	318
	Temp Lieut (A/Captain)	F.A. KENDRICK MC	1st	07.01.1919	318
32500	Sgt	W.LYCETT	1st	07.01.1919	318
16895	Sgt	G. PHILLIPS Bilston	1st	07.01.1919	318
	2Lieut (Temp Captain)	E. de TRAFFORD MC	1st	26.05.1917	5201
Bronze Medal for Valour					
41622	L/Cpl	R. CURTIS Grantham	1st	07.01.1919	318
8/12279	Pte	A. FORD		26.05.1917	5203
13266	Sgt	H. GREEN Walsall		12.09.1918	10742
9569	A/Cpl	A. HARRISON MM Wednesbury	1st	07.01.1919	318
	Lieut	A. Jerrard VC	5th	02.11.1918	12978
	Lieut (A/Captain)	F. A. KENDRICK MC Wolverhampton	1st	17.05.1919	6200
6893	A/Sgt	S. MANTLE MM	1st	07.01.1919	318
9674	LCPL (A/CPL)	A. ROSEWARNE	7th	26.05.1917	5205
	2 Lieut	J. SALT	1st	29.11.1918	14098
Croce di Guerra					
	Temp Lieut (A/Captain)	H.BARKWORTH MC	9th	17.05.1919	6201

No.	Rank	Name/Residence	Battalion	London Gazette	Page
32992	Pte	W. Beardsley Derby	1st	17.05.1919	6205
	Brevet Major (T/Brig General)	A.B. BEAUMAN DSO	1st	11.03.1919	3284
8479	CQMS (A/CSM)	T. BILLS DCM, MM W Bromwich	1st	29.11.1918	14100
	Captain (Temp Lt Col)	C.S. BURT DSO	1st	29.11.1918	14099
	Lieutenant (Temp Major)	C.C. HARLAND MC	7th	07.10.1919	12404
13949	Pte	J.HINTON MM Heathtown	1st	29.11.1918	14100
	Lieut	A.W. LEE MC	1st	17.05.1919	6203
41265	L/Cpl	H. MOLYNEUX (Wigan Lancs)	9th	17.05.1919	6207
	Lieut (A/Captain)	Fred ROBINSON MC	1st	17.05.1919	6204
	Lieut (A/Captain)	R.H. SPROAT		17.05.1919	6204
	Lieut	G. STARK		17.05.1919	6204
	Captain (Temp Major)	Lionel Fenton STEPHENSON	9th Bn	07.10.1919	12414
	Temp Lieut Colonel	R. STEPHENSON DSO		17.05.1919	6204
12388	Pte	R. THOMPSON (West Bromwich)	1st	17.05.1919	6208
	Lieut (T/Captain)	Edward de TRAFFORD MC	1st	17.05.1919	6204

JAPAN

Japanese Order of The Sacred Treasure 3rd Class

	Rank	Name/Residence	Battalion	London Gazette	Page
	Major & Brevet Lt Colonel	S.S. BUTLER CMG, DSO	1st Bn	07.10.1919	12415

No.	Rank	Name/Residence	Battalion	London Gazette	Page

PANAMA

Medal of La Solidaridad
2nd Class (with Rosette)

	Major & Brevet Lt Col	B.H.W. TAYLOR CBE		17.02.1920	1937

PORTUGAL

Military Order of AVIS 2nd Class

	Brevet Major	G. de C. GLOVER DSO, MC	2nd	10.10.1918	11951

Military Order of AVIS 3rd Class

	Temp Captain	R.HOLLOCOMBE MC	6th	10.10.1918	11951

ROUMANIA

Croix De Virtute Militaria 2nd Class

19068	Cpl	W. PADMORE (Wolverhampton)	7th	20.09.1919	11752

Medaille Barbatie si Credinta 3rd Class

44667	Pte	J.WHITTLE (Blackburn)	1/5th	20.09.1919	11758

RUSSIA

Order of St Stanislaus 3rd Class (with swords)

	Lt (Temp Major)	W.H. CARTER DSO MC	2nd & 7th Att Middlesex Regt	15.02.1917	1600
	Lt Col (Temp Brig Gen)	R.M. OVENS CMG	1st	15.02.1917	1600

Cross of St George 3rd Class

6874	Cpl	J. HUNT	2nd	25.08.1915	8506
8689	CSM (Acting RSM)	F. PARR	1st	15.02.1917	1601

Cross of St George 4th Class

8860	CQMS	F. BYTHEWAY	1st	25.08.1915	8506
6330	L/Cpl	H.COTTERILL	2nd	25.08.1915	8507
2561	CSM	J.DUGGAN	1/6th	25.08.1915	8507
3336	Pte	T. PRICE	6th	25.08.1915	8508

No.	Rank	Name/Residence	Battalion	London Gazette	Page
Medal of St George 2nd Class					
8362	Sgt	A.BUSBY	2nd	25.08.1915	8510
Medal of St George 3rd Class					
11509	Pte	B. HESSON	2nd	25.08.1915 Now R.E.No 86137	8513
2137	L/Cpl	F.PAYTON	1/6th	25.08.1915	8513
Medal of St George 4th Class					
7072	L/Cpl	B.FITZPATRICK	2nd	25.08.1915	8515
39442	Private	J. LINDSEY	RAMC	15.02.1917	1603
1982	Pte	A. MAYO	1/6th	25.08.1915	8516
9579	Private	G. PRICE	1st	15.02.1917	1603

SERBIA

No.	Rank	Name/Residence	Battalion	London Gazette	Page
Serbian Silver Medal					
9880	Pte (now LCPL)	G.TAYLOR		15.02.1917	1614

DIVISIONAL CARDS

No.	Rank	Name	Battalion	Date
240681	Private	Bishop W.H.	2/6th	01.11.1917
242322	Private	Catewell W.G.	2/6th	01.11.1917
242313	L/Corporal	Chapman A.	2/6th	09.05.1918 Att 176th Inf Bde
202791	Private	Coleman F.	2/5th	01.01.1917
9746	Private	Cowell A.	2/5th	01.11.1917
242271	Private	Cox W.J.	2/6th	01.11.1917
40760	Private	Crowther H.	2/5th	01.11.1917
242157	Private	Cutts J.	2/6th	01.11.1917

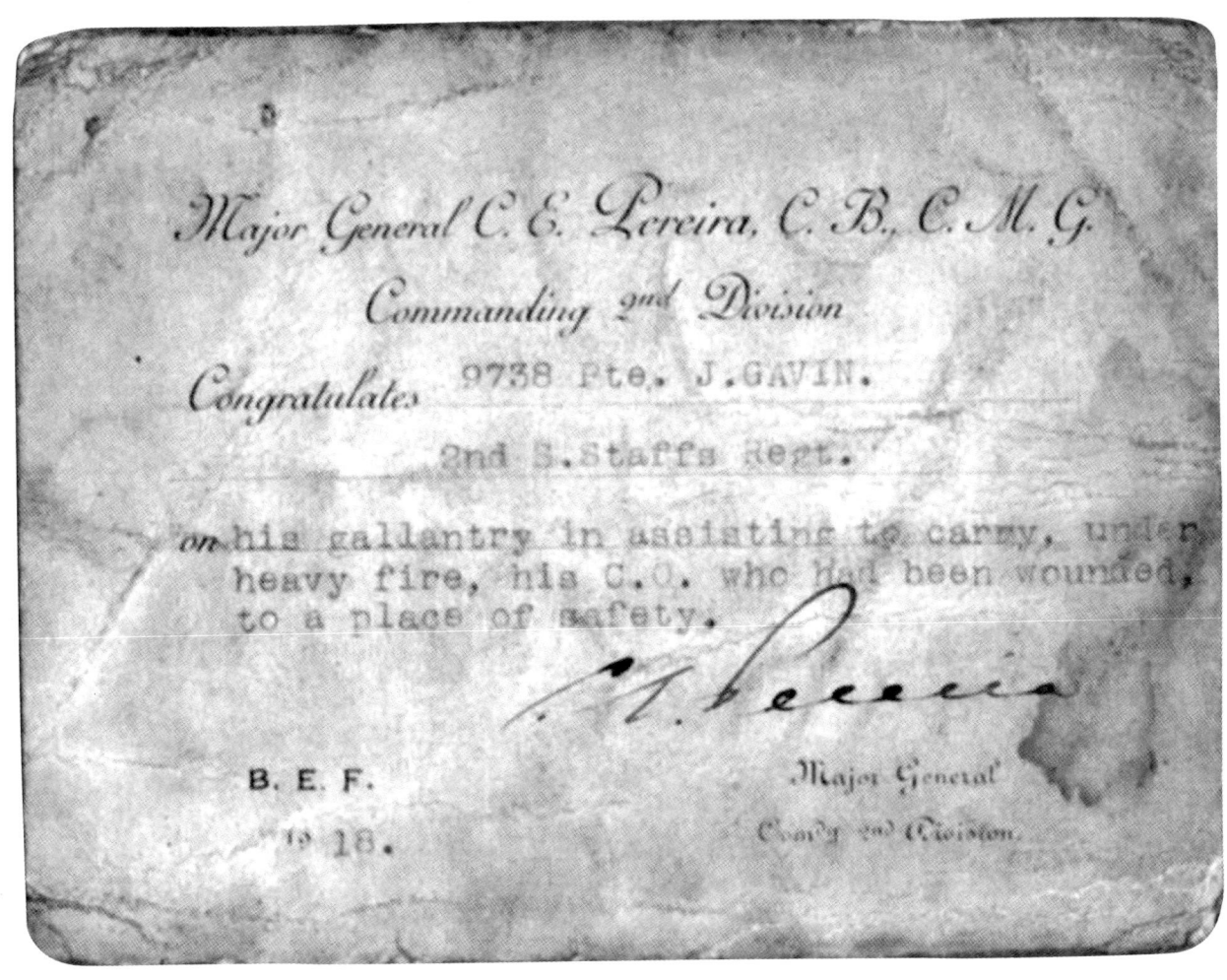

Divisional Card for Private 9738 James GAVIN MM & 2 Bars

No.	Rank	Name	Battalion	Date
10123	Private	Dibble J.	2/5th	01.11.1917
9172	L/Corporal	Dodd J.	2/5th	01.11.1917
242129	L/Corporal	Everton A.	2/6th	01.11.1917
241244	Private	Fernyhough J.	2/6th	01.11.1917
9738	Private	Gavin J.	2/6th	1918
40468	Private	Hammond O.	2/5th	01.11.1917
200337	L/Corporal	Hickman L.	2/5th	01.11.1917
241819	Private	Hickman D.	2/6th	01.11.1917
240130	Private	Keating	2/5th	04.01.1918
9597	Private	Philpot W.H.	2/6th	09.05.1918 Att 176th Inf Bde
201355	Private	Plant O.	2/5th	01.11.1917
242131	Private	Sperry A.	2/6th	01.11.1917
202602	Private	Vanner F.	2/5th	01.11.1917
201356	L/Corporal	Wood T.	2/5th	01.11.1917

BREAKDOWN OF AWARDS

THE table of awards shows up some interesting points, of the 5 VC's mentioned in the book, three were awarded to men whilst serving with the South Staffordshire Battalions, the other two were men who had previously served with or had been attached to the 1/5th Battalion South Staffords. The high number of awards of the DSO, MC, DCM, MM shows the intensity of the fighting during WW1.

VC	5
KBE	1
CB (Civ)	1
CB (Mil)	2
KCMG	1
CMG	8
CBE	6
DSO	58 plus 6 1st Bar and 1 2nd Bar awards
OBE	13
MVO	1
MC	143 plus 16 1st Bar
DCM	166 plus 3 1st Bar
MM	645 plus 27 1st Bar and 1 2nd Bar awards
DFC	1
MSM	67
MID	416 (34 (2x), 13 (3x), 6 (4x), 6 (5x), 3 (6x))
MBE (M)	7
MBE (C)	2
AM	1
TD	8

Foreign Awards By Country

Belgium	21
Egypt	1
France	33
Hedjez	1
Italy	38
Japan	1
Panama	1
Portugal	2
Roumania	2
Russia	16
Serbia	1

BIOGRAPHICAL DETAILS

This section deals with additional information that has been located from different sources, such as newspapers and private collections; it gives an insight to "the man behind the medal" The entries are alphabetical, some quite lengthy, others just a couple of lines.

2nd Lieutenant J. Baker MC

2nd Lieutenant J. Baker MC

Second Lieutenant John Baker, son of Mr John Baker JP, C.C, Cannock Chase Miners agent, has been awarded the Military Cross for conspicuous bravery on the 29th, on the occasion of the storming of the canal at Bellenglise, by the 46th North Midland Division. "I would not have missed it for the world. The men were splendid, and we are all proud of them", said Lieutenant Baker. Before joining the colours in August 1914, Lieutenant Baker was an assistant to Mr R. Blanchard, surveyor to the Cannock Urban Council. He served in France with the Oxford and Bucks Light Infantry, being wounded on one occasion, and was gazetted to the Staffords on June 26, 1917.

Captain G.H. BALL DSO, MC

"BIRMINGHAM OFFICER'S DOUBLE DISTINCTION"

Captain G.H. Ball whose name appears in the list of those recently awarded the D.S.O., and the M.C., is an old pupil of King Edwards's High School, Birmingham, and the son of the Headmaster of King Edward's Grammar School, Camp Hill. He was a member of the O.T.C., and received a commission in the South Staffordshire Regiment in October 1915, just after reaching his 18th birthday. He went to France in May 1916, and has seen continuous service since. He has been previously mentioned in despatches for continuous daring and valuable work. The D.S.O. was awarded for operations on the St Quentin Canal on September 28th, and the M.C. for fighting in the Riqueval Wood, on October 12th last. (6.12.18)

Private Thomas BARRATT VC

"THE COSELEY VC"

At a meeting of the Coseley Education Committee, held on Tuesday night, it was announced that the brother of Private Thomas Barratt, the Coseley V.C. had received a letter from the King, in which he was asked if he would go to Buckingham Palace to receive his brothers award, or whether the medal should be sent to him at Coseley. The committee discussed the question of providing a suitable memorial to commemorate the heroism of Private Barratt. It was agreed that the matter of a public memorial was one to be dealt with at a council meeting, but Mr T.K. Fellows (chairman) said, that in his opinion, apart from any public memorial, which they would certainly support, some action should be taken by the committee with a view to establishing a suitable memorial to the hero in the schools of the district. No definite line of action was, however, formulated by the committee.

Brevet Major (Acting Lieutenant Colonel) Archibold Bentley BEAUMAN DSO

Gazetted Brigadier General at the age of 29. The son of Mr A.A. Beauman, at one time Conservative MP for Peckham, he joined the 2nd Battalion South Staffordshire Regiment on February, 22nd 1908, and served with the battalion in South Africa and at Lichfield, where he was well known as an excellent cricketer, giving many brilliant displays on the Lichfield Garrison and Lichfield cricket grounds. He was posted to the 1st Battalion on November 15th, 1914, with the temporary rank of captain, and gazetted to full rank on March 1st, 1915. He was wounded in the following June, and in September 1915, he was made Companion of the Distinguished Service Order in recognition of his gallantry and devotion to duty in the field. (14.9.18)

Sergeant John Thomas BIRCH DCM

"DCM FOR WEDNESFIELD SERGEANT"

Sergeant John Thomas Birch, son of John and Emma Birch, 12 Graisley Lane, Wednesfield, has been awarded the Distinguished Conduct Medal for leading his platoon in action (in the absence of his officer) at the river Piave. The gallant sergeant is 21 years of age and has been on active service for 4? years. He was once wounded and was previously recommended for gallant service in the field. Sgt Birch joined his majesty's Forces at the age of 17.

Sergeant W. BIRCHALL DCM, MM

"WEDNESFIELD HERO SECURES MILITARY MEDAL AND D.C.M."

Sergeant W. Birchall second son of Mr and Mrs George Birchall, of 64 Neachell's Lane, Wednesfield, has brought distinction to his native district by meritorious achievements in the field. He has just secured the Military Medal and the D.C.M., and we are informed he is the first Wednesfield man to obtain the dual honour. Twenty-seven years of age, Sergeant Birchall was abroad with the South Staffords when the war broke out and was sent to France in 1914. He has seen some strenuous engagements, but has escaped injuries. At the present time he is on sick leave at Eastbourne. Sergeant Birchall comes from a fighting family. Mr George Birchall has three sons and a son in law. His eldest served for two years and eight months in the South African War, and the youngest after being in France for sixteen months was discharged. The son in law who has five children enlisted at the outbreak of hostilities. Prior to joining the army Sergeant Birchall worked at the Patent Axle Box Works, having been employed there from a boy as a chipper and filer. (4.1.17)

Corporal Charles BOARDMAN MM

"HEDNESFORD"

Presentation- On Saturday evening Corporal Charles Boardman, South Staffordshire Regiment was presented with a wallet containing £12 in notes in recognition of his having gained the Military Medal for bravery at Poelcappelle in October 1917. Mr J Smithhurst made the presentation on behalf of the officials and workmen of the West Cannock Colliery where Boardman was employed prior to joining the Colours in August 1914. Short speeches were also made by Mr S. Underwood and the Rev W.J. Kinchington. Solos were conducted by Lieutenant H. Jones and Bandmaster R. Laycock. (23.3.18)

Lieutenant Colonel S. BONNER DSO

Lieutenant Colonel Singleton Bonner, DSO, South Staffordshire Regiment, attached Royal Fusiliers, who died May 1 of wounds received in action on April 23, was the youngest son of the late Mr John Bonner of the Falkland Islands, and was 37 years of age. He was educated at Harrow, and served in the South African war, receiving both medals with five clasps. He was three times mentioned in despatches during the present war, and was awarded the DSO after the battle of Festubert, 1915. During March and April of that year he commanded the 1st South Staffordshire Regiment, and returned to England after being gassed at Loos. Shortly after his return to the front last month he assumed command of a battalion of the Royal Fusiliers, which he was commanding when he was mortally wounded. (8.5.17 BDP)

Corporal W.A. BROTHERS MM

"BIRMINGHAM MILITARY MEDALIST"

The Military Medal has been awarded to Lance Corporal W.A. Brothers, Signal Section, South Staffordshire Regiment, eldest son of Mr A.E. Brothers, of Carpenters Road, Lozells, Birmingham. Lance Corporal Brothers, who is twenty years of age, was educated at Aston Higher Grade School, Whitebead Road, and before enlisting two years ago was wages clerk at Messrs Brandauer's, New John Street West, Hockley. (2.10.17)

Private W. BRUERTON MM

"MILITARY MEDAL FOR WOLVERHAMPTON SOLDIER"

Another Wolverhampton man has been honoured for services in the field. We refer to Private W. Bruerton, of the South Staffords whose home is in Compton Street. To him has been awarded the Military Medal for helping to reorganise his platoon in the midst of battle after his sergeant has been wounded. Private Bruerton was formerly in the employ of Messrs W. Chatham and Son Ltd, Ablow Street, Wolverhampton, and joined the army on August 8th 1914. He was present at the landing in the Dardanelles, and remained there until the evacuation. He was then sent to other parts of the battle area, where he has seen much service and has ably performed every duty.

Lieutenant Colonel W. Burnett DSO

Lieutenant Colonel W. BURNETT DSO

"BRAVE AND STRAIGHT"

Lieutenant Colonel William Burnett of Hednesford has not lived long to enjoy the honour of the D.S.O. conferred upon him several weeks ago for gallant conduct. Official news was received on Wednesday that Cannock

Chase's premier fighting man had died from wounds received in action two days previously. His death is a great loss to Cannock Chase, and all over the district the news will be received with deep regret.

For 17 years the late officer had been employed at the Chase and Rugeley Colliery, and in his capacity of underground manager had earned an enviable reputation among the miners as one who was "as straight as a pin". He was very popular with everybody and when at the outbreak of war he marched away at the head of his men, the Hednesford Company of Territorials, to fight for King and Country he was as proud of his men as they were of him.

Honours came upon him by reason of hard work and meritorious achievements. Commencing with the rank of captain, he progressed to the position of commanding officer of his battalion and was ultimately gazetted to the command of another battalion with the rank of Lieutenant Colonel. Prior to succeeding Major R. Holton as officer in command of the Hednesford Territorials, Lieutenant Colonel Burnett had charge of the Bloxwich Company.

The deceased officer was a keen sportsman. For several years past he had held the presidency of the Hednesford Town Football Club, and as playing captain of the Cannock and Rugeley Colliery C.C. He was always enthusiastic in the pursuit of the popular summer pastime. The annual show of the Cannock and Rugeley Colliery Workman's Horticultural Society was an event in which he took a great deal of interest and into which he threw tremendous enthusiasm. No one had more pleasure out of the pit pony competition than he.

Lieutenant Colonel Burnett, who leaves a widow, a Walsall lady and one son, was 36 years of age, and was a native of Burton.

25745 Corporal Acting Sergeant J. CROWTHER

D.C.M. WINNER

Joseph Crowther, who is 23 years of age and belongs to the South Staffordshire Regiment, has been awarded the DCM. His home is at Temperance Cottage, John Street, and Ettingshall. Enlisting in January 1913, he was at Aldershot at the time war broke out, and went abroad on Aug 9, 1914. He has been wounded four times and mentioned in despatches. His latest distinction was awarded for dressing about thirty wounded men under shell fire and getting them to a place of safety. Before joining the Army, Sergeant Crowther was employed at the Sunbeam Works and prior to that attended Ettingshall Council Schools.

S.G. CUXON

South Staffs, regiment, son of Mr and Mrs John Cuxon, Aldridge Road, Perry Barr, has been awarded the Military Cross. Lieutenant Cuxon who is twenty-four years of age, and was educated at the King Edward's High School, Birmingham, obtained his commission in November 1914, and in the following June obtained his first lieutenancy. He served in Egypt and France, from where he was invalided afterwards being sent to Italy, where he has been eleven months.

Lieutenant R. T. DANIELS

"WOLVERHAMPTON OFFICER WINS M.C."

Lt R.T. Daniels MC

Lieutenant Raymond T. Daniels, South Staffordshire Regiment, who has been awarded the Military Cross for conspicuous gallantry and devotion to duty whilst in charge of a trench mortar battery, is the only son of Mr and

Mrs Daniels, The Lodge, Codsall, near Wolverhampton. He joined the army on the outbreak of war, and has been twice wounded. He is 22 years old, and was educated at the Higher-Grade School, Wolverhampton, the Wolverhampton Grammar School, and Harper Adams College, Newport, Salop. When war broke out he was engaged in the Land Valuation Office, Dudley District.

Corporal J. DYAS MM 1st Battalion

Joined 7th August 1914. Discharged 7th June 1919. Holds MM, 1914 Star British War and Victory medals. One Wound stripe.

Sent to France, November 11th 1914, and was in many battles, viz: Ypres, Somme, Loos, Bullecourt and Ancre, where he was awarded the Military Medal for conspicuous bravery, on 11th January 1917. He went to Italy and was badly wounded by shrapnel at the battle of Piave November 1st 1918.
Home address 67 Blewitt Street, Hednesford.

Sergeant F.H. EDWARDS MM, MSM 1/6th Battalion

Joined July 1915, discharged January 1919, Holds MM, MSM 1914-15 Star, British War and Victory medals. Two wounds stripes.

Sent to France, November 1915, and saw active service at Neuve Chapelle. Later, despatched for Egypt, where he remained for a short time and then returned to France and saw further active service at Vimy Ridge, where he received serious wounds to the chest. Received hospital treatment in France and later, despatched home. On recovery, returned to action in France and was engaged on the Somme and La Bassee, where he was gassed and later, was wounded on the Somme. Finished his military career in France and was discharged after the cessation of hostilities. Home address Watling Street Brownhills.

Captain A.F. ENNALS MC 5th Battalion att K.O.Y.L.I.

Joined 3rd September 1914. Discharged 29th January 1919. Holds Military Cross, 1914-15 Star, British War and Victory medals.

Landed in France, 1st March 1915 to 17th November 1915, with 1/5th South Staffs. With 3/5th South Staffs in England to March 1918; in France from March 1918 to January 1919. Attached to 9th Kings Own Yorkshire Light Infantry from July 1918 as Signal Officer, Adjutant etc. Home address "Walden" Mellish Road, Walsall.

Lance Corporal W. FORSBURY

"WEDNESBURY SOLDIER PRESENTED
WITH MILITARY MEDAL"

At Wednesbury Town Council meeting yesterday, the Mayor (Alderman Pritchard) presented the Military Medal to Lance Corporal W. Forsbury, of the 4th South Staffordshire Regiment, which had been awarded for gallantry at Kemmel Hill in April last. The recipient, who lives at St James's Street, Wednesbury, was warmly congratulated by the Mayor and his colleges.

Sergeant T.M. GARNER

"A TETTENHALL MILITARY MEDALIST KILLED"

News has been received by Mrs T.M. Garner, of 80 Aldersley Road Tettenhall, of the death in action of her husband, Sergeant T.M. Garner, South Staffordshire Regiment, killed on the 21st. Sergeant Garner joined the "Non-Manuals" in August 1914 and was later posted to the South Staffords. He had served for three years at the front, and was due home on leave at the time of his death. His commanding officer writing to Mrs Garner says: - "During our last tour in the line your husband won the Military Medal for digging out one of his men under heavy shell fire, who had been buried by a heavy shell. He was my bravest sergeant and did not know what fear was. He repeatedly did acts of bravery, and was a grand example to his platoon. I shall miss him, and it must be a comfort to you to know he died fighting for his King and country. As his Company Commander, I can testify to his keenness and his great ability to lead men" His brother, Private J.R. Garner of the same regiment, was reported "missing" and later "presumed killed" on October 13th, 1915. Another brother Private J.E. Garner is also serving at the front. Sergeant T.M. Garner is the third Tettenhall man who has won the Military Medal.

Private G.E. GUEST

"MILITARY MEDAL FOR WEDNESBURY SOLDIER"

At Wednesbury Town Council on Monday the Mayor said he had received a Military Medal for presentation to Private G.E. Guest, of the South Staffordshire Regiment, whose home was in the borough. He had intended making the presentation last Friday, but the medal had not arrived, and, unfortunately, the soldier that morning had to return to his unit. On behalf of the town they as a Corporation congratulated Guest upon the award and hoped he would be spared to return after the war and settle among his friends again.

Lieutenant F.J. GIBBS

"A BRAVE STAFFORDSHIRE OFFICER"

In a further list of awards of the Military Cross for gallantry and devotion to duty appears the name of Temp Lieutenant F.J. Gibbs, South Staffordshire Regiment and R.F.C., who has been awarded the Military Cross. Lieutenant Gibbs is the elder son of Mr and Mrs J. Gibbs, of Chasetown. He is an "Old Boy" of Walsall Grammar School. When war broke out he was a student at Saltley College, Birmingham, and a member of the Territorial Battalion of the Royal Warwickshire Regiment. He was immediately mobilised, and after 10 months service received a commission in the South Staffordshire Regiment in June 1915. In April 1916, he went to Egypt, and was attached to the Welsh Fusiliers, serving with them in the desert before El Arish. He gained his certificate as a pilot in the Royal Flying Corps in October 1916, training at Aboukir. The award of the Military Cross was gazetted on Sept. 27, 1917. He had then been in France since April.

Sergeant R. HANDY 8th Battalion

Joined 7th September 1914, discharged 26th December 1918. Holds DCM, French Croix de Guerre, 1914-15 Star, British War and Victory medals.

Sent to France June 1915, served at Ypres, The Bluff, Somme, Arras and Armentieres. Awarded the D.C.M. and Croix de Guerre on 23rd April 1917, at Arras, for conspicuous bravery and devotion to duty, in reorganising his company and leading them into a second attack.

Home address 5 The Lot, Cheslyn Hay.

Sergeant W.T. HARRISON DCM 2nd Battalion

Joined 8th December 1914. Discharged 21st April 1920. Holds DCM, later 1914-15 Star, British War and Victory medals. Two wound stripes.

Went to France, 23rd May 1915, and was in action at Givenchy, 26th September 1915. Went to the Somme, July 1916, and received his first wound. Delville Wood. Sent to Rouen, and rejoined battalion in September 1916. Was sent to the Ancre and afterwards Arras, and was in the taking of Hoppy Wood. Afterwards went to Ypres and from there to Cambrai, and awarded the DCM for bombing a post. Received a second wound, 1st December 1917, sent to Tooting hospital.

Home address 28 Anglesey Street, Hednesford.

2nd Lieutenant B.D. Hatchett MC

2nd Lieutenant B.D. HATCHETT

"WOLVERHAMPTON OFFICER HONOURED"

Second Lieutenant Basil Dudley Hatchett, South Staffordshire Regiment, awarded the Military Cross for conspicuous gallantry and devotion to duty when in command of two guns, is the son of the late Mr Henry Hatchett, who was secretary to the old South Staffordshire Tramways Company, and Mrs Hatchett, of Tettenhall Road, Wolverhampton. He is a nephew of Mr J. Billingsley, JP, of Smethwick. He was educated at Hurstbier Point College, where he was a member of the O.T.C. He afterwards joined the staff of the Metropolitan Bank at Wolverhampton, where he was well known, and as a member of the Staffordshire Yeomanry, was mobilised on the outbreak of war. Being anxious to get to the front quickly, he transferred to an infantry regiment.

Private E. HATHEWAY 2nd Battalion

Joined August 1914. Discharged 8th February 1919. Holds DCM, 1914-15 Star British War and Victory medals. Served in France from May 1915, until January 1919, and was engaged in the following battles: Loos where he was mentioned in Despatches and received the DCM, The Somme 1916 and all engagements in which the battalion took part until the Armistice. Discharged from Clipstone Camp. Home address Northwood Villas, Aldridge.

2nd Lieutenant J. HENNEY 1/5th Battalion

Joined 31st August 1914, discharged 21st March 1919. Holds 1914-15 Star, British War and Victory medals.

Went into training at Lichfield (promoted to Lance Corporal), then to Aldershot and on to Folkstone, where he was again promoted, to Sergeant. Embarked for France and went into action near Estares, Ypres, Souschay, the Somme, where he was Mentioned in Despatches for attending wounded whilst under fire; onto Vimy Ridge, back to Ypres (6 months), after which he was sent to England to the Cadet Battalion, Oxford to train as an officer. After obtaining his commission he joined the 3rd South Staffords at Newcastle-on-Tyne. Returned to France, Sept 1918, on the way to the line, had a narrow escape from death in a train smash near Roshelle. Again went into action at Riqueval Wood with the 1st South Staffords. He was posted to the 137th Brigade Headquarters, as Brigade Transport Officer until discharge.

Home address Swan Inn, Longdon, near Rugeley.

Lieutenant J. HERRINGTON 2nd Battalion

Joined 21st April 1915, discharged 1st January 1919. Holds Military Cross, Military Medal, British War and Victory medals.

Training in Jersey, saw service in France, Belgium, Armentieres, St Eloi, Vermelles, Dumbarton, Vimy Ridge, and Somme (1st Battle). Awarded the Military Medal for bravery on the field during the Somme action. Recommended for Commission. Afterwards posted to 9th Staffs, saw service in Italy, in charge of defences on Asiago Plateau and San-Sisto Ridge. Mentioned In Despatches at San-Sisto Ridge. Awarded Military Cross for work on defences, was present throughout the whole attack made on the Piave and subsequent advances, and then demobilised.

Home address 15 Glover Street, Wimblebury.

Sergeant F. HULME South Staffs & Tank Corps

Joined 28th August 1914, discharged 25th February 1919. Holds British War and Victory medals. Two wound stripes.

Sent to France February 1916, and was in action at Armentieres, then sent to the 1st July offensive on the Somme. Afterwards sent to Arras, Passchendaele and Cambrai. He was wounded and sent convalescent to Rouen. He was sent again to rejoin his unit, stayed with them 2 months and was then transferred to the Tank corps and was in action at Cambrai, St Quinten and the crossing of the Canal, where he was wounded and mentioned in despatches for pluck and soldiering conduct. Sent to Rouen Hospital on recovery then went to rejoin the Corps and stayed until the armistice was signed.

Home address 3 Chapel Square, Cheslyn Hay.

Private John JONES

"BILSTON SOLDIER"

Mr W, Hughes (Chairman of Bilston Council) on Thursday evening presented the Military Medal to Private John Jones, of Free Street, Bilston, and was pleased to learn that he was connected with the 6th South Staffordshire Regt,- which formed part of the 46th Division. The record of which the award had been granted showed that during operation on the morning of April 23, in front of Lens, Jones acted as company runner and made six journeys from his company commander to battalion headquarters, which entailed passing through a heavy artillery barrage. He rendered invaluable services in keeping touch between his company and platoon commanders, displayed the greatest courage, and was always cheerful and anxious to do further journeys. From midnight till 11pm he was constantly on his feet, and after his battalion was relieved he again went to the firing line to search for three missing men, returning at 8 am, after 30 hours continuous work under fire.

Mr Hughes stated there was a scheme in hand to recognise the services of all Bilston men who had gained decorations in the war.

Private Samuel JONES

"A COSELEY MEDALLIST"

Private Samuel Jones, of Ladymoor, Coseley, has been awarded the Military Medal for Bravery and devotion to duty. He has a unique record, having been in the Army for sixteen years. A member of the original Expeditionary Force, he took part in the retirement from Mons, fighting rearguard actions at Charleroi, Le Cateau, Sissons, Maux, Ham, St Quinten and Chassney. When the tide turned he fought at Richeburg, Levautie, the Marne, Neuve Chapelle, La Basse, Aubers Ridge, The Aisne, 2nd battle of Ypres, Dickbush, Kemnel, Neuve Gleece, 3rd battle of Ypres, the Somme, Ancre, Albert, Arras, St Jean, Passchendale and Bapaume.

2nd Lieutenant W.H.R. LLOYD

Second Lieutenant Walter Harry Richardson Lloyds, South Staffordshire Regiment, is the nephew and adopted son of Mr H. Richardson, the executive officer of the Birmingham Food Control Committee, of 5, Somerset Road, Handsworth Wood. He is 19 years of age, and was educated at Handsworth Grammar School and Denstone College, and at both establishments he was a member of the O.T.C. On leaving college he entered the automatic department of W & T Avery (Limited), and continued his military training in connection with the Birmingham University O.T.C., and also B Company of the Handsworth Volunteers. As soon as he was old enough he joined the Inns of Court O.T.C., and obtained his commission in the South Staffords about 12 months ago. He went to France in April last.

Captain H.L.B. Lovatt MC

Captain H.L.B. LOVATT MC

"MILITARY CROSS FOR CAPTAIN LOVATT"

Captain H. Leslie B. Lovatt, son of Mr Wilson Lovatt, of Wightwick House, Wolverhampton, joined the South Staffordshire Regiment in August 1914, was transferred to the Royal Engineers in 1916 and appointed D.A.D.L. to the 4th Corps in the early part of 1917. He was educated at Wellington college, Berkshire and is one of the recipients of the Military Cross mentioned in the New Years Honours List.

Captain A.E. MACHIN 1/5th Battalion

Joined September 1914, discharged Feb 1919. Holds 1914-15 Star, British War and Victory Medals. Three wound stripes.

Enlisted, as a Private, rose to the rank of Corporal then Sergeant, and saw action at Loos, afterwards was Commissioned and saw action as Officer. Wounded at Gommecourt he was invalided home to hospital at Manchester, and upon recovery again embarked for France, and was in action at Lens and St Quinten. Again wounded at La Basse. After recovery, saw service at St Quinten, where he was wounded a third time, but remained with his unit until discharged. Mentioned in Despatches 1918.

Home address 93 Persehouse Street, Walsall.

CSM E. MARTIN DCM 1/5th Battalion

Joined 3rd March 1912, discharged May 1919. Holds DCM, Medal Militare, Croix de Guerre, 1914-15 Star British War and Victory medals. Two wound stripes.

Went to France February 1915, with the 46th Division and went into action at Armentieres, moving from there to Messines Ridge. Wounded at Hulloch, October 1915, arrived in England, sent to a hospital in Bedfordshire. Sent to France again and arrived with his old battalion. Was recommended and received the D.C.M. For recovering wounded under shell fire. Afterwards was recommended and received the Medal Militare and Croix de Guerre for doing very useful patrol work for his battalion. Took part in the principal engagements in which involved his battalion until finally discharged.

Home address 23 Heath Gap Road, Blackfords, Cannock.

Private T. MOORE MM

Private Thomas Moore, South Staffordshire Regiment, of Coronation Road High Heath Pelsall, has been awarded the Military Medal for bringing in a wounded officer during a gas attack.

2nd Lieutenant S.G. MAITLAND S. STAFFS R.

Second Lieutenant Stewart Gordon Maitland is 21 years of age, and is the son of Mr F.W.R. Maitland, 13 Trafalgar Road, Moseley, and a nephew of the vicar of Dudley. He was educated at Hele's School, Exeter, and at the outbreak of the war was an apprentice at Vickers (Ltd) Birmingham. He was in the 2nd City of Birmingham Battalion in September 1914, went to France in November, 1915 and served with his battalion until May 1917, when having attained the rank of sergeant, he came home to train for his commission. He was gazetted to the South Staffordshire Regiment in November 1917, and returned to France in January last. At the time of the action for which he has been decorated this young officer was acting as adjutant of his battalion, the adjutant having become a casualty, and when the King visited that part of the line the next day Mr Maitland was presented to him as a "bit of a marvel" having come through without a scratch.

Captain E.J.H. MEYNELL

Mr Hubert Meynell of Wolverhampton has received from the War Office the Military Cross awarded to his son, the late Captain E.J.H. Meynell, South Staffordshire Regiment. The Military Secretary expresses to Mr Meynell the Secretary of State's regret that the gallant officer, who gave his life for his country, did not survive to receive his reward from the hands of his Majesty the King. It may be noted that Captain Meynell who was only 22 years of age, died on October 4, 1918, of wounds received in action the previous day.

Brigadier General L. BOYD-MOSS, CMG

Brig Gen Lionel Boyd-Moss C.M.G., who has been reported wounded, is an officer whose promotion has been remarkably rapid. Between Oct 25 and Nov 10 1915, he was promoted to temporary Lieutenant Colonel and then to the rank of Brigadier General, with command of the Brigade. Brig Gen Boyd Moss belongs to the South Staffordshire Regiment, with which he has served throughout the war until his promotion to Brigadier General, and has distinguished himself by gallantry and devotion to duty, having been mentioned in despatches and awarded the C.M.G. He joined the South Staffords from the Militia in 1896, and spent 20 years with the regiment. His first active service was in the operations in Sierra Leone in 1898-9 for which he obtained the medal with clasp. He served in the South African War from 1900 to 1902, was mentioned in despatches, given the brevet rank of major, and awarded the Queens medal with three clasps and the Kings medal with two clasps.

Acting Captain E.W. Page MC

Acting Captain E.W. PAGE MC

Acting Captain E.W. Page is the third of four sons of the official Receiver of Wolverhampton, all of whom hold commissions in the Army. He is a well known hockey player, having played for the Midlands for some years and as an international for England in three successive seasons. He is also a fine cricketer and golfer. By profession he is a chartered accountant. One of his brothers, Captain H.A. Page, has just been promoted to the rank of balloon commander in the Royal Flying Corps.

CSM A. PEARCE 1/5th Battalion

Joined 4th August 1914. Holds 1914-15 Star British War, Victory and Territorial Efficiency medals.

Sent to France March 2nd, 1915, being in reserve for battle of Neuve Chapelle, afterwards serving in the trenches at Messines for three months, was in the first battle of Ypres, battle of Loos October 13th, 1915, battle of Somme 1st July, 1916 and served in Egypt for a short time. Afterwards returning to France served with the Regiment until Armistice was signed. Demobilised November 1918. Mentioned in Despatches August 8th, 1918. Home address 36 Bradbury Lane, Hednesford.

CSM W. PEARCE 1/5th Battalion

Joined 1st March 1910, discharged 1st May 1919. Holds 1914-15 Star, British War and Victory and Territorial Efficiency medals. Two wound stripes.

Awarded the Royal Humane Certificate on parchment for gallantry in saving life at sea, 2nd September 1917, and was sent to France 1915. Was wounded at Messines Ridge, came to England and on recovery went into action, and was again wounded at Hill 60, and came again to England, returned for a third time, sent back to England and was made Sergeant Instructor until discharged. Now rejoined again.

Home address 70 Mount Street, Hednesford.

2nd Lieutenant H. Piggins MC

2nd Lieutenant H. PIGGINS MC & BAR

"WALSALL OFFICERS ACHIEVEMENT"

Lieutenant Piggins, who is 25, is the son of Mr & Mrs E. Piggins, of 67 Mount Street, Walsall. He joined the Army on August 8th, 1914, and went to the Dardanelles, where he was slightly wounded, and also had a severe attack of dysentery. He gained his commission in October 1917, won the Military Cross on March 9th last, and 21 days later so distinguished himself that he was awarded the bar. A letter received from him by his parents a week ago stated that he was all right.

Sergeant J.W. PITT DCM 1st & 5th Battalions

Joined 6th October 1914, discharged 16th January 1919. Holds DCM, 1914-15 Star, British War and Victory medals. Two wound stripes. Went to France with the 46th Division February 1915, holding the line at Armentieres for a while, then went into action at Hohenzollern Redoubt, October 13th, 1915. Afterwards going to Egypt, being there a short time, returning to France, March 1916, took part in the offensive of the Somme, 1916, being in the taking of Gommecourt. Was recommended and awarded the D.C.M., for taking charge of trenches (which were being heavily shelled) at Messines, 6th May 1915. Was in all the engagements in which his battalion took part until the armistice, being finally discharged.

Home address 504 Stafford Road, Cannock.

Pioneer Sergeant W. POSTANCE

An interesting presentation, by permission of the military authorities, took place in the Tettenhall Institute on Friday evening, when Pioneer Sergeant W. Postance, South Staffords, of Tettenhall was presented by Colonel Alex McBean with the Military Medal, awarded to him for bravery in the field in October 1915, on the occasion of the attack on the Hohenzollern Redoubt. Colonel McBean in making the presentation explained that the gallant sergeant had up to date only received the ribbon, but he (the Colonel) had now great pleasure in presenting the more tangible decoration. Colonel McBean, who was supported by Mr Samuel Bayliss, JP., Mr Muras, Mr Douglas Graham, Miss Thornycroft, Miss Florence Thornycroft and others explained that Sergeant Postance had been on short leave and was returning overseas on Saturday. The speaker referred to Tettenhall's contribution to the war, and stated that 487 men from the village and immediate neighbourhood had joined the colours.

Sergeant W. READ

"MILITARY MEDAL FOR LANGLEY SOLDIER"

Sergeant Walter Read, of Rood End Road, Langley who belongs to the South Staffordshire Regiment, has been awarded the Military Medal. The official account of his bravery being as follows. "Though only recently promoted he had on several occasions shown great coolness under fire. On the night of June 10 his platoon was detailed to dig a trench in the captured area at———. There was a heavy fire, and he set a good example by his coolness and courage and was of great assistance to his officers in getting the work completed. He is 28 years of age, was formerly in business as a butcher. He has been on active service for two years.

2nd Lieutenant S. Rubery

2nd Lieutenant S. RUBERY

Second Lieutenant Rubery is a son of the late Mr Samuel Rubery, who was an iron merchant carrying on business at Darlaston and who lived at Oaken, and subsequently in Wolverhampton. His uncle Mr J.T. Rubery J.P., Melish

Road, Darlaston, and he is a nephew of Miss Alma Rubery, Hon Sec to the Church Mission for the Deaf and Dumb in Staffordshire and Shropshire. At one time he was associated with newspaper work in Wolverhampton, and afterwards became an architect. He joined the colours at Walsall as a private, since which he has been granted a commission.

Lieutenant Colonel SAVAGE-ARMSTRONG DSO

"CASUALTIES AMONG MIDLAND OFFICERS"

Lieutenant Colonel Francis Nesbitt Savage-Armstrong, DSO, South Staffordshire Regiment, attached to the Royal Warwickshire Regiment, who has been killed in action, served with the South Staffords in the South African war, and had five bars to his two medals. In the present war he was mentioned four times in despatches, first by Viscount French and afterwards by Sir Douglas Haig. He went to France in November 1914, and was with his own regiment at Fromelles, Neuve Chapelle and Festubert, being severely wounded at the last mentioned battle on May 16, 1916. After recovery he was ordered on "light duty", but in September last he returned to the front and was appointed to the command of a service battalion of the Rifle Brigade, and afterwards of a battalion of the Royal Warwickshire Regiment, of which he was in command of when he was killed. (B.D.P. 8.5.17)

2nd Lieutenant Samuel SAUNDERS

"MILITARY CROSS FOR WOLVERHAMPTON OFFICER"

Among the officers to receive the Military Cross and Bar at Buckingham Palace on Wednesday was Second Lieutenant Samuel Saunders. The award was made for gallantry and devotion to duty in action. Second Lieutenant Saunders is the youngest son of the late Alderman James Saunders, a former mayor of Wolverhampton, and he is a partner in the firm of James Saunders and Sons iron merchants, Darlington Street, Wolverhampton. As an early member of the Volunteer Force he gained useful knowledge, and joined the army in September 1915. From February to April 1916, he was commanding a brigade of the R.F.A. He went to France in January 1917, and was wounded in May.

Private T. SCREEN

"WOLVERHAMPTON MILITARY MEDALLIST"

The soldier whose home is in Dimmock Street, Parkfield, Wolverhampton, distinguished himself on the 30th November and on the 1st December. As a leader of a bombing party he held at bay a horde of German raiders until the arrival of reinforcements. Private Screen has already received at the hands of his Commanding officer the red, white and blue ribbon, and steps will be taken to arrange for the presentation of the medal by the Chief Magistrate of his native town.

Corporal ROBERT SHELDON

Corporal Robert Sheldon, of the South Staffordshire Regiment, who has been awarded the Military Medal, is the youngest son of Mr and Mrs J. Sheldon, of 22 Wilkinson Street, Aston. He joined the colours in May 1915, and was sent to France on Christmas day, 1916. The award was made for gallantry on the night of June 24-25, when he established and maintained a forward post, showing great initiative and a good example to his men under shell fire.

Captain SILVERS

We have pleasure in announcing that Captain Silvers, son of Mrs Silvers of the Talbot Hotel, Wolverhampton, has been awarded the Military Cross. The officer who is only 24 years of age, together with a brother joined as a private the South Staffords at the outbreak of war, and has seen much service. He rose to the rank of lieutenant in 1915, and was given his captaincy about six months ago. Captain Silvers was wounded during September and

Captain Silvers MC

was recently home on leave. An old scholar of the Wolverhampton Grammar School, he was serving his articles with Mr Johnston, chartered accountant when he enlisted. At one time Captain Silvers was captain of Penn Fields Football Club, and was also associated with tennis.

L/Cpl D. SLATER

"HOW A DUDLEY SOLDIER WON THE MILITARY MEDAL"

The Military medal has been awarded to Lance Corporal David Slater (South Staffords), of Springfield, near Dudley. According to the official record Lance Corporal Slater was patrolling with three privates to locate new positions of the enemy. After advancing about 300 yards he came suddenly upon a party of the enemy, 25 to 30 in number, hidden in the corn. His party was fired on with rifles and grenades. Two jumped into a dyke, and the third who was badly injured, was assisted by Lance Corporal Slater. They were pursued by the enemy, with the result that Lance Corporal Slater had his clothes and equipment torn in four places by bullets, but he continued to help the wounded man back to his post. Five minutes later the man died, but if it had not been for Lance Corporal Slater's pluck he would have fallen into enemy hands.

Captain P.J. SLATER

"WALSALL OFFICER WINS
DISTINGUISHED FLYING CROSS"

Captain Percival J. Slater, of the South Staffordshire regiment, has been awarded the Distinguished Flying Cross. Captain Slater is the eldest son of Mr S.M. Slater, ex mayor of Walsall. He went out to France with the 46th North Midland Division early in 1915, and was severely wounded in the following October in the attack on the Hohenzollern redoubt. Being incapacitated for further infantry service, he was transferred to the Balloon wing of the Royal Air Force and went across to France again about a year ago. He has previously been mentioned in despatches.

Sergeant Bert SMITH

D.C.M. And Military medal Winner. Sergeant Bert Smith, of the South Staffordshire Regiment, who formerly worked at the West Cannock Colliery, Hednesford and was a prominent footballer in Hazel Slade Institute and Rugeley Albion, has been awarded the D.C.M. and Military Medal for distinguished service in action in France. Sergeant Smith's wife and children live at Walsall Road, Cannock, but his parents live at Hazel Slade and it was from the latter mining village that he joined the colours nearly three years ago. Sergeant Smith was wounded in the recent fighting, and is now in hospital in Manchester.

Corporal John SMITH DCM 2nd Battalion

Corporal John Smith of the 2nd South Staffords has been at the front for some time has been awarded the DCM, he has for some years lived at Darnford Cottages between Lichfield and Whittington Barracks, but is a native of Walsall and his parents Mr & Mrs E. Smith, live at 11 Littleton East Street. For over thirteen years he has served in the Army and took part in the concluding stages of the Boer War, when he acted as an officer's servant. Scant though the details are regarding how he earned the DCM, it is evident he acted with great bravery. The Staffords were occupying a well advanced trench not far from the German lines, when an officer fell severely wounded. Moments were precious, and with scarce a thought for himself, Cpl Smith clambered out of the trench to fetch an ambulance. Luck seems to have favoured him, for although shells and bullets were whistling all around, he managed to cross the fire swept zone in safety and bring the ambulance back. Naturally in such a risky venture he had several narrow shaves, the concussion from one shell knocked him down, while a bullet grazed his flesh. (Walsall Observer 20.2.1915)

He has no known grave and is commemorated on the Le Touret Memorial to the Missing, Pas de Calais, France, Panel 21 and 22.

Lieutenant L.C. SMITH

"WEDNESBURY OFFICER WINS THE MILITARY CROSS"

A Wednesbury officer in Lieutenant Leslie Coleman Smith, of the South Staffordshire Regiment, but lately attached to the Lincoln's has been awarded the Military Cross. He is the youngest of five soldier sons of the late Colonel C.E. Smith, of Wednesbury, and has recently passed his 19th birthday. He was educated at the Grammar School, Solihull, where at the time of joining the Army he was head prefect, and captain of the first XI, cricket and football teams. He played for Warwick County and made his first century in one of their fixtures. His military training with the O.T.C. in connection with the school proved very helpful in preparing him for taking his commission in June last year, and proceeding to the front in the autumn, he has taken an active part in the severe fighting. Of the other sons, two have given their lives for their country, one is serving in Egypt, and the other has been invalided home after two years at the front.

Private G. SPRUCE

"ANOTHER LOCAL MILITARY MEDALLIST"

Private George Spruce, the South Staffordshire Regiment, who resides at 65 Willenhall Road, recently returned from the front, has been awarded the Military Medal under the following circumstances: -

During the advance from Le Catelet to Le Cateau, from 5th to 10th October inclusive the work of this man as stretcher bearer was characterised by absolute fearlessness and untiring energy. He bandaged in the open, and carried in many of our wounded. On the 9th October he was personally responsible for saving the lives of three wounded men who had fallen into a stream, and who would have drowned but for his timely aid, rendered under machine gun fire. Spruce enlisted on Monday, September 7th 1914 in the South Staffords. He went to France in July 1915 and was wounded July 30th. He rejoined the regiment on October 16th, and was wounded at Armentieres on May 14th 1916, and was subsequently transferred to the 11th Sherwood Foresters. In July 1916, he was on the Somme and next at Ypres. He went with the division to Italy in October 1917, and came back in September 1918 to France. He has now been demobilised.

Corporal C.E. STOKES

"HONOUR FOR A WARLEY SOLDIER"

Corporal C.E. Stokes, of George Road, Warley (South Staffordshire Regiment), who has been awarded the Military Medal, is 39 years of age, and served nine years in the Royal Warwickshire Regiment, taking part in the South African War. Joining the colours soon after the outbreak of hostilities, he saw considerable service in Gallipoli, where he was wounded. Subsequently transferred to France, where he was twice wounded.

L/Cpl A. STYCH MM 1/5th Battalion

Joined 22nd April 1913. Holds MM, 1914-15 Star British War and Victory medals. One Wound stripe.

Saw service with the 1/5th South Staffords in France from 3rd March, 1915 until wounded in both arms at Gommecourt on 1st July, 1916, was awarded the Military Medal for gallantry at Neuville St Vass, when his company were blown up by a mine. Returned to France on 27th September 1916 and was transferred to 7th Suffolk's in which battalion he was killed on April 23rd, 1917, at Arras.

Home address 102 Parker Street, Bloxwich.

Private Samuel THOMAS

"WALSALL SOLDIER PUBLICLY HONOURED"

The business of the Walsall War Pensions Committee was interrupted for a short time on Thursday night in order that the mayor (Councillor S.M. Slater) might publicly present to Private Samuel Thomas, of the South Staffords, the Croix de Guerre, which was recently awarded to him by the French War Office. The mayor remarked that Private Thomas, who is 22 years of age, and whose home is in GreenLane, Walsall, joined the South Staffords in January 1915. The deeds for which the medal had been awarded were done in Delville Wood, where the French and British Armies were at the time in close touch and where Private Thomas was acting as a "runner". It was for the bravery displayed in the performance of those dangerous duties that the French War Office had conferred upon him this honour. Though we had been at war with the French, we were now fighting side by side in this tremendous historic conflict, and it was very pleasing to see one Army recognising the bravery of men in the other Army. On behalf of the town, he congratulated Private Thomas on the honour he had won, and wished him a safe return to his native town when the war was over. The Mayor amid applause then pinned the decoration on Private Thomas's breast. Councillor E. Evans, who responded for Private Thomas, said the latter told him that he would rather fight than talk.

Lance Corporal J. THOMPSON

Lance Corporal Joseph Thompson, of the South Staffordshire Regiment, a stretcher bearer, has been awarded the Military Medal for conspicuous bravery. Before enlisting he was a member of the Bearwood Harriers, and has been at the front a year and nine months. His wife resides at 109, Cheshire Road, Smethwick.

Private A.J. TIMMINS 9th Battalion

Joined 11th October 1914. Discharged 6th February 1919. Holds 1914-15 Star British War and Victory medals.

Went to France 23rd August 1915 and was in action at Armentieres, which front he was on 6 months. Afterwards went to the Somme and was in the engagements of July and August. Also in the taking of some of the Salient points. Was sent to Ypres, and was in the third battle. Afterwards sent to Italy and was there 12 months during which time the armistice was signed. Mentioned in Despatches by General Earl of Cavan KP. KCB MVO, 18th January 1919. Home address 18 McGhie Street, Hednesford.

Corporal J. TIMMINS

"CANNOCK MILITARY MEDALLIST KILLED"

Corporal James Timmins, South Staffordshire Regiment, of Heath Hayes, Cannock, who was awarded the Military Medal a few months ago, has been killed in action. A miner at the Coppice Colliery, he was assistant scoutmaster at Heath Hayes and was also a member of the Cannock Fire Brigade. Three brothers of deceased are still with the colours.

Lieutenant & Quartermaster E. Walker DCM

Lieutenant & Quartermaster E. WALKER

"A LITTLE HAYWOOD DCM WINNER"

In the Council House on the 16th inst, a Distinguished Conduct Medal won by Lieutenant & Quartermaster Eli Walker, while serving as a non commissioned officer with the South Staffords at Gallipoli was presented to him by Lieutenant Colonel Phelps. The Mayor (Councillor S.M. Slater) presided, a number of public men and representatives of the military authorities being present. Among the latter were Mayor Brace and Lieutenant Nat Bishop, from the local recruiting office; and Mr Fausett Osbourne and Mr F.R. Clarke, military representatives at the Local Tribunal. A number of wounded soldiers attended.

Lieutenant Walker is a native of Little Haywood, Stafford, but his home is now Freer Street, Walsall. He has a record of nearly 29 years service in the Army. He had been acting as sergeant major to the Territorials, and was on pension when the war broke out. He rejoined and was sent out to Gallipoli in July 1915, taking part in the severe fighting at Suvla Bay and it was there he won the medal. After the evacuation he was stationed for a time in Egypt, proceeding thence to France in July of last year. The mayor said that it was right such presentations should take place in public, because the honours won were not alone the possession of the man who gained them, nor even his battalion and regiment, but also of the nation, and especially of the town with which he had been associated.

Lieutenant Colonel Phelps, in making the presentation, said the medal was not awarded for any one particular act, but for continuously carrying on important work under the most difficult and dangerous conditions. It was not less well deserved on that account; indeed he was not sure that such work did not better merit recognition than acts that were done on the impulse of the moment. One of the most splendid things about Englishmen in the present war was the way they carried on under all kinds of circumstances; it was the spirit that was winning the war. Colonel Phelps said that the occasion was particularly interesting to him because he also took part in the fighting at Sulva Bay, and at the end of the three days only two officers, besides himself, and 120 men were left out of 1,050. He believed the South Staffords to which Lieutenant Walker was attached suffered just as severely.

Lieutenant Walker responded, modestly observed that he would have preferred to receive the medal through the post. He was returning to France the next day, and hoped he would be spared to carry on for some time longer.

A vote of thanks was passed to Lieutenant Colonel Phelps, on the proposition of Mr J. Parker, MP for Halifax.

2nd Lieutenant G.S. WALKER

Second Lieutenant George S Walker, of the South Staffordshire Regiment, is the elder son of the late David Walker, of Corngreaves, Cradley Heath, and Mrs Walker of 325 George Road, Erdington. He enlisted in September 1914, going to France early in March 1915. In June 1916, he was wounded and invalided to England. He returned to France in October 1917, and was dangerously wounded at Cambrai while performing the deed for which he was awarded the Military Cross.

Colonel Waterhouse DSO

Lieutenant Colonel WATERHOUSE

Lieutenant Colonel Waterhouse of the South Staffordshire Regiment, who has been awarded the D.S.O. Was formerly in command of the 3rd Volunteer Battalion South Staffordshire Regiment, and on the formation of the Territorial Force in 1908 he was transferred to the command of the 6th Battalion South Staffordshire Regiment.

In October 1915 Colonel Waterhouse was severely wounded, and for some time his life was in danger. He recovered, however, and in 1916 and the following year he was mentioned in despatches. Last May he returned to the Western font on staff duties, where he has since remained. Colonel Waterhouse, who is a Deputy Lieutenant of Staffordshire, is Magistrates Clerk at Wolverhampton and at Sedgley.

SOLDIER WITH MANY DECORATIONS. 13. 12. 18

Company sergeant-major F. Webb, South Staffordshire Regiment, is, with regard to war decorations, a record holder. Earning the Mons Star and ribbon in 1914, he was awarded in 1917 the Belgian Croix de Guerre. Since then he has served in Italy, where he gained the Military Medal and the Italian Croce de Guerra. Sergt.-major Webb has served in the Army for about twelve years. His home is at 10, St. Mary's-terrace, Wolverhampton.

CSM F. Webb

Private G. WILLETT MM 6th Battalion

Joined October 1915, discharged February 1919. Holds MM, British War and Victory medals.

Sent to France June 1916, saw active service at Berles, Lens, La Bassee, Loos was also engaged in the battle of the Somme, and the crossing of the St Quinten Canal, underwent medical operation in France, on recovery was sent to England for further treatment. Later returning to France, where he remained until after the cessation of hostilities, and finally discharged. The Military Medal was awarded for capturing a machine gun north of Sequehart in October 1918. "North of Sequehart, on October 3rd 1918, this man spotted a machine gun firing on our troops, and at once got his Lewis Gun into action, wounding several of the team. Together with another man he then rushed the post and captured it. During the whole time, he showed great bravery and initiative"

Sergeant I.L. WILLIAMS MM

Sergeant. Issac Leonard Williams, South Staffs, whose mother resides at High Street, Swindon, Dudley, has been killed in action. Sergeant Williams, who joined the Army four years ago, had been on active service for two years. He was 22 years old and received his first wound in June 1915. He fought through many battles.

Photo J.J. Woolley

2nd Lieutenant J.J. WOOLLEY

Second Lieutenant J.J. Woolley of the South Staffordshire Regiment whose home is at 24 Oxford Street, Bilston, has been awarded the Military Cross. Lieutenant Woolley, who joined the Army in October 1914, is now lying ill in France.

AWARDS NOT LOCATED

L ISTED below are the Honours and Awards that I have been unable to locate in the London Gazette. I would be most grateful for any of the details that are not shown, in order that my master copy and the working copy held at the Staffordshire Regimental Museum may be amended.

Distinguished Service Order

Lt Col	A.M. Morris	SSR	War Diary June 1918

Military Cross

Lt	A.J. Hull	USA	Medical Officer Att SSR
2nd Lt	S. Saunders	SSR	Regt History 25.2.1917

Territorial Decoration

Lt Col	F.W.B. Law	6 SSR
Lt Col	T.F. Waterhouse	6 SSR

Military Medal

	L/Cpl	R. Borton	SSR	
40925	L/Cpl	J. Cook	SSR	War Diary 30.11.1917
242075	Cpl	H.G. Cox	6 SSR	
18374	Pte	T. Davies	SSR	
53028	Cpl	G. Donald	SSR	War Diary 31.12.1917 Bar
	Pte	W. Evans	SSR	
7022	L/Sgt	A.E. Foulkes	SSR	
242080	Sgt	P.N.V. Gower	6 SSR	
61639	L/Cpl	W. Harrison	1 SSR	War Diary 18.04.1918
	Sgt	J.E. Harvey	SSR	
40123	Pte	S. Hill	4 SSR	
	Pte	J. Humphreys	SSR	
15966	Pte	J.H. Lewis	SSR	
30049	Sgt	A.W. Morrell	1 SSR	War Diary 31.05.1917
12531	Pte	W. Myner	1 SSR	War Diary 28.10.1917
493	Sgt	J. Preece	6 SSR	
	L/Cpl	D. Robin	SSR	
	Pte	G. Spruce	1 SSR	
630824	Pte	B. Tate	SSR	Is this 36107 4th SSR
	Cpl	R.J. Timmins	SSR	
	Sgt	G. Wain	SSR	
9339	L/Cpl	J. Watson	1 SSR	War Diary 31.01.1917
	Sgt	R. Webster	SSR	
	Pte	A.J. White	SSR	

Mentioned In Despatches

Capt		H.S. Blockley	1 SSR	Regt History 25.02.1917
Capt		A.F.G. Kilby VC	2 SSR	Regt History 30.11.1915
Brig Gen		R.M. Ovens CMG	1 SSR	Regt History

Foreign Awards

6911	Sgt	W.G. Gasgoine	2 SSR	French Medaille Militaire
	T Major	C.C. Naylor		French Croix de Guerre
	T Capt	F. Le Sueur		Italian Silver Medal For Valour
	Rev	Parker		Italian Croce di Guerra
	CSM	F. Webb	SSR	Italian Croce di Guerra

THE LAST POST

Members of the Ypres (Iper) Fire Brigade
Sounding The Last Post

They shall grow not old, as we that are left grow old
Age shall not weary them, nor the years condemn.
At the going down of the sun and in the morning
We will remember them.